In Pursuit of Foresight

In Pursuit
of Foresight

Disaster Incubation Theory
Re-imagined

MIKE LAUDER

Routledge
Taylor & Francis Group

LONDON AND NEW YORK

First published 2015 by Gower Publishing

Published 2016 by Routledge
2 Park Square, Milton Park, Abingdon, Oxon OX14 4RN
711 Third Avenue, New York, NY 10017, USA

First issued in paperback 2017

Routledge is an imprint of the Taylor & Francis Group, an informa business

British Library Cataloguing in Publication Data
A catalogue record for this book is available from the British Library

Library of Congress Cataloging-in-Publication Data
Lauder, Mike.
 In pursuit of foresight : disaster incubation theory re-imagined / by Mike Lauder.
    pages cm
 Includes bibliographical references and index.
   ISBN 978-1-4724-6889-5 (hardback) -- ISBN 978-1-4724-6890-1 (ebook) -- ISBN 978-1-4724-6891-8 (epub) 1. Risk management. 2. Disasters--Prevention. I. Title.

  HD61.L3767 2015
  658.4'77--dc23

                                                                    2015023102

ISBN 13: 978-1-138-49632-3 (pbk)
ISBN 13: 978-1-4724-6889-5 (hbk)

Contents

List of Figures

List of Tables

Acknowledgements

I would like to express to Dr Frank Stech and Dr Zvi Lanier my deepest appreciation for their generosity in allowing me the unrestricted use of their work on the Yom Kippur War. Their generosity enabled me to do two things. The first was that I was able to contrast the way Dr Stech used Turner's model to explain failure with my use of it as a catalyst to *foresight*. The second was to use Dr Lanir's work, that provided a very interesting perspective on a number of important missteps by the Israelis in their build up to that war and to show how they may have been identified by use of my proposed framework. These two works provided the rich detail I required to illustrate my case. These authors' generosity enabled me to concentrate on making my case in the best way I was able rather than having to construct my argument while consciously counting the number of their words that I used. For this I will be forever grateful.

I would also like to acknowledge my wife Marian and friends Stuart Harper and Roger Carter for the helping me shape my script and making it more readable: for this my publishing editor should be eternally grateful!

Chapter 1

In Appreciation of Barry Turner

Introduction

Many inquiry reports blame managers for the *failures of foresight*. These reports are founded on the premise that, with a little more thought, these oversights which enabled the *crisis* to occur, would have been avoided. Is it really that simple? These inquiry reports then go on to offer recommendations that, in hindsight, may have prevented the events from occurring, but may also be the genesis of the next crisis. In many cases these recommendations have failed to avoid the *reverse fallacy*. I have described the *reverse fallacy* in more detail elsewhere.[1] For the purpose of this book, it is sufficient to define the *reverse fallacy* as an action or omission that is seen as being significant in the context of one particular tragedy, but then leads to a recommendation that is not universally appropriate. This may then result in *unintended consequences* at some point in the future. Such recommendations are just another type of *failure of foresight*.

The really important question however is whether, without *hindsight*, it is possible to avoid such failures. An important enabler when trying to avoid such *failures of foresight* is to be able to identify in advance the factors that might lead to such failure. Traditionally this is done through the means of a *risk assessment*. However this procedural approach has a number of significant drawbacks. The first is that *risk assessments* are generally conducted at the lower levels of an organisation. The risks identified, that are then collated into a risk register, become dominated by low-level safety issues. While important, these risks tend to distract managers from looking at what is strategically important. The second issue with this process is that it tends to exclude from consideration risks that would have significant consequences for the organisation because they are only likely to occur very rarely; these types of risk have become known as *Black Swans*.[2] If the volume of *Black Swans* identified within inquiry reports is a guide, they occur more often than

---

1   Lauder (2013:146–147)
2   Taleb (2007)

we would like to think. The third issue is that because busy managers are presented with detailed risk registers containing a plethora of problems that need to be addressed, they forget to assess for themselves what is important to their business. This final issue has been identified within the developing practice labelled *Enterprise Risk Management* (or *ERM*). ERM now requires a twin approach to be taken to *risk assessment*. One approach maintains the bottom-up method that is more generally used. The second approach requires a top-down assessment of the strategic risk; this approach has also been given the label *risk governance*. However, as this high-level approach to *risk assessment* is relatively immature, there is comparatively little written about it and, therefore, for practitioners, it may be difficult to see what this approach might look like. In this book I look to help close this gap.

The desire to close this gap has led to the quest for alternative or complimentary methods of generating *foresight* of failure. Attributed to Eric Hollnagel is the sentiment that, "What you look for is what you find; what you find is what you fix".[3] Hollnagel is warning us that we often have to know that a problem exists, what factors are at play, before we will find evidence for it in a particular case. Based on this premise I have conducted an extensive search of academic and other literature in order to identify these factors.[4] This research identified over 200 factors that others suggested are associated with failure. In my earlier work I grouped these factors into 20 categories for ease of their management. In this work I have gone further and, based on the idea behind the "magical number seven, plus or minus two", I have reduced the number of categories to seven. Throughout this book, you will find that I have used italics for the specific purpose of identifying these factors. Terms found in italics are the labels being used to signify that the term has a defined academic meaning. These signify a much richer meaning than the words used would appear to have in themselves. I italicise these phrases to warn my reader that they should resist any temptation to give such phrases new meanings or to use these terms in new ways not previously implied.

Aim

The aim of this book is twofold. These will be addressed in its two parts. The first goal is to take a theory of disaster originally used to understand the causes of a failure and then refine and re-imagine it as a tool for *foresight*. In Chapter

---

3　Hollnagel (2008)
4　Lauder (2011)

2 I will explain why I have chosen to use Turner's much quoted but under-utilised *Disaster Incubation Theory* rather than any of the other contenders. I will explain how I have seen it used by others and then conclude the first part of the book by re-imagining it as a catalyst for *foresight*. While conducting my analysis it became clear that it was essential to be able to identify which phase of the model an organisation was in. This dividing line evolved to be the *onset* of the *crisis*/disaster. In the simplest terms, organisations should know that they are either in a *crisis* or in the period during which a *crisis* is incubating; the issue becomes, "which *crisis*?"

For the purpose of generating *foresight*, once a *crisis* starts then it is too late. The second part of this book therefore looks at action that might be taken during the *incubation period*. This action is focused around the issues of prevent and prepare: that is, to prevent from happening that which the organisation must avoid and prepare the organisation to react to unwanted occurrences should they occur. I use the analysis of *complex* but well-known examples as the vehicle to develop my theoretical ideas. For the purpose of this book the terms disaster, accident, *crisis* and the like will be considered as synonymous and, for clarity, will just be referred to as unwanted events[5] (or, for ease of reference, "events"). This rule will only be broken if such terms are used as part of a technical term or a quote. In the end, the purpose of this book is to provide a theoretical construct that will form the basis for future empirical work. For managers, a more selective reading of this book may provide them with ideas of how to assess more effectively what the future may hold for them.

In the remainder of this section I endeavour to explain Turner's *Disaster Incubation Theory* and will use examples of how it has been applied to broaden our understanding of it. As a result of my original analysis of Turner's theory, I started to imagine how it might be used to promote *foresight* and this may be by a reshaping of its configuration. I conclude this chapter by describing the new form.

Disaster Incubation Theory Described

As originally written, *Disaster Incubation Theory* consisted of a six-stage process (see Table 1.1). The issue being addressed in this book is one of how to use generic disaster theories such as this one as a tool to prevent future disasters, to generate *foresight*. As this book is concerned with how existing knowledge

---

5   Lauder (2011:Ch2)

of the mechanisms that may lead to events might be used to prevent or reduce the effects of such events, it might therefore be assumed that this book is only concerned with the stages up to the emergence of the full event. This is not the case. We need to examine the whole model because someone else's future is our past: if we just concentrate on passing our insight to the next generation we may forget that those before us were trying to do the same for us. If we do not learn from the past, why should the next generation?

DISASTER INCUBATION THEORY STAGES

Turner's *Disaster Incubation Theory* stages are outlined in Table 1.1 and then described in more detail.

Table 1.1   *Disaster Incubation Theory*

Stage I – *Notionally Normal Starting Point*:
Allows the context to be set, enables beliefs about potential hazards to be articulated and the precautions that are considered normal to be articulated.

Stage II – *Incubation Period*:
Explains the accumulation of an unnoticed set of events which are at odds with the accepted beliefs about hazards and the norms of their avoidance. All of these events must fall into one of two categories: either the events are not known to anyone or they are known but not fully understood by all concerned.

Stage III – *Precipitating Event*:
The event "forces itself to the attention and transforms general perceptions of stage II". Such an event arouses attention because of its immediate characteristics, for example: the train crashes, the building catches fire, or share prices begin to drop.

Stage IV – *Onset*:
The *precipitating event* is followed immediately by the *onset* – Stage IV. The *onset* starts when "the immediate consequence of the collapse of cultural precautions becom[es] apparent". These are the direct and unanticipated consequences of the failure, an *onset* which occurs with varying rate and intensity, and over an area of varying scope.

Stage V – *Rescue and Salvage*:
First stage adjustment: the immediate post-collapse situation is recognised in ad hoc adjustments which permit the work of *rescue and salvage* to be started.

Stage VI – *Full Cultural Readjustment*:
An inquiry or assessment is carried out, and beliefs and *precautionary norms* are adjusted to fit the newly gained understanding of the world.

Stage I is described by Turner as "the set of culturally held beliefs" at a *notionally normal starting point*.[6] He expands this by talking of "initial culturally accepted beliefs about the world and its hazards" and the "associated precautionary norms set out in laws, codes of practice, mores, and folkways". This is interpreted to mean that before any analysis starts it is necessary to establish a point of departure, to establish the point at which the organisation felt that it was based on solid foundations. While it is accepted that this will be a social construct, its apparent arbitrary nature is legitimised by the explanation of why the point was chosen. Once the point has been chosen and justified, it is necessary to set the context for the subsequent analysis. From Turner's perspective the context was not only to include details of the hazards those involved believed they faced but also the precautions that they considered normal at that point and, by implication, appropriate. The essence of Stage I is to establish when (if ever) the system believed it had the *foresight* to manage the world it faced.

Stage II is described by Turner as the *incubation period* when a "disaster or a cultural collapse takes place because of some inaccuracy or inadequacy in the accepted norms and beliefs (where) there is an accumulation of a number of events that are at odds with the picture of the world and its hazards represented by existing norms and beliefs".[7] This is the period where the norms are eroded and factors are at work that led (directly or indirectly) to the subsequent events. This period is critical to the avoidance of *failures of foresight*. Turner's work also identified seven *issues of interest* identified within previous literature reviews.[8] *Issues of interest* are the main factors that have previously been identified as potential sources of system failure at whatever level they may occur. For example, the *issues of interest* identified by Turner, which I will explain in more detail in a later chapter, are:

- rigidity of perception and beliefs;
- decoy phenomena;
- information difficulties;
- *organisational exclusivity* (neglect of outside complaints);
- exacerbation of the hazards by strangers;
- failure to comply with regulations;
- the tendency to minimise emergent danger.

---

6   Turner (1976:381)
7   Turner (1976:381)
8   For example see Lauder (2011)

Stage III is described by Turner as the *precipitating event* (or what Lagadec called *the brutal audit*[9]) and states that "such an event arouses attention because of its immediate characteristics. For instance, the train crashes, the building catches fire, or share prices begin to drop".[10] These illustrations provided by Turner offer the idea of a "moment in time". This idea is reinforced by Turner when he says, "The precipitating event is *followed immediately* (emphasis added) by the *onset* – Stage IV – of the direct and unanticipated consequences of the failure." This *precipitating event* is therefore taken to be the moment when those involved perceive that they have lost control of events.

Stage IV is described by Turner as the *onset* and how it "occurs with varying rate and intensity, and over an area of varying scope".[11] This is interpreted to mean that such events may be over relatively quickly, such as happens in a plane crash, or may rage out of control for some time, such as a forest fire. The *onset* is taken to be the main body of the event. During the *onset* phase the *failure of foresight* might still occur if there had been a failure to foresee how the events might escalate or where this could or should have been prevented. *Onset* can be seen as a component of *crisis management*.

Stage V, what Turner labelled *rescue and salvage*, is the first stage of adjusting to the crisis that emerged at Stage IV, the *onset*. It is also a component of *crisis management*, "in which rapid and ad hoc redefinitions of the situation are made by participants to permit a recognition of the most important features of the failure and enable work of rescue and salvage to be carried out. When the immediate effects have subsided, it becomes possible to carry out a more leisurely and less superficial assessment of the incident, and to move toward something like a full cultural adjustment". This may be seen as covering both the acute and chronic stages of the *crisis management* process.

Stage VI, *full cultural readjustment*, is the final stage in Turner's model. This is the stage in which Turner sees us learning from such events. Turner says, "When the immediate effects have subsided, it becomes possible to carry out a more leisurely and less superficial assessment of the incident, and to move toward something like a full cultural adjustment ... of beliefs, norms, and precautions, making them compatible with the newly gained understanding of the world." Here we see the "definition of new well-structured problems and appropriate precautions in inquiries following the disaster". We see "the establishment of a new level of precautions and expectations" but he warns

---

9   Lagadec (1993:54)
10   Turner (1976:382)
11   Turner (1976:382)

Stage I – Notionally normal starting point	Stage II – Incubation period	Stage III – Precipitating event	Stage IV – Onset	Stage V – Rescue and salvage	Stage VI – Full cultural readjustment

Figure 1.1　Basic Turner model

that "this full cultural readjustment is limited by the amount of disagreement which prevails among groups about the effectiveness of any new precautions adopted".[12] He warns that local politics may interfere with the learning process.

In summary, Turner's stages are:

- Stage I – *Notionally normal starting point*
- Stage II – *Incubation period*
- Stage III – *Precipitating event*
- Stage IV – *Onset*
- Stage V – *Rescue and salvage*
- Stage VI – *Full cultural readjustment*

These stages may be depicted in a basic linear model: see Figure 1.1. This model illustrates a basic equity between the stages that follow each other in a chronological sequence. This provides my starting point.

These descriptions provide distinction between stages as an aid to future analysis.

Case Studies

The next step is to evaluate Turner's framework against case studies in order to develop a fuller appreciation of it. This is not an attempt to provide any new understanding about the case studies used nor does it wish to impart any judgement or comment on these papers' declared purpose. These cases are simply being used as three data sets to explore the types of questions that may help to refine our understanding of Turner's work as we move towards a tool to facilitate *foresight*. The data were chosen for the variety of contexts in which they were set, the variety in the scope of the events and, most importantly, the detail in which they described the development of the events. Two of the cases use Turners Model as their analytical method but the first one does not.

12　Turner (1976:764); Turner (1978:92)

The first data set is provided by Moore, Beck and Buchanan[13] and is a paper submitted to the Fifth Annual Seminar on Improving People Performance in Healthcare. The paper describes the occurrence of a twin *never event* during a surgical procedure. For UK NHS a *never event* is an event that should never occur. The paper focused on barriers to learning from such events.

The second data set was provided by Panos Constantinides' paper[14] on an explosion at the Mari Naval Base that occurred in the Republic of Cyprus on 11 July 2011. According to the author, the case starts in February 2009. It runs through to the production of the inquiry report in September 2011 and its consequences. While the paper used *Disaster Incubation Theory* to layout the events, the paper presents "a framework of decision-making across three layers, namely, operational, collective-choice, and constitutional".[15]

The third and final data set was provided Richard Oloruntoba's paper[16] on the 2009 bushfires in the State of Victoria, Australia. Again the paper used *Disaster Incubation Theory* to layout the events. The paper's focus was to suggest improvements that might be incorporated into the forest firefighting system in the future. Of the three papers this one sticks closest to my interpretation of Turner's method.

As the purpose of this book is to enhance understanding of how Turner's *Disaster Incubation Theory* stages may be used as part of *risk governance*, this section will describe the insight provided by each data set. While I have set out the data by stages, readers may, as an alternative, follow each data set through each stage in order to see more easily the thread of each story.

STAGE I – *NOTIONALLY NORMAL STARTING POINT*

Stage I lets us examine the culturally held beliefs about the hazards that exist and normal precautions that are deemed to be adequate. These are the precautions that have been taken at a specific point in time. This specified time is then deemed to be the *notionally normal starting point* for the subsequent discussion.

---

13   Moore, Beck and Buchanan (2013)
14   Constantinides (2013)
15   Constantinides (2013:1672)
16   Oloruntoba (2013)

Data set 1

In terms of laying out "beliefs about the world and its hazards", data set 1 indicates that the UK Department of Health have designated 25 hazards as *never events*. This list includes the events described in this paper. The paper also explains, as for *precautionary norms*, that there was a role for the procedures known as "the London protocol" and the World Health Organisation's checklist procedure.

Data set 2

While the narrative of data set 2 states that Stage I starts in February 2009, it goes on to describe how the events were the result of action to enforce two UN resolutions (1747 (2007) and 1803 (2008)). This would suggest that the case, when seen through the lens of *Disaster Incubation Theory*, actually should have started with UN Resolution 1747 in 2007 as this will have generated its own associated jeopardy/threats and these should have had their own linked *precautionary norms*. For his purpose the author went back to 20 January 2009 and told of a cargo ship's detention by the US Navy on the grounds that it was breaking UN sanctions against Iran. He then laid out the events leading to the ship's cargo of munitions ending up being stored at the Mari Naval Base. The paper did not, however, directly discuss the perceived hazards that this presented to those involved or the *precautionary norms* in place at the time. What analysis of this paper did demonstrate was that without this context it proved impossible to come to any view about the subsequent events except that the outcome was definitely unwanted by any normal standards. Without this context, all other judgement could be seen to be heavily loaded by *hindsight*.

Data set 3

Data set 3 provided an interesting contrast to the other two. Data set 3 used Stage I to describe how those involved perceived the effectiveness of their *precautionary norms*. The point made by Oloruntoba was that officials in the organisations "at the heart of bushfire prevention, planning and mitigation activities … seem to have (had) confidence in the planning and mitigation processes".[17] However it was not possible from this work to determine how they perceived the threats and hazards, how these hazards were matched by the *precautionary norms* and therefore whether the plans were anything more than *fantasy documents*.[18]

---

17 Oloruntoba (2013:1684)
18 Clarke and Perrow (1996)

Summary

Analysis of the data sets demonstrates that without a clear context that establishes a baseline, it is not possible to understand fully the forces at work in any situation. Analysis also showed that great care needs to be taken when selecting a *notionally normal starting point* and this selection needs to be fully explained. As a tool for *foresight* the selection of the *notionally normal starting point* would provide the first important debating point. This baseline needs to establish both what the problem is, what the hazards might be, and how the system plans to respond either by preventing the hazard manifesting itself or how the system intends to respond should it occur. In practice, when fully understood, situations rarely present simple choices. Any analysis that does not factor in this complexity is therefore likely to be flawed. As a *foresight* tool, this complexity and the resulting ambiguities and uncertainties need to be established at this point.

STAGE II – *INCUBATION PERIOD*

Stage II examines the unnoticed set of events and errors that accumulate as the situation evolves. This is seen to put the new context at odds with the beliefs about hazards and the normal precautions put in place to avoid them that had previously been accepted. This may, in turn, result in the accepted *precautionary norms* being inadequate. The data sets were examined from two perspectives. The first concerns chronology and layering and the second is for evidence of the *issues of interest* used to enhance or direct the analysis.

Data set 1

Data set 1 provides a relatively simple and abbreviated scenario over a very limited timeframe (a day). This lack of complexity requires very little collation and analysis in order to understand the sequence of events. Taken at an undifferentiated level (without defining *micro* to *mega levels*), situations may always seem simpler than they actually are. This data set highlights the need to develop a rich understanding of events. This may be done by layering the activity so that it can be fully understood. In this case the layers might have differentiated between roles within the surgical process and where decision-making responsibilities lay. The authors of the paper do, in the end, refer to Rasmussen's layering approach;[19] the layers were given as: 1) government, 2) regulators, 3) organisation, 4) management, 5) staff, 6) infrastructure

---

19 Rasmussen (1997)

and equipment and 7) processes and procedures. Their interpretation of Rasmussen's original theory only goes to show how flexibly it can be used. The paper does not use *issues of interest* to enhance its analysis.

Data set 2

In the case of data set 2, for Constantinides, the *incubation period* starts when the explosives are moved into storage at the Mari Naval Base on 6 March 2009 and this period runs through to 4 July 2011. The case provides a rich stream of data within a single narrative, based over a set timescale, which lays out the discussions about what to do next with the cargo of explosives. It is accepted that this might be part of the author's device to make his case for a multi-layer decision-making framework: by separating the narrative into the four defined layers, that interaction (or demonstrable lack of interaction) between the layers can be seen clearly. In this case the layers were: 1) the operational layer, 2) collective-choice layer and 3) the constitutional layer. He explains that the operational layer is the "layer of action and … is directly linked with operational responsibility". The second layer is one collective-choice that "explains the layer of authoritative decision-making". It is directly linked with political responsibility. The final layer is constitutional, this is "where collective-choice mechanisms are designed".[20] This would suggest that, as the use of layers helps post-incident analysis then, the use of layers may also be useful when applied to *foresight* tools. The paper does not discuss how the baseline *precautionary norms* for the safe storage of explosives were ignored and why this occurred during the period that the problem was incubating. The paper does not use *issues of interest* to enhance its analysis.

Data set 3

Data set 3 also provides a rich stream of data. Data set 3 divides Stage II into three main issues. These issues are: 1) unpredictable people in high hazard areas, 2) land-use planning failures and 3) unprecedented weather patterns. These issues were developed and explained using a defined chronology. While each proposition offered was substantiated by the evidence provided, it did not, however, elucidate the gaps and dysfunctional interactions between the various structural layers inherent at any set of organisation boundaries. This would suggest that any *foresight* device needs to explore and explain any such gaps and dysfunctional interactions.

---

20 Constantinides (2013:1668)

Oloruntoba acknowledges Turner's *issues of interest* and can be seen to use them in imaginative ways in order to enrich his understanding of this *crisis*. He says that:

> ... *often, more than one unknown source of danger begins to accumulate either because (a) erroneous assumptions were made, or (b) one problem may have acted as a decoy, or (c) complaints of danger from non-experts from outside the organization are simply dismissed ..., or (d) the natural human instinct of reluctance to fear the worst overtakes evidence or common-sense, or (e) there are challenges regarding information handling in complex situations.*

The author then uses these ideas to structure his argument.

Summary

These data sets show the utility of both layering and using *issues of interest* in order to develop a richer understanding of a problem area. For *foresight*, this reinforces the notion that by advocating the use of layers, those involved in the *risk discourse* can be stimulated to think more deeply about how their organisation interacts both internally and with external agents. This debate, if candid enough, may then reveal where these interactions are dysfunctional. The way Oloruntoba has used Turner's *issues of interest* also provides an interesting twist to the debate. Rather than using Turner's ideas literally, Oloruntoba has interpreted them for his context. As a tool for *foresight*, this suggests that any set of *issues of interest* should only provide a starting point in the *risk discourse*. The *issues of interest* provide a stimulus that enables the group to explore their own knowledge and experience to determine what is critical to them.

STAGE III – PRECIPITATING EVENT

Even in hindsight identifying the event that constitutes Stage III presents a problem. Stage III is described by Turner as the event that "forces itself to the attention and transforms general perceptions of stage 2". He explains that such an event arouses attention because of its immediate characteristics. The examples he gives are train crashes, buildings catching fire or when share prices begin to drop. However, as we shall see, this point is not as easy to identify as it might initially seem to be.

Data set 1

Data set 1 starts to demonstrate the difficulties that might occur when trying to identify the *precipitating event*. In this case there were two occurrences that constituted a *never event*. In this case "the operating surgeon did not check Mr Mitcham's wristband, and selected the implant lens based on the original theatre list".[21] One *never event* was the use of the wrong implant and the second was the misidentification of the patient. For the first to happen the second must have already occurred. Therefore, the issue becomes one of determining when the first occurred for, up to this point, it would have been possible (however unlikely the corrective action may have been) to have prevented the *never event* from occurring.

The *precipitating event* can therefore be seen to be the point at which the misidentification took place. The question of "who was responsible" is, in this case, only coincidental in that it sets the time the event happened. The fact that it is not clear who had the final responsibly to correctly identify the patient should have been a red flag for the surgical process overall as this danger is recognised as being the *fallacy of social redundancy*.[22] The point is that each *never event* will happen at a moment in time. At this point in time a Rubicon will have been crossed and so there can be no reversal of this new state. If this point of no return in a process is recognised then it would provide a *point for reflection*.[23] This is a point at which *mindfulness* should be specially exercised leading to reflections such as "we are about to step over this point of no return, is every necessary condition in place to enable us to proceed safely?" This should be compared with the rather mindless way in which these two Rubicon moments seem to have been crossed in this instance. In this case the *precipitating event* can be seen to be a *micro* level (a *sharp end*) issue.

Data set 2

Constantinides is very clear as to what he sees as being his *precipitating event*. He explains that on the night of 4 July 2011, the officers in charge on site found that containers had deformed. The officer informed the Commander of the Naval Base who, in turn, went to inspect the site. The officer is quoted as saying, "The way the container expanded … I realized (it) … may have been caused by an internal combustion."[24]

21 Moore et al. (2013:14)
22 Snook (2000:210)
23 Barton and Sutcliffe (2009)
24 Constantinides (2013:1664)

As the officers were concerned with the dangerous state of the explosive materiel, they perceived that they had a *crisis* which they now needed to prevent from turning into a disaster. The event had brought itself to their attention and transformed general perceptions of Stage II. In that the event (the visit) had "transform(ed) general perceptions", the night of the 4 July can rightly be seen to qualify as the *precipitating event.* However, also as stated earlier, Turner said that "such an event arouses attention because of its **immediate characteristics**" [bold added for emphasis]. Compared with what was to come on the 11 July, the visit on the 4 July might just be seen as an early warning of an impending *crisis*. This case has therefore stimulated other thoughts about how *Disaster Incubation Theory* may be used.

Here I see there being an issue of what an academic might refer to as the level of analysis and what the practitioner might see as a boundary issue. At different levels of analysis different people have different perception of what is a *crisis* (this subject will be covered in more detail later in this book). Putting it more simply, this is a question of "who cares about what at what level of the organisation"? In this case where are the boundaries to be drawn? I question whether this is a *micro level* case (the issue being the safe local storage of explosive materiel) or whether it is a *mega level* issue of how political interference at governmental level can jeopardise the safe storage of explosive materiel. From what Constantinides says, there is evidence that the events of the 4 July had not "force(d) itself to the attention and transform(ed) general perceptions of stage 2" at the top government level for it took two days to set up a committee to decide what to do and another day before any action was taken on the ground. This does not suggest the urgency triggered by a perceived *crisis*!

This case also raises the issue of identifying "points of no return" raised by the first data set. The question that I would have is whether those involved found themselves in a position that was recoverable or not. With rapid and appropriate action, could the explosion have been prevented after the 4 July discovery? Had the cultural precautions collapsed or were they only temporarily degraded? If the position was recoverable, this would lend weight to the argument against 4 July providing the *precipitating event*; if the position was not recoverable this would lend weight in favour of selecting 4 July as the *precipitating event.*

To determine the *precipitating event* in this case it is necessary to determine the point at which control of the situation was lost. Data set 2 provides a dilemma. By 03:40 hrs on the 11 July 2011 some of the containers had caught fire. At 05:50 hrs there was an explosion estimated to be in the order of 1.5 kiloton. It killed 12 people and destroyed a major power station. It is important to note that, at this point, the continuing safe storage of the munitions was no longer an issue. The event had precipitated a *crisis* of a quite different nature. Clearly control had been lost at 05:50 hrs on 11 July when the explosion occurred. The question is, had control been lost earlier? For example, had control been lost at the point that the fire was identified (03:40 hrs)? It should be noted that the attempts made to fight this fire were against established procedures (providing an example of *practical drift*); this would lend credence to the case for 03:40 hrs being the key time. Finally, there must be a question as to whether control had actually been lost by the 4 July 2011. As the author of the data set (Constantinides) included the events of 4 July within Stage III, this would suggest that he seems to think so. Within this data set there is no discussion of what else might have been done during the period 4–11 July 2011 that might have prevented the fire and explosion occurring.

From the data available it is not possible for me to determine the actual *precipitating event* but the case does highlight the problems. In this case, as written by Constantinides, the *precipitating event* can be seen to be a *micro level* (a *sharp end*) issue. However, when you change the level of analysis to the *mega level*, it might also be seen to be a *blunt end* issue. This discrepancy reminds us of the importance of setting the unit and level of analysis and then consistently following this throughout the analysis.

Data set 3

In the case of the 2009 Victoria Bushfires, data set 3 provides a similar dilemma to the one identified within data set 2. "Ignition of bushfires … seems to have largely been caused by over-heated electricity cables (although) some other fires seem to have been deliberately lit by arsonists".[25] The initial bushfires broke out on 28 January 2009 at Delburn. Another bushfire broke out on 4 February at Burnyip. In themselves, bushfires in the State of Victoria are seen as normal occurrences and are managed at a local level in most circumstances. While these local fires may produce a *crisis* at the local (*micro*) level, they are unlikely to register as a *crisis* at higher levels (the *macro* being district and *mega* being State levels). At the time, and when seen at a local level, there was probably no discernible pattern in these early fires. In this case, however, the potential *crisis* was identified at the *mega level*. While still ambiguous, weather forecasts had warned that the 7 February 2009 was likely to be an extremely hot day and therefore the State's particular vulnerability to bush fires was recognised.

---

25 Oloruntoba (2013:1690)

Oloruntoba states:

> *As many as 400 large individual fires were recorded on 7 February, 2009*
> *and spreading fast ... The onset of the consequences of ignition, and the*
> *failure of existing belief systems unfolded at a high rate and intensity,*
> *and over a large area ... other bushfires sprang up as temperatures rose*
> *and wind speeds increased "spotting" or the distribution of embers.*[26]

By the end of the day over 200 people were dead. The loss of control in this case was not only experienced at the *micro level* but at the *mega level* as well. In this context, any temporary loss of control at the *micro level* is, however, considered to be less relevant than the loss of control at the higher levels. While teams at the *micro level* might be able to suppress individual fires, at the *mega level* the overall picture of bushfires was clearly out of control. For this reason I place the *precipitating event* as being the *macro level* (a *blunt end*) loss of control that occurred on 7 February 2009.

Summary

The *precipitating event* for any such events is seen to be the moment that control is lost at the level deemed critical. While to some this definition may seem ambiguous, to others it provides flexibility. In terms of *foresight*, I would argue that it is up to those involved to use the flexibility it provides to remove any ambiguity in their case. While *precipitating events* are normally pushed down to the *micro level* (the *sharp end*), they may also occur at the *macro* or *mega levels* (the *blunt end*).

One of the key difficulties in determining the *precipitating event* is the dividing line between what is normal and what is abnormal. It is recognition of the abnormal rather than the normal that provides a warning of failure. In common usage the term *chaos* suggests complete disorder and confusion. *Chaos* theory provides a different perspective; this body of work suggests that the confusion or apparent disorder is due to the patterns inherent in an activity being too *complex* for the viewer to recognise or understand. In simpler terms, a perception of *chaos* occurs when the world around you does not make sense. In this context, *chaos*, which is often transitory, can be seen to be normal. It is therefore *abnormal chaos* that we are trying to identify. (I examine this idea in more detail in the next chapter.) *Normal chaos* can be seen as the multiple small changes needed to keep any plan of action on course; this state is seen to be

---

26   Oloruntoba (2013:1691)

normal while, to outsiders, it may look *chaotic*. The transition to *abnormal chaos* is when the situation reaches the point that loss of control is perceived by those affected. *Organisational oscillation*[27] means that they are in constant flux around this threshold, which makes the time they actually trip that threshold more difficult to spot.

One way to resolve these difficulties is to see the incident that precipitates the event as "the point of no return" where control is recognised as being lost and when it is not possible to return to the present state but only to one that becomes recognised as the new normal. This point is not when the event is deemed to be inevitable but when those involved sense their powerlessness to prevent it happening or escalating.

If this revised *Disaster Incubation Theory* framework is to be used as a *foresight* tool it will, however, not have quite the same problems. The issue would not be to identify when the *precipitating event* occurred but to decide what might constitute a *precipitating event*. With the use of tools such as *premortems*,[28] it may be possible to *anticipate* the emergence of unwanted events (whether they manifest themselves at the *micro* or *mega levels*) and to insert *points for reflection* designed to disrupt any *dysfunctional momentum* towards disaster.

STAGE IV – ONSET

The *onset* stage consists of the main body of any event that goes past the initial moment of *crisis* and lasts as long as those involved do not feel that they have the situation under their control. As noted earlier, Turner described *onset* as "the immediate consequence of the collapse of cultural precautions becoming apparent". During this period the situation may escalate or it may be contained depending on how it is managed.

Data set 1

In the case of data set 1, the nature of *never events* (in this case the misidentification of the patient and the implanting of the wrong lens) mean that they are binary; the event either has or has not occurred. *Onset* was minimal as the *never event* cannot escalate; it could only morph into another type of *crisis* such as the death of the patient. In this case the *never event* was immediately recognised and corrected.

---

27 Reason (1998:4–5)
28 Klein (2007)

Data set 2

As written by Constantinides, the *Onset* stage within data set 2 starts on 5 July 2011. He outlines how the "custodian" officer briefed the Chief of Staff of the National Guard and how they went together to brief the Minister of Defence. At that meeting, the "custodian" officer recommended that a red alert be declared and that the base should be evacuated immediately. However the Minister of Defence ignored this remark and instructed that an expert panel be set up to examine the issues. The expert panel report was finalised on 6 July 2011. The expert panel recommended that the containers be hosed with sea water and that the deformed container be removed. However, he points out that no officials from the Cyprus Electricity Authority were informed about the potential risks to their nearby power plant. On 7 July 2011, the report was sent to the Ministry of Defence and on 8 July 2011 a fire engine of the National Guard went to the Naval Base and hosed the containers with water.

This section of Constantinides' work provides an interesting insight into how the author used Turner's work. During the *onset* stage the situation both escalated and morphed into a political *crisis*. The explosion destroyed the adjacent power station and started fires in the area that had to be contained and subdued. As the authority regained control of the local situation (the fires and the casualties) the *crisis* turned from an issue of whether, where and how to store munitions into a *crisis* of power generation, finance and politics. This data set illustrates how the nature of the boundaries set will inform the overall nature of the *crisis*. Initially the issues were limited to the storage of potentially hazardous material; only later did the issues expand to include wider political considerations. This means that the form of the events is shaped by individual perceptions of those involved and so may misidentify the true nature of the most critical part of the coming *crisis*.

Data set 3

Within data set 3 under the *onset* stage it describes "the immediate and unanticipated consequence ... was that as many as 400 large individual fires were recorded on 7 February 2009".[29] These crises of continuing fires then continue to evolve as bushfires flared up for about a month perpetuated by forces such as the high temperatures and increased wind speeds; this in turn increased "spotting" (a label given to the distribution of burning embers that cause more fires). As with the previous case, the extent of the events examined

---

29 Oloruntoba (2013:1691)

is defined by how the boundaries were set. In this case the events escalated and continued until the weather turned in favour of the firefighters. Unlike previous examples, where the transition between Stages IV and V can be seen as being abrupt, in this case the transition we see is an overlap as the forces that perpetuate the forest fires are countered by the energy and resource employed to suppress them. We can therefore depict the relationship between these two stages as being a *force field*.[30] In terms of *foresight* this leads to the conclusion that *failure of foresight* may also contribute to ways the duration of a *crisis* may be extended. This highlights the need to examine how any event may escalate or change after the *precipitating event* and consideration is needed to *anticipate* these changes or how the system may be given the capacity to absorb them.

Summary

The *onset* stage is seen to last for the duration of the *crisis* event and might be characterised as being part of the *crisis management* phase. *Crisis management* is a discipline in its own right; in general the details of this discipline are outside the scope of this book. I would therefore characterise the *onset* stage as covering the forces that look to perpetuate the *crisis*. From the perspective of *failure of foresight*, the issue here is to foresee how the *precipitating event* may escalate further. This would encompass what these forces might be, to *anticipate* how these may be countered and to develop the capability to be ready to do so.

STAGE V – RESCUE AND SALVAGE

The *rescue and salvage* stage is said by Turner to be when "the immediate post-collapse situation is recognized in ad hoc adjustments which permit the work of rescue and salvage to be started".

Data set 1

The events described in data set 1 were not allowed to escalate further and so the situation moved into rescue, salvage and readjustment processes. "The surgeon detected the error when completing the operation notes after the procedure. Mr Mitcham was informed, and was returned to theatre where the implant was replaced with the correct lens. He suffered no harm."[31] *Rescue and salvage* was quickly achieved. In this case we do see the linear relationship between *onset* and *rescue and salvage* as depicted in Figure 1.1.

---

30 Johnson and Scholes (1997:459)
31 Moore et al. (2103:14)

Data set 2

In data set 2, Constantinides again is clear about how he sees this phase being used. However, as Turner labels this *rescue and salvage*, it is difficult to reconcile Constantinides' use of Stage V with "the immediate post-collapse situation" articulated in Turner's original work. Constantinides used the Stage V label to cover the events of 11 July 2011. He describes how around 03:40 hrs, officials heard explosions and how the commanding officer saw that containers had caught fire. He describes how, at this point, they immediately sounded the alarm. He describes how all personnel on duty at the base were mobilised, how key personnel were alerted and how fire engines were dispatched to site. He states that at 05:17 hrs the Chief Commander of the Navy ordered everyone to evacuate the base and how around 05:50 hrs there was a large explosion. This explosion was estimated to consist of between 80,000 and 160,000 kg of explosives. The result was the deaths of 13 people, injuries to 62 more and a complete destruction of the neighbouring power plant. Also, damage was caused to the infrastructure of the Naval Base, buildings and other premises in nearby villages, and the A1 highway.

To me this is a description of a *precipitating event* as it finished with an explosion and it does not seem to cover either rescue or salvage operations. I would see the *rescue and salvage* stage starting after the explosion. Constantinides' work does not, however, cover any aspects of the rescue or salvage on site but does cover the subsequent *onset* of the political *crisis* that then enveloped the nation's President.

Data set 3

Within data set 3 Oloruntoba agrees that "Stage 5 is the first phase of necessary post-disaster ad hoc adjustments which permit the work of rescue, relief, and salvage to be initiated". He recognises that this is when the immediate *crisis* situation is recognised and how ad hoc assessments of the situation enable quick short-term adjustments to be made. He sees how, in their turn, these enable rescue, relief and salvage activities to begin. He also sees how that, at the heart of this activity, command, control and incident management challenge the systems data collection and dissemination processes.

While Oloruntoba concurs that this stage is about the rapid and ad hoc definitions and redefinitions allowing participants to resolve the problem of emergency rescue, his focus is on what should have happened rather than how this emergency was resolved. He concentrates on information challenges, evacuation and disaster declaration issues. It is therefore not possible from the data available to develop any real understanding of the *force field* in play between the *onset* and *rescue and salvage* stages.

Summary

Each data set provides a different way of describing the *rescue and salvage* stage. Data set 1 provides the clearest description of how the surgical team rescued the situation. The other data sets did not make this so clear. In terms of generating *foresight* we can see that Stage V provides the opportunity to debate how the *resilience* of their organisation can be enhanced and what needs to be done to supplement the current capability.

STAGE VI – *FULL CULTURAL READJUSTMENT*

Stage VI, the *full cultural readjustment* stage, is the period during which the organisation can learn from this particular *crisis* control. During this stage we see inquiries or other assessments being carried out whereby organisational beliefs and *precautionary norms* are assessed and then adjusted to fit the newly gained understanding of the world.

Data set I

Data set 1 states that, the next month, "A Serious Incident Management Group was convened … They agreed that, as a 'surgical placement of wrong implant', and as a 'misidentification of patient', this incident met the criteria for a never event".[32] This stage was the main focus of the original paper and therefore the paper makes some points on the learning process worth noting. The key amongst these is that the authors use theory to divide the learning process into two phases. These are the *passive learning* and *active learning* phases. *Passive learning* consists of the investigation, the inquiry deliberations and the production of recommendations. The *active learning* phase consists of all the analysis, training and change management required to implement the inquiry's recommendations. However, in this case, the practice did not use this dividing line as the learning process seems to have been disrupted by other political considerations, as Turner foretold. As a result the author resorted to telling the chronological sequence of the subsequent learning.

---

32 Moore et al. (2103:14)

Data set 2

Data set 2 summed up the *full cultural readjustment* by describing how, in the aftermath of the explosion the Minister of Defence, the Minister of Foreign Policy and the National Guard Commander-in-Chief resigned. Constantinides states how the opposition parties demanded the resignation of the President and how, on 20 July 2011, the Government appointed an independent committee to report on the events that led up to the disaster and how the Cyprus Police also launched a criminal investigation. He explains how there was initial criticism from the opposition parties and the general public because the key investigator allegedly had a close relationship with the President of Cyprus who appointed him. However the report released on 3 October 2011 concluded that the President held the principal responsibility. The investigator requested that the Attorney General look into the possibility of serious crimes being committed. The President rejected the results of the investigation, denying any personal responsibility and accusing the key investigator of exceeding his mandate.

From this case we can see Turner's point that the learning process will be politically biased, however the case does not develop or provide evidence for societal and *organisational learning*.

Data set 3

Within data set 3 Oloruntoba agrees that this stage describes the efforts involved in assessing the causes of the disaster, and how the culturally approved beliefs and precautions that were in place turned out to be so ineffective and failed disastrously when needed. Oloruntoba stays close to Turner's construct in that he sees that at this stage the pattern of events that developed in the *incubation period* becomes clearer and reveals how other events contributed at other stages. He outlines the role played by "formal investigations and informal personal reflections" and how it is hoped that these lead to the necessary adjustments to beliefs, assumptions, statutes and laws in order to prevent future recurrence.

In this case the formal inquiry was conducted by the Victorian Bushfires Royal Commission chaired by The Hon. Bernard Teague AO. The commission made 67 recommendations. Whether these lessons were learnt and by whom are not covered within Oloruntoba's paper.

Summary

Learning from a *crisis* is a major consideration for the public and so for politicians; we hear the often-used phrase "this should never happen again". Unfortunately it is probable that such events will, as society still has a long way to go before it is able to learn effectively from these incidents. In terms of stimulating *foresight*, these data sets do suggest two considerations. The first is the separation of *passive learning* (the investigation or inquiry) from *active learning* (that is the implementation of the inquiry recommendations). Directly linked to the first is the second consideration. This is the fact that *passive learning* relates to the past incident and *active learning* relates to future incidents. This in turn would suggest a major deficiency in Turner's model. Turner's model, like many models that have followed, put learning at the end of the process. The *active learning* phase, however, relates to the next *crisis* and not the one that has just passed and so the model needs to include learning as part of the incubation stage.

Reshaping Turner's Model

The case studies enable us to have a clear understanding of how Turner's stages may be used to create *foresight*. In Turner's earlier work he used Roman numerals to number his stages as I have done up to this point. To help differentiate the re-imagined stages I will annotate these using Arabic numerals.

- Stage 1 enables the perceived hazards and the normal associated precautions to be defined at a set time. This forms a baseline against which the *drift* or event *incubation* can be assessed.
- Stage 2 covers the period during which the event incubates up to the point at which control of the situation is lost. The case studies suggest that these events may be more easily understood if the chronology is separated into *micro*, *mezzo*, *macro* and *mega* layers.
- Stage 3 is seen to determine when control of this situation is lost and whether this happens at the *micro* or another level.
- Stage 4 is seen to be concerned with the forces that escalate or perpetuate the event.
- Stage 5 encompasses the forces and resources that can be used to counter the forces that are escalating or perpetuating the event.
- Stage 6 is the drawing of lessons both passively and actively.

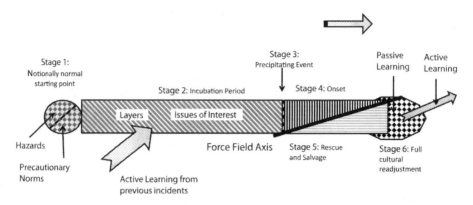

Figure 1.2   *Disaster Incubation Theory* **schematic**

While the first two stages concern *foresight* when it comes to the prevention of an event, the latter stages (3, 4 and 5) concern *foresight* when it comes to preparing to reduce how an event might escalate. Finally, whereas most *crisis* and disaster models show learning as an outcome of an event, its importance as an outcome might be viewed as being far less significant than the ability to learn lessons from the past. When compared with the body of knowledge that already exists, the new lessons learnt from any particular new incident are of minimal significance. Research shows that few new lessons are now identified from inquiry reports; the lesson that is now revealed is that what is already known has not been absorbed by the organisation concerned.

The data provided by the case studies has enabled me to re-imagine Turner's *Disaster Incubation Theory* model. In Figure 1.2 we can see the revised model. The refinements to Turner's work are made in *italics* in the following tables of refined stages.

STAGE 1 – NOTIONALLY NORMAL STARTING POINT

Stage 1's purpose is to set a baseline against which the *incubation* of the event can be seen. In order to establish the required baseline the *risk discourse* needs to articulate the boundaries for the debate, the hazards perceived, the perspective taken by those involved and associated norms for the precautions to be taken (whether these are formal or informal). It is also seen to be important that the key assumptions on which all judgements are based are articulated. Stage 1 is redefined in Table 1.2.

Table 1.2   Stage 1 redefined

Stage 1 – *Notionally Normal Starting Point*:
The set of culturally held beliefs and assumptions about the hazards faced and the formal or informal precautions required and taken at a notionally "normal" starting point. This articulation needs to include the perspective held by those involved and it needs to identify their associated priorities.
    This articulation needs to consider:

- The potential consequences of non-delivery of a defined output, of any barrier to delivery, any unexpected occurrence, any unknowns and any *unintended consequence* that may emerge from the delivery process.
- Setting, explaining and justifying the geographic, temporal and organisational boundaries for the discussion.
- Defining victim categories (based on Perrow's four types: operators, voluntary, involuntary and intergenerational) in order to assess who cares, how much about what.

STAGE 2 – *INCUBATION PERIOD*

Stage 2 describes the period during which the event emerges as (or incubates into) something unwanted (see Table 1.3).

Table 1.3   Stage 2 redefined

Stage 2 – *Incubation Period*:
- The period during which there is an accumulation of an unnoticed set of events and when it is necessary to test for changes in assumptions, practices and beliefs which are at odds with the originally accepted beliefs about hazards and the norms of their avoidance and how this may stress the system.

STAGE 3 – *PRECIPITATING EVENT*

Stage 3 is seen as defining the moment when those involved are seen to have lost control of the situation: it is seen to be the point of no return (see Table 1.4). Prior to this moment there were options, no matter how unlikely, that if taken, could have prevented the event from occurring. This test is chosen as it is seen to correspond with the testing made during post-event public inquiries.[33]

---

33 Lauder (2013)

Table 1.4   Stage 3 redefined

> **Stage 3 – *Precipitating Event*:**
> • The event that forces those involved, at whatever level they operate, to appreciate that they have lost control of their situation and that they have crossed the threshold between normal and *abnormal chaos*.

STAGE 4 – ONSET

Stage 4 should be used to examine how a perceived event may escalate and develop (see Table 1.5). This would be designed to provide *foresight* and thereby enable mitigation efforts to be planned. Stages 4 and 5 may be considered in a similar way to a *force field analysis*[34] where the forces that may cause the event to escalate (Stage 4) are contrasted with the forces that may be used to control and mitigate the effects of the event (Stage 5).

Table 1.5   Stage 4 redefined

> **Stage 4 – *Onset*:**
> • *Onset* immediately follows the *precipitating event* and may, through unanticipated consequences of the failure or inability, *or the failure to intercede appropriately in a timely manner*, escalate with varying rate and intensity, and over an area of varying scope.

STAGE 5 – RESCUE AND SALVAGE

Stage 5 provides the second half of the *force field analysis* (see Table 1.6).

Table 1.6   Stage 5 redefined

> **Stage 5 – *Rescue and Salvage*:**
> • First stage adjustment: the immediate post-collapse situation is recognised in ad hoc adjustments which permit the work of *rescue and salvage* to be started. The stage starts with ad hoc adjustments that enable the initial *crisis* to be managed and evolve into more carefully planned measures as control of the situation is regained. This stage continues until those involved feel that they have established a new normal state.

---

34 Johnson and Scholes (1997:459)

STAGE 6 – *FULL CULTURAL READJUSTMENT*

Stage 6 provides the opportunity for an organisation to adapt and adjust to a new situation (see Table 1.7). While organisations may espouse learning from such *crisis*, "unfortunately, the typical reaction to organisational disasters is to create more and more precise external controls. In most instances, this is an excellent formula for undercutting productivity and, at the same time, increasing the likelihood of future disasters".[35] We see the organisation trying to learn from the events (*passive learning*) and to put those lessons into practice (*active learning*). It does, however, have to be recognised that an organisation's ability to learn and adapt will be affected by the politics, local and otherwise. Politics start with the inquiry that may only use a very limited amount of the knowledge available to the wider community; this is typified by judge-led inquiries that only look at the circumstances directly related to the incident and often ignore much of the relevant knowledge developed by researchers and practitioners.[36] As Turner warns us, "this full cultural readjustment is limited by the amount of disagreement which prevails among groups about the effectiveness of any new precautions adopted".[37]

Table 1.7   Stage 6 redefined

Stage 6 – *Full Cultural Readjustment*:
- An inquiry or assessment (*passive learning*) is carried out, challenging any new understanding against the existing knowledge base, in order to identify the key lessons and to make recommendations, filtered by reality, how beliefs and *precautionary norms* are adjusted to fit the newly gained understanding of the world. The *passive learning* is followed by *active learning* which includes the change management necessary to implement the proposal that will prevent or mitigate the next *crisis*.

Conclusion

In this chapter I have looked at how Turner's model, originally designed to explain disasters, might be developed into a tool to promote *foresight*. Having considered a number of options, which I explain in my next chapter, it was Barry Turner's original *Disaster Incubation Theory* that seemed to not only to provide a good basis for a *foresight* framework but also to be amenable to the changes deemed necessary. Having selected the model I explained it in more

35 Bozeman (2011:136)
36 Lauder (2013)
37 Turner (1976:764); Turner (1978:92)

detail based on Turner's writings. To increase our understanding of the model, I have used three case studies, two of which have used Turner's model as their analytical method. One of the first issues when using this model is to be able to identify where in the process you sit. In broad terms, it is important to realise if you are not in a *crisis* then you are in the period in which one is incubating. The issue is to identify which *crisis* this is!

From the data we saw how important it was to use Stage 1 to establish a clear baseline for future deliberations. From Stage 2 we saw how layers and *issues of interest* can be used as a starting point for *risk discourse*. From discussion of Stage 3 we saw the potential difficulties that can be encountered when trying to identify the *precipitating event* and how this can be confused by a careless use of levels of an analysis. This is what you are trying to prevent during Stage 2. We also saw how Stages 4 and 5 do not follow each other but form a *force field* between the forces that look to perpetuate the *crisis* and those being employed to resolve it: these latter forces need to be prepared in advance as part of the *foresight* exercise. Finally, as part of Stage 6, we learnt of the need to differentiate between *active* and *passive learning* and to realise that what we learn from others' previous experience is probably more important for society than the lessons we will provide society. Finally I have re-imagined Turner's model and elaborated on the purpose of each stage. In my next chapter I look to go into more detail about the issues that need to be addressed when in pursuit of *foresight*.

Chapter 2
Selecting a Framework for Foresight

Introduction

Most current approaches to strategy and planning are based on the premise of selecting objectives and working out how these will be delivered. This is a basic and conventional approach and, as many would argue, is generally successful. Here I have to acknowledge the existence of what Mintzberg and others call "the learning school"[1] that sees strategy formulation as an emergent process; this is not, however, quite the same as looking at how strategy formulation manages emergent properties of the system. We still have some way to go before we really understand the relationship between strategy and *chaos*. In the conventional approach it is assumed that the object will be achieved if the steps are envisaged correctly and enacted successfully. However, a richer understanding of such issues can be generated by looking at the issue from a different perspective. As leading authors agree that "if one accepts the premise that the dynamic of success is chaotic (then) all forms of long-term planning are completely ineffective",[2] we have to find an alternative way to look at this subject. An alternative and frame-breaking approach is required.

In this chapter I will explain why I chose *Disaster Incubation Theory* as my basic framework for promoting *foresight*. There are many models that purport to explain the origins of crises and disasters. The first task is to explain why I chose to use Turner's model as my aid to promoting *foresight*. I will also look at the main ideas that stimulated the development of my approach to generating *foresight* and why *chaos* rather than order should be considered to be the normal state.

---

1   Mintzberg, Ahlstrand, and Lampel (1998:175–232)
2   Lissack (1997:206)

Selection of a Framework

My interest primarily focuses on the period during which *foresight* can be exercised and to see whether oversight can be avoided. That is, my focus is on preventing *failures of foresight*. This might suggest that my analysis should stop at the point the event occurs. If this was the case then my analysis would stop after Turner's stage four. However, for reasons that I will explain later, I found it necessary to review the complete cycle depicted within these frameworks. This review revealed some major issues with these models when they are used to promote *foresight*. I will now explain why I eliminated the alternative and counter some of the criticism made of Turner's work.

ELIMINATING ALTERNATIVES

In selecting a framework for *foresight*, I started with Turner's *Disaster Incubation Theory*[3] as it was one of the first that addressed the causes of accidents. Theories developed after 1976 would therefore have had *Disaster Incubation Theory* to provide a base upon which to build, whether they used it or not. This set the first of my criteria, which was whether the model, as an alternative to Turner's, enhanced it. The second of my criteria concerned use of *hindsight*. As these models were developed to help our understanding of the ways crises and disasters unfold, they are able to use *hindsight*. The use of *hindsight* would include the employment of any data only available after the event or where the event made clear which of the data already available should have been given a higher priority. Should the model require the use of *hindsight* then it is not suitable for my purpose. The third of my criteria is the need to be able to identify the stage that you are in. Without being able to identify where you are in the cycle, it would not be possible to confirm what has or has not been done and what is necessary to do in preparation for the future.

In contrast to Turner's work there is the work by Fink[4] who uses a different set of terms. Fink lists the stages as *prodromal*, acute, chronic and *crisis resolution*; these do not, however, give as much differentiation as Turner's and so will not be used. In the end it was decided to superimpose Rous-Dufort's *Processual Theory of Crisis* and Ibrahim-Razi's *Sequence of Technological Disasters* on top of Turner's model in order to enrich the picture available.

---

3   Turner (1976 and 1978); Turner and Pidgeon (1997)
4   Fink (1986:20)

Having reviewed a selection of models, my preference was to continue to user Turner's framework. I will now explain why. I examined, for example, Barry Bozeman's[5] disaster life cycle. Bozeman asks whether we can "identify the life cycle of an organization disaster". He thought that we could but that the stages were not linear, singular or mutually exclusive. In his view, "depending on the particular components of the disaster, the stages can occur in virtually any combination". His stages were:

1.   **The generation stage**: The period in which the factors that ultimately cause the disaster gather together.
2.   **The proximate cause stage**: At this time, the factors causing the disaster coalesce and the event(s) that constitute the disaster occur.
3.   **The secondary cause stage**: During this period, various disaster events may occur and spread negative outcomes to parties not previously affected and perhaps generate a snowball effect of one disaster leading to the next.
4.   **The recognition stage**: The period during which the organisation and its members recognise the disaster and begin to have an appreciation for its full effect.
5.   **The vetting stage**: During this period, the organisation and its members attempt to identify causal factors.
6.   **The response stage**: A self-conscious strategy for mitigating the effects of the disaster.
7.   **The inculcation stage**: Once the disaster has passed. This refers to the organisations' and its members' interpretation of the meaning of the disaster for the organisation. It may involve long-term changes ... and it may even involve a shared denial.

Bozeman's recognition that his stages were not linear, singular or mutually exclusive only reinforces the idea that *chaos* is normal. This does not however help when seeking *foresight*. I have set out seven alternatives to Turner's model in Table 2.1.

I now eliminate each: neither Fink,[6] Shrivastava et al.,[7] Silverstien,[8] nor Pearson and Mitroff[9] really added anything significant in terms of the structure

---

5   Bozeman (2011:128–129)
6   Fink (1986)
7   Shrivastava, Mitroff, Miller and Miglani (1988)
8   Silverstein (1992)
9   Pearson and Mitroff (1993)

Table 2.1   Alternative models

Disaster Incubation Theory	Fink, 1986	Industrial Crises Model	Silverstein, 1992	Pearson and Mitroff, 1993	Systems Failure and Cultural Readjustment Model	Sequence of Technological Disaster	A Processual Theory of Crisis
Turner, 1976		Shrivastava et al., 1988			Toft and Reynolds, 1999	Shaluf et al, 2002, Ibrahim-Razi	Roux-Dufort, 2009
Stage I – "Notionally normal starting point"			(1) quiescent (ready to reiterate the cycle)				
Stage II – Incubation Period	Prodome Greek for "running before"	Phase I – Pre-crisis conditions	(2) prodromal (more obvious warnings or indicators of the impending disaster)	(i) signal detection	Stage 1 Incubation	Phase 1: Generation of errors, Phase 2: Accumulation of errors	Phase 1: Anomalies and inattention
				(ii) preparation/ prevention	Stage 2 The operational socio-technical system	Phase 3: Warnings, Phase 4: (Failure of) correction, Phase 5: Impending disaster ("Unsafe conditions")	Phase 2: Vulnerabilities and attribution
Stage III – Precipitating event:	Acute crisis	Phase II – Trigger event			Stage 3 Precipitating event	Phase 6: Triggering event, Phase 7: Emergency state (defences)	Phase 3: Disruptions and denial of reality
Stage IV – Onset:	Chronic Crisis	Phase III – Crisis extension	(3) disaster	(iii) containment/ damage limitation	Stage 4 Disaster	Phase 8: Disaster	Phase 4: Crisis and escalation
Stage V – Rescue and salvage:	Resolution	Phase IV – Crisis resolution	(4) rescue (attempt to attain some level of stability) and (5) recovery (clean-up)	(iv) recovery	Stage 5 Rescue and salvage		
Stage VI – Full cultural readjustment:				(v) learning	Stage 6 Inquiry and reports, Stage 7 Feedback		

that helps *foresight*. While Toft and Reynolds[10] did add significantly to the structure of the model, their main focus was on "generating hindsight" (rather than *foresight*) and preventing valuable lessons being lost; this loss they termed the *failure of hindsight*.

This emphasis on *hindsight* makes their model unsuitable for my purpose. The final two models (produced by Shaluf et al. and Roux-Dufort[11]) were eliminated because, only with hindsight is it possible to delineate between the phases and, even then, to delineate them as clear phases, is an act of wilful selectivity. Such phases can only be a post-hoc construction. For all its limitations, I determined that Turner's model provides me with the most appropriate starting point for my *foresight* framework.

IN DEFENCE OF TURNER

Turner' work on *Disaster Incubation Theory* does not seem to have received the wide recognition that some think it deserves. Others have already noted that the "first edition went largely ignored".[12] It was not until 1996 when Diane Vaughan cited Turner in her work on the Challenger disaster[13] did others follow suit. In 1998 Karl Weick[14] wrote "an appreciation of Barry Turner"; he said "that Barry Turner is one of the best minds ever to have tackled this nest of issues". As part of my research I have now found over 100 books and academic articles that cite Turner or his constructs of the *man-made disaster* and the *incubation period*. The majority of these writings (56 occasions) have either just cited Turner or his idea of *incubation* without further explanation. Most of the remainder of the works describe all or part of *Disaster Incubation Theory* in order to set up their own argument rather than expanding on Turner's ideas. In addition to these papers, the ideas central to *incubation* can now be found frequently within related academic literature without any attribution to Turner. Finally, I have found only four articles that use *Disaster Incubation Theory* as an analytical methodology; I will use these cases to examine the way Turner's model can be, and has been, used.

Turner's work has also received some criticism. Some[15] see Turner's work as coming from an information-processing perspective, which they seem to

---

10 Toft and Reynolds (2005)
11 Shaluf et al. (2002); Roux-Dufort (2009)
12 Rijpma (2003:43)
13 Vaughan (1996)
14 Weick (1998)
15 Manning (1998); Yang and Haugen (2014)

suggest limits its utility. Shrivastava, Sonpar and Pazzaglia[16] look to diminish the value of Turner's work when they say "DIT concentrates (in hindsight, one might add) on what goes wrong in the lead up to organizational accidents". They cite Rijpma in order to justify their claim. In his turn, Rijpma sums up *Disaster Incubation Theory* as "a theory of unnoticed accumulation of hazards". In this statement I think that he misses its richness. This comment overlooks Turner's statement within his original 1978 book that it was the "intention of this book to consider whether there may be some general principle which could be formulated to deal with at least some ill structured problems before they are sharply defined by the disaster, to seek an understanding of the origins of disaster".[17] While Turner accepted that his work used *hindsight*, his intention was to generalise lessons learnt so they can be used for *foresight*. This principle is central to this book as well.

Approach

The premise behind this work is that it should provide *practical utility*[18] to academic knowledge.

> *Practical utility is seen as arising when theory can be directly applied to the problems practicing managers and other organizational practitioners face … through "the observation of real-life phenomena" … Thus, theory directed at practical importance would focus on prescriptions for structuring and organizing around a phenomenon and less on how science can further delineate or understand the phenomenon.*[19]

This work should be seen to be based within the "scholarship of application"[20] and the related practices of "engaged scholarship".[21]

The accusations of *failure of foresight* that are at the centre of this research are often directed at senior members of organisations who are at, in James Reason's terminology, the *blunt end*. Of interest is an understanding as to why people, such as these, make the decisions they do and whether they are seen as logical, rational and justifiable at the time. The issue for this research is whether there

---

16 Shrivastava, Mitrodd, Miller and Miglani (2009:1371)
17 Turner (1978:75)
18 Corley and Gioia (2011)
19 Corley and Gioia (2011:18)
20 Boyer (1990)
21 Van de Ven (2007)

might have been a way of framing the issues differently that might lead to a different understanding and therefore to different decisions. As a mechanism designed to prevent or mitigate adverse consequences, this issue of framing the problem may be seen as being part of the organisation's *risk management*, or more accurately, the *risk governance* process. Conventional *risk management* tools have a number of weaknesses when it comes to *risk governance*. Key in these weaknesses is the rather mechanistic processes and bottom-up approach used.[22] The proposed framework would look to reverse this process by capitalising on the knowledge and experience of the senior executive by encouraging and enabling them to debate what is critical to their organisation.

The method that I proposed for the pursuit of *foresight* is based on a number of considerations. These considerations are central to my thinking and therefore provide a foundation to the rest of the book. These considerations are *exploratory response*, the use of questions, *risk discourse*, the use of multiple *analytical levels* and the role of *postcards*.

EXPLORATORY RESPONSE

In what Edmondson and his colleagues[23] called the *recovery window*, which is akin to Turner's *incubation period*, they say that there are two possible responses. These they call the *confirmatory response* and the *exploratory response*. The *confirmatory response* is thought to "reinforce accepted assumptions and acts in ways consistent with established frames and beliefs" while the *exploratory response* "involves constant challenging and testing of existing assumptions and experimentation with new behaviours". They go on to advocate an *exploratory response* approach as it recommends that leaders should "assume the presence of a threat" leading them to "ask 'what if ...?'", to be proactive and to direct their efforts towards problem-solving. They believe that this promotes open-mindedness and learning.

QUESTIONS NOT ANSWERS

Central to this research is the idea that "good questions" will provoke an animated *risk discourse*. While academics may wish to see the purpose of their work as being to describe, explain, predict and test,[24] it may not have the greatest *practical utility*. After the fall of Singapore, Sir Winston Churchill is

---

22 Black and Baldwin (2007)
23 Edmondson, Roberto, Bohmer, Ferlins, and Feldman (2005:235 and 238)
24 Yin (2003)

reported as having said: "I ought to have known … I ought to have asked."[25] In a speech to the Academy of Management by their "Executive of the Year, 1999", John S. Reed stated:

> We (as managers) have to do two things: we decide what to do, and we try to make it happen. If you boil down all of the practice of business, it is the combination of those two things and the interaction between them that defines the world in which we live.[26]

He goes on to explain that:

> All … research can do is inform us. It certainly does not give us answers.

Karl Weick[27] sees utility in academic work that "provokes" discussion (it "gets us talking, digging, comparing, refining, and focusing on the right question"). Peng and Dess[28] state that scholarship "can help managers frame issues, ask the right questions, and question their underlying assumptions". In terms of the two key practitioner questions posed above by John Reed ("what to do" and "how to make it happen"), there is seen to be a need for researchers to broaden their scope in order to produce the pertinent questions which stimulate informed debate rather than deliver packaged answers. However, in the end, all this work can do is to provide a catalyst to others so that they talk, dig, compare, refine and focus on the issues of "what are the right questions?"

RISK DISCOURSE

This brings us to the idea of *risk discourse*; this is about talking, digging, comparing, refining and focusing on the right question where they pertain to the risks their organisation faces. This phrase was taken from work by Ortwin Renn.[29] In 2001 he wrote a paper[30] with Andreas Klinke in which he identified three major strategies for the management of risk. These strategies were labelled "risk-based, precautionary and discursive strategies" and are all part of the "deliberative processes actors need to agree on norms and procedures to manage risks". They see these *discursive strategies* being required

---

25 Weick and Sutcliffe (2007:84)
26 Huff (2000)
27 Weick (2004)
28 Peng and Dess (2010:287)
29 Renn (2008:56–66)
30 Klinke and Renn (2001:159)

"for consciousness and confidence building".[31] To be true to Renn's work, I have to point out that he recommends the use of *discursive strategies* for issues with a high degree of ambiguity and a precautionary strategy for times where there is a high degree of uncertainty. However from my academic perspective (the *scholarship of application*), I feel that this approach in its pure form is too prescriptive.

Klinke and Renn say that a *discursive strategy* "is essential if ... the potential for wide ranging damage is ignored ... What is needed is the involvement of affected people so that they are able to integrate the remaining uncertainties and ambiguities into the political deliberation".[32] This would seem appropriate for board-level discussions. They suggest that a strategy of discourse should encompass: 1) consciousness building, 2) confidence building, 3) introducing substitutes, 4) improving knowledge and 5) contingency management.[33] They see the result of such a strategy as "the design of the cooperative discourse model for resolving risk conflicts".[34]

For Renn a *discursive strategy* is a "Habermasian discourse based on the competition of arguments".[35] The assumption here must be that the best arguments will prevail. However, as all practitioners are well aware, politics and expediency often also have a role to play. Renn acknowledges this when he talks of various different types of discourse. He speaks of the need to "differentiate between three different types of discourses. These discourses are all necessary to deal with the issue ... first, a discourse among experts on the risks and benefits of different ... options ... second, a political discourse on the future ... and third, a procedural discourse on the most appropriate decision-making process".[36] Elsewhere Renn further enriches that idea of discourse when he discusses other types of discourse such as *reflective discourse* which questions "how much uncertainty and ignorance one is willing to accept".[37] What we have to acknowledge here is the discourse does not provide an easy solution. If it is to be effective, it will require great effort and perseverance. A basic assumption of this work is that there are no general and universally binding answers or solutions. What is suggested is that the greater the involvement of those who are affected, the greater the transparency in decision-making, the

---

31 Klinke and Renn (2001:166)
32 Klinke and Renn (2001:168)
33 Klinke and Renn (2001:169)
34 Brown and Heyman (2012:422)
35 Renn (2008:931)
36 Hocke and Renn (2009:931)
37 Renn (2008:196)

more rational and non-hierarchical the discourse, the more open and two-way is the risk communication, then the more likely it is that potential effect and acceptable solutions will appear.[38]

With *risk discourse* there are the principles of communication, inclusion and reflection. These principles hold that various actors taking part in this reflective discourse discuss how decisions could and should be made in the face of irresolvable uncertainty, complexity and ambiguity. The reflection principle emphasises that there are important difficult issues (uncertainty, complexity, ambiguity and a balancing act) that need repeated consideration by all actors throughout the process.[39] From a *risk governance* perspective, I would suggest that an executive needs to discuss these issues in order to fully understand their complexities, uncertainties and ambiguities before they decide on what action it would be appropriate to take.

ANALYTICAL LEVELS

Cohen and Gooch[40] refer to a *fallacy of homogeneity*. This is "the habit of speaking of a large organisation as a unitary whole". Within the safety science literature, for example, in 1997 Jens Rasmussen[41] produced the idea of the multi-level analysis; his basic model used six levels. He justified his layered approach by saying:

> *Many levels of politicians, managers, safety officers, and work planners are involved in the control of safety by means of laws, rules, and instructions that are formalised means for the ultimate control of some hazardous, physical process. They seek to motivate workers and operators, to educate them, to guide them, or to constrain their behaviour by rules and equipment design, so as to increase the safety of their performance.*[42]

These ideas were developed by Nancy Leveson who expanded them into the STAMP (Systems Theoretic Accident Modelling and Processes) methodology over a series of papers. The first was published in 2004.[43] She supports Rasmussen's justification for this approach. She says:

---

38   Renn (2004)
39   van Asselt and Renn (2011:443)
40   Cohen and Gooch (1990:37)
41   Rasmussen (1997)
42   Rasmussen (1997:184)
43   Leveson (2004)

> *... accident causation must be viewed as a complex process involving the entire socio-technical system including legislators, government agencies, industry associations and insurance companies, company management, technical and engineering personnel, operations, etc.*[44]

I will provide a number of examples to illustrate this point. This error is often exhibited when non-United Kingdom citizens refer to all UK nationals as being "English"; they do not seem to recognise the existence of the Scottish, Welsh and Northern Irish national sub-groups that make up this nation. We also view large corporations as a single entity, as we conflate their boards with the corporations they are meant to control. Even at board level we often see evidence that the board is seen as a single entity representing a single view when, in fact, they are a collection of individuals trying to come to a common view. Even when considering a single individual it may be a mistake to view them as a homogenous being when there may be a number of facets of their character and psychology that are in conflict, thereby creating uncertainty and ambiguity of outcome.

Rather than specifying specific levels, there is seen to be merit in providing generic terms that can be adapted to the prevailing circumstance. Not only are generic levels more flexible, they also require those involved in the discussions to start to think and debate about what levels are the most appropriate to their issue. An example of where this method has been used can be seen in the Donaghy report.[45] This was a report into "the Underlying Causes of Construction Fatal Accidents" for the Secretary of State for Work and Pensions and it stratified issues into *macro*, *mezzo* and *micro levels*. Any revised model for *foresight* will need its stages to be stratified. The stratification proposed is a four-level system using the labels *mega*, *macro*, *mezzo* and *micro*. These will be applied to the layers starting at the *blunt end* and moving towards the *sharp end* of any issue.[46]

Those at the *sharp end*, the *micro level*, will need further delineation. Another example of where homogeneity is broken down is Charles Perrow's division of victims. He divides them into four categories.[47] These have been labelled "operators", "voluntary", "involuntary" and "intergenerational". To Perrow, the first group were those who actively controlled and operated the system. The second group consists of those who are part of the system but have no

44 Leveson (2004:247)
45 Donaghy (2009)
46 Reason (1997:113)
47 Perrow (1999:67)

influence over the operations: they include non-operational personnel (such as delivery drivers) or system users (such as passengers). The third group consists of bystanders (that is someone with no connection and only random alignment; they were in the wrong place at wrong time.) The final group Perrow referred to as "intergenerational"; Perrow stated that "for the most part (these are) victims of radiation and toxic chemicals", these are foetuses and future generations. Since Perrow first wrote these words in 1984, public attitude to such *normal accidents* have changed. There is now far greater recognition of the effect that such events might have on the families of those directly involved.[48] I have interpreted the idea of "intergeneration" to now include the victim's wider family and friends in order to provoke discussion about how they might be affected and then, in turn, might affect the post-incident world. This final category has therefore been expanded to include "those not involved in the event but affected by it". In more colloquial terms, those involved would be looking for potential sources of "blow-back". They would need to debate "whose cage was being rattled" and "how loudly could the beast roar?"

Therefore, as part of any analysis, I would suggest using the construct of *"micro, mezzo, macro* and *mega"* to differentiate layers within a perceived entity (either vertical or horizontal) and as it applies to the context. In my previous book[49] on public inquiries, I found that I needed to use this construct because these inquiry reports seem to conflate issues of personal training (a *micro* issue) with issues of government policy (a *mega level* issue) and a number of layers in between. I found that such differentiation helped to bring clarity to any discussion of risk.

A POSTCARD

Finally, we come to the idea of providing catalytic frameworks. Unlike many other academic models, these frameworks are not intended to offer explanation of causality. They are meant to stimulate debate. Debates or arguments often start because two people disagree. Therefore it is not important to me that people agree with the way that I have represented issues within this book. If the result is that it stimulates them to think again about an issue and to come up with, what is for them, better answers, then I have achieved my aim. Here again I have been stimulated by an idea espoused by Karl Weick. He says that "rich comparisons breed further richness":[50] he suggests using a *postcard*

---

48   Lauder (2011:101)
49   Lauder (2013)
50   Weick (2007:17)

to help an observer appreciate a painting. He says "(t)he postcard essentially alerts you to features of the painting you might otherwise have overlooked. The imperfect reproduction serves as a clue to sites where the artist's genius is more evident ... Go into inquiry clear about what you expect, what you believe. That is your postcard". The imperfect frameworks offered within this book should be thought of as such a postcard. The more detailed construct of the proposed framework can be used as a catalyst for thinking rather than being just a normative or predictive model.

Much of existing academic literature on crises and accidents looks to determine why such events occur and how the recommendations made following such events can be implemented more effectively. In the terms used by Toft and Reynolds,[51] this work is about how to turn *passive learning* into *active learning*. To use a sporting analogy, the desire to provide academic knowledge with *practical utility*, is akin to turning post-match pundits into productive members of the coaching staff. This is because, rather than just commenting, they provide the players with the practical skills and knowledge necessary to play the game rather than just commenting on the outcome. Rather than apply *hindsight*, they take what they know and try to use it to produce a better outcome in the future and thus providing *foresight*. In summary, my approach to generating *foresight* is to stimulate those who are concerned, those who know and those who must act to bring together what they know and to have a continuous reasoned discussion in order to generate the most appropriate solutions.

Chaos as the Norm

One of the dominant themes that emerges from inquiry reports is that order is taken as being the norm. Any breakdown of that order is deemed, by those conducting the inquiry, to happen because of sloppiness at best and negligence at worst. However, we have to consider whether the basis of this paradigm is correct. For the purpose of this work I have made the basic assumption that the world is *chaotic* and that we only have a very limited ability to gain and maintain control over our surroundings and our future. We need to consider that where we think we are in charge of the situation, this may just be an *illusion of control*[52] and that such illusions induce potential jeopardy into the situation.

---

51 Toft and Reynolds (2005)
52 Durand (2004:109–130)

Dooley and Van de Ven have pointed to the interest expressed by organisational scholars in "the notion that at times an organization may be viewed as behaving chaotically (and the) implications of chaos – that the system is deterministic and hypersensitive to small perturbations".[53] They point out that "in the vernacular the term *chaos* implies a state of disorder and confusion", however, this is not correct when the term is applied to system dynamics. In the case of system dynamics "chaotic dynamics imply a causal system that is orderly (albeit unpredictable) and clear in its determination of the future from the past".[54] What is relevant here is that, in general, the orderliness of these systems is difficult to recognise or even perceive. So what do I mean by the term *chaos*? The *chaos* is defined here as "the inability to see any pattern within an activity or series of events". This inability to see potential future outcomes that are the consequence of the same series of inputs are seen as them being unpredictable.[55] Here we need to differentiate between random events (to which there is no pattern) and *chaos* (where there may be a pattern) to see if we have the ability to do so.

Both (at one end of the scale) *chaos* theorists and James Reason's "Protection/ Production Oscillation" (at the other) can be used to suggest that what is considered to be normal is fairly *chaotic*. This may, therefore, be one of the reasons why organisations fail to spot potential failures. What in hindsight may seem clear may, in fact, be part of an actual pattern that is *chaotic*. This might mean that there is a highly ambiguous boundary between *normal chaos* and *abnormal chaos*. Here we will examine two aspects of this threshold relevant to this case. First is Reason's "Protection/Production Oscillation" and the second is Rasmussen's Boundary of Acceptable Performance. However, before we explain these constructions, I feel I must first explain some of the precepts that underlie them. These precepts are: 1) the idea of "benefits" derived from conducting business, 2) our desire to *tame* complexity, 3) why failure should be considered to be inevitable and finally 4) the idea of zones of vulnerability.

BUSINESS BENEFITS

Organisations have different purposes; these are many and varied. Theses purposes range from child care to national defence and from bookkeeping to exploring far regions of our universe. Each purpose will bring with it an associated level of acceptable harm. The level of harm acceptable for each

---

53   Dooley and Van de Ven (1999:358)
54   Dooley and Van de Ven (1999:359)
55   Singh and Parikshit (2002:49)

organisational purpose may be explicitly stated within regulations; it may be clear what is acceptable to the public or the organisation may have to feel its way in order to find this out. Adding greater complexity to this problem are the changing levels of what is acceptable to the public, whether they be directly involved or not. In a paper written in 1976, Barry Turner states that:

> When a trawler is lost in Arctic fishing grounds, or when a wall collapses onto a firefighting team, there is much less comment than when an accident kills passengers on a suburban commuter train.[56]

This may no longer be the case. There have been recent cases in the UK where members of the coastguard,[57] the fire service[58] and the police[59] have been prosecuted or have modified their action for fear of prosecution under Health and Safety regulations. This has had, and is having, a significant effect on the way these services can now be provided. Some would argue that seeking to protect the providers of a service means that these providers are becoming unable to provide the service expected by the public. This issue comes down to one of risk transfer which sits alongside the issue of risk reduction; reducing the risk to one party may well entail an unacknowledged increase in the risks to others, and hence we see the emergence of *unintended consequences* within various *risk management* processes. These issues mean that senior management face ambiguities created by being unclear how society views the jeopardy they face and that the view is changing over time. In this scenario we see the boundaries of what is acceptable being both unclear and mobile.

TAMING COMPLEXITY

We are told that the world is becoming more complex. The first reaction to complexity is to try to simplify the issues. In order to understand this complexity we subdivide and categorise. We break *complex* issues down into simpler parts and then assume that if we understand the parts we will understand the whole. Society seems to be obsessed with Newtonian rationality and seems to live by the premise that all things are quantifiable and predictable given the collection of enough information. Inquiry reports seem

---

56 Turner (1976:380)
57 "Cliff hero resigns in safety row", http://news.bbc.co.uk/1/hi/england/tees/7183017.stm, accessed 6 November 2010
58 *Scotsman Newspaper* Report dated 13 March 2010, http://news.scotsman.com/news/Firefighters-told-to-39use-common.6149249.jp, accessed 5 November 2010
59 "Boy drowned as police support officers 'stood by'", http://www.guardian.co.uk/uk/2007/sep/21/1, accessed 5 November 2010

to be based on this premise despite evidence that the information necessary is often available to the organisation and that too much information can be as debilitating as too little. This premise is however now being challenged.

When writing on the subject of leadership, Snowden and Boone suggest there seems to be "a fundamental assumption of organizational theory and practice: that a certain level of predictability and order exists in the world. This assumption, grounded in the Newtonian science that underlies scientific management, encourages simplifications that are useful in ordered circumstances. Circumstances change, however, and as they become more complex, the simplifications can fail".[60]

A prominent writer on aviation and other safety issues, Sidney Dekker[61] and his colleagues explored some of the weakness in this Newtonian approach. They warn that "many still equate 'scientific thinking' with 'Newtonian thinking'" and its reductionist approach. They relate this to accident investigation which they see as being based on a premise that "the functioning or non-functioning of the whole can be explained by the functioning or non-functioning of constituent components. Attempts to understand the failure of a *complex* system in terms of failures or breakages of individual components" leads us to see that finding this broken part then becomes their "eureka part". They go on to say that while "the mechanistic paradigm is compelling in its simplicity, coherence and apparent completeness and largely consistent with intuition and common sense",[62] it is false. They then go on to "explore what that means for safety science and work towards a post-Newtonian analysis of failure in complex systems".[63] They conclude:

> When accidents are seen as complex phenomena, there is no longer an obvious relationship between the behavior of parts in the system ... and system-level outcomes. Instead, system-level behaviors emerge from the multitude of relationship and interconnections deeper inside the system, and cannot be reduced to those relationships or interconnections ... The complexity perspective dispenses with the notion that there are easy answers to a complex systems event.[64]

---

60 Snowden and Boone (2007:1)
61 Dekker, Cilliers and Hofmeyr (2011:940)
62 Dekker et al. (2011:940)
63 Dekker et al. (2011:939)
64 Dekker et al. (2011:944)

Despite the prominence of thinking about linear relationships between phenomena (such as *"cause and effect"*), writers have been warning us for some time of the danger of overlooking non-linear relationships within systems. Charles Perrow has been warning since 1984[65] about the potential for *normal accidents* and the role played by *interactive complexity* and, through complexity, to *chaos* theory.

Anna Goldoff has looked at complexity in decision-making. She states that "risk assessment and risk management is one subfield of decision-making … Another is chaos theory". She goes on:

> *"Chaos" theory, nonlinear dynamics and related models (quantum theory, the science of complexity, "fuzzy logic" and fractuality) are influenced by the new thinking in science which sees the world as made up of complex systems that are nonlinear, dynamic, unstable and unpredictable. In contrast, Newtonian science defined observed phenomena in an ordered, stable, linear and predictable way.[66]*

She also says that:

> *While chaos theory provides a different perspective of the world in contrast to Newtonian science, it doesn't completely disprove Newtonian thinking as a reflection of reality. It tells us that Newtonian science is only "part of the picture".[67]*

At this point we run into a problem of definitions and the interplay between three terms. The terms are complicated, *complex* and *chaotic*. Within the literature that covers this subject area we find a range of definitions for these terms. I will therefore explain how I differentiate between these terms. Complicated systems "(1) are understandable by studying the behaviour of their component parts, (2) can be deduced on the basis of cause and effect, and (3) can be determined independent of the observer, that is, deduced only from 'objective' empirical observations".[68] An aircraft is an example of a complicated system. Dekker sees that "complicated systems become *complex* because they are opened up to influences that lie way beyond engineering specifications and reliability predictions".[69] This understanding is akin to Perrow's *interactive complexity*.

---

65 Perrow (1984)
66 Goldoff (2000:2019)
67 Goldoff (2000:2019)
68 Aven, Vinnem and Wiencke (2007:447)
69 Dekker et al. (2011:942)

Ortwin Renn believes that complexity "refers to the difficulty in identifying and quantifying the causal links between a multitude of potential causal agents and specific observed effects".[70] Peter Massingham says that, "The most complex knowledge is idea creation and problem-solving involving ill-structured and unknown cause and effect relationships. Examples include business process improvements, large scale investments, or new business initiatives".[71] Charles Perrow sees *complex* interactions as "those of unfamiliar sequences, or unplanned and unexpected sequences, and either not visible and not immediately comprehensible".[72] Central to all these definitions is that interaction between components is difficult to foresee.

From the idea of *complex* we move to the idea of *chaotic*. While *complex* describes the interaction, in this context the term *chaotic* describes the acknowledgement that we probably cannot foresee how a cause will affect an outcome and how minor, often unperceivable, changes are likely to produce vastly different results. Weick and Sutcliffe, when talking about managing the unexpected, espouse three principles of *anticipation*. Alongside "preoccupation with failure" and "sensitivity to operation", they talk of a "reluctance to simplify". They say that "expectations simplify the world and steer observers away from the very disconfirming evidence that foreshadows unexpected problems ... (and that) early warning signs lie buried in those heterogeneous details". One way to maintain the richness of a *complex* problem is to be able to differentiate between *complex* and less *complex* issues.

Rittel and Webber[73] started the differentiation between simple and *complex* problems. They used two categories, those of "*tame*" (or "benign") and "*wicked*". They say:

> The problems that scientists and engineers have usually focused upon are mostly "tame" or "benign" ones. As an example, consider a problem of mathematics, such as solving an equation; ... the mission is clear. It is clear, in turn, whether or not the problems have been solved.
>
> Wicked problems, in contrast, have neither of these clarifying traits; ... The information needed to understand the problem depends upon one's idea for solving it. That is to say: in order to describe a wicked-problem in sufficient detail, one has to develop an exhaustive inventory of all

---

70   Renn (2008:371)
71   Massingham (2010:472)
72   Perrow (1999:78)
73   Rittel and Webber (1973:160 and 161)

conceivable solutions ahead of time. The reason is that every question asking for additional information depends upon the understanding of the problem and its resolution.

Keith Grint applies the idea of *tame* and *wicked* problems to management. He sees *tame* problems as being those that can be resolved. These issues allow problem-solving techniques to be used. On the other hand he sees *wicked* problems as those that are unresolvable. These problems can only be managed. This implies that constant adjustment is required to navigate a line between two or more conflicting goals. We also see how "pressure to act decisively often leads" people to try find solutions that do not exist to such problems.[74]

David Hancock[75] goes one step further in developing these categorisations. He uses a matrix with the dimensions of social and technical complexity. His four quadrants are labelled *tame, messy, wicked* and *wicked mess*. *Tame* problems are those that are the least socially and technically complex. *Messy* problems are those that are the less socially but more technically complex. *Wicked* problems are those that are more socially but less technically complex. *Wicked messes* are problems that are both socially and technically complex. Related to *tame, messy, wicked* and *wicked mess* problems is the idea of *elegant* and *clumsy solutions*.

Grint describes *elegant solutions*[76] as the ones where there is a single resolution (or mode). These might also be seen as being scientific solutions such as the resolution of a mathematical problem. Grint calls multi-mode *clumsy solutions'*.[77] He sees these as using the skills that pragmatically engage with the most *complex* problems. Bricoleurs are described as using whatever comes to hand, whatever needs to be stitched together, to ensure practical success. LaPorte and Consolini[78] refer to a number of pieces of work that discuss variations on the idea of the *clumsy solution*: alternative terms are "disjointed incrementalism", "partisan mutual adjustment",[79] "*compounded abstraction*"[80] or "*Plowman effect*".[81] Lindblom started the discussion with his concept of *successive limited comparison* and this led to the idea of *muddling through*.[82]

---

74 Grint (2008)
75 Hancock (2004); Hancock and Holt (2003)
76 Grint (2008)
77 Grint (2008:11 and 14)
78 LaPorte and Consolini (1991:26)
79 Lindblom (1983:523)
80 Irwin, R. (1977)
81 Plowman (2007)
82 Lindblom (1959)

A dictionary definition of *muddling through* cited by Hollnagel[83] is "to push on to a favourable outcome in a disorganised way". He goes on to state that it "proposes that people usually achieve their goals ... by actions which are more like stumbling than the deliberate execution of a well-defined procedure". David Hancock[84] sees *muddling through* as a strategy where project teams deal with problems as they arise on whosoever "shouts the loudest" or who makes the "strongest argument" basis. "The project meanders through the process until it 'arrives' at a solution. Advantages are typically short lived and the disadvantages are that the problem is never 'fully' resolved as the solution is constantly changing."

The temptation when faced with a *complex* problem is to try to deal with them a bit at a time. While this is quite understandable, it does mean that events may meander as they respond to existing pressures. The result is that the organisations may not end up in the place they expected to be. In addition, while some problems may be suitable for resolution, this may not always be the case. Many political problems, such as the allocation of budgets, setting priorities or when faced with deciding on the least-worst option, require judgement rather than scientific management. The danger when confusing issues that need to be managed rather than resolved is that a perceived solution may turn into the source of the next *crisis*. When faced with complexity, as Weick and Sutcliffe warned, we should be "reluctant to simply" such problems.

INEVITABILITY OF FAILURE

Linked to the issue of *messy problems* is the question of whether failure is inevitable. This is central to much of the debate that pits *normal accident* against *high reliability organisation*. In his construct of *normal accidents*, Charles Perrow is seen to suggest that accidents will happen in *complex* systems that are closely coupled. This has been characterised as being fatalist[85] or as being pessimistic.[86] I would suggest that this is just pragmatic. I shall explain why.

Charles Perrow does not offer the construct of *normal accidents* as a theory of accident causation (as others have tried to characterise it) but as a warning.[87] He was trying to warn those considering creating facilities that might potentially

---

83 Hollnagel (2009:44 and 45)
84 Hancock (2010:9)
85 Pidgeon (2012:20)
86 Sagan (1993:13)
87 In a private email of 1 November 2010, Professor Perrow kindly confirmed that this reading correctly represented his views

be very hazardous to those who use them, to society, or even to mankind in general. He was trying to warn that complexity makes failure difficult to prevent and close coupling could make the hazard rapidly escalate causing great jeopardy to those involved. He was asking those planning such endeavours to think twice before they embarked on such a course. In this context the phrase "accidents are inevitable" can be seen as a shorthand reference to a more subtle concern. This therefore brings us to semantic debate over the meaning of the term "inevitable".

The definition of the term inevitable is "certain to happen; unavoidable; totally predictable".[88] I see two mechanisms that describe the course to the inevitable. The first is based on a *cause and effect* relationship. As academic work often looks to explain why something happens, it is easy to understand why academics, when looking at the relationship between *interactive complexity* and close coupling (which are fundamental building blocks of *normal accidents*), make the assumption that what Perrow was describing was a *cause and effect* relationship. There is a second route to "inevitability" in probability and the law of large numbers. For example, if you have six die and you roll them enough times then, inevitably, one roll will produce six sixes. Therefore we can see that *interactive complexity* and close coupling by themselves may not lead to failure; however if there are enough systems that are interactively *complex* and close coupled then some will fail. If one of the systems that fails has severe consequences, Perrow suggests that we should think carefully before embarking on that project.

The reverse of failures being inevitable is that they are not inevitable. Both statements however can be seen to be equally inaccurate. Just as not every endeavour will fail, it may not be possible to ensure that no endeavour will ever fail. In addition, constructs such as *entropy* are used to suggest that, if unattended, systems become unordered. This disorder may lead to the failure of the organisation delivering its planned outputs. Therefore it could be argued that unless close attention is paid to a system it will, at some time, fail. To put this statement another way, failure is inevitable unless efforts are made to ensure it does not fail; *chaos* is therefore normal. The question then becomes whether these efforts can ensure that the system does not fail. Scott Sagan[89] posited that the construct of a *high reliability organisation* provided a more optimistic approach. However, few writers who endorse this idea would suggest that even this approach can ensure failure-free operations. The most

---

88   As given in the Oxford Dictionary (1985)
89   Sagan (1993:13)

common definition of a *high reliability organisation* includes the notion of "near error free"[90] which, under the law of large numbers, would lead to an inevitable failure. The question of which one of a number of comparable systems will fail is therefore a more difficult pattern to identify.

ZONES OF VULNERABILITY

During every day routine operations we see activities that momentarily put the participants at greater risk of being harmed. These periods might be seen as *zones of high vulnerability* where special care needs to be taken. For example, within Federal Aviation Administration (FAA) regulations there is a rule called "the Sterile Cockpit Rule". This rule requires pilots to refrain from non-essential activities during critical phases of flight. The phases deemed critical include all ground operations (taxi, takeoff and landing) and all non-cruising flight operations conducted below 10,000 feet. This rule prompts pilots to consider their flight as a series of phases rather than a homogeneous whole. A similar idea can be seen in the notion of *operational modes*.

Some authors[91] have used the term *operational modes* to delineate changes of tempo in the way tasks are performed. The context of their research was the control room on a naval warship during combat operations. They use the label *routine* to refer to steady state operation or what is considered to be the norm. They use the label *high tempo* to refer to times when the pace of work becomes so hectic that additional resources or new ways of working are required to enable the organisation to cope with the evolving situation. Finally, they use the label *crisis* to denote when the organisation is close to potential collapse which again requires different resources or ways of working. It is important to highlight that *high tempo* indicates "much more of the same things" are happening and so additional resources are required; in *crisis* the organisation is on the cusp of a paradigm shift which requires different skills and therefore different resources.

Roe and Schulman[92] take a slightly different perspective when they use the term *operational modes*. The context of their research was the control of an electrical power distribution company; compared to the military context, the situation they were describing can be seen to be far more stable and bounded. Their delineation is based on the organisational routines required to cope with the prevailing situation. They divide the modes into four categories. The first is

---

90 Weick (1987:122); Roberts and Rosseau (1989); La Porte and Consolini (1991:23)
91 Rochlin (1991)
92 Roe and Schulman (2008:48)

the *just-this-way* mode that enables those conducting the tasks to perform them in accordance with very specific detailed procedures; this requires the context to be very stable. The second category they label the *just-in-case* mode; in this mode those conducting the tasks are able to adopt organisational routines that accord to wide-ranging established (broader) rules and procedures. This mode is required when the core routines no longer match the specific tasks; it is where the stability of the situation has been disturbed. Their third mode is labelled *just-in-time*; this mode requires greater flexibility than the first two. This mode requires experience and judgement as the situation has to be assessed on its own merits as "many situations (are) not covered by procedures". The final mode, labelled *just-for-now*, is akin to *crisis*; Roe and Schulman saw tasks being performed reactively and that the people waited for something to happen.

If we look at the *micro level* we also see *zones of high vulnerability*; Roe and Schulman labelled these as *precursor zones*. Referring to their own research they say that "each performance mode has its own precursor zone in which reliability skills and their match to tasks becomes endangered".[93] Some see the modes as being "characterized by unknown *conditions* that challenge operator skills and lay the groundwork for more fundamental error or failure.[94] In this zone operators encounter situations not informed by their prior experience", I see this interpretation as being mistaken. Roe and Schulman see that "each performance mode has its own precursor zone"; it is therefore the transition between modes where additional vulnerability lies because while an action may be appropriate within one zone it may not be in another. It is the recognition that the mode (or paradigm) has changed that is the issue. It is the recognition that a new set of rules governs the situation and what you have done before is no longer appropriate. This view can be seen to be consistent with those who define *operational mode* in terms of tempo. The same operators are required for the *routine* and *high tempo* – it might be that the control room needs to escalate from minimum to full manning in order to monitor all the systems; this is not a skills issue but one of workload. In this context the *crisis* may require a person with additional authority to those routinely necessary.

The point here is that operations should not be seen as a homogeneous activity. Operations have modes and, while different modes may have different intrinsic levels of jeopardy associated with them, the move between modes also produces a *zone of vulnerability*. If we look at *zones of vulnerability* in terms of *micro* to *mega levels*, we might depict them as follows:

---

93 Roe and Schulman (2008:115)
94 Skogdalen, Utne and Vinnem (2011:1188)

- At the *micro level* a *zone of vulnerability* is created by the transition between *operational modes*.
- At the *mezzo level* a *zone of vulnerability* is created by different *operational modes* having different intrinsic levels of jeopardy associated with them.
- At the *macro* and *mega levels* a *zone of vulnerability* is created by the failure to distinguish between being in the pre-*crisis* phase and being in a *crisis*.

While it may seem to be a simple task to differentiate being in the pre-*crisis* phase and being in a *crisis*, in practice, this is found not to be so. Beside the different terminology and different definition produced by different writers and besides the different levels of *crisis* (what may be a *crisis* to the worker on the shop floor might not be a *crisis* to a member of the executive board, and vice versa), there may be confusion caused by polar opposite views of the issue. While Turner talks of the *incubation period* as "the accumulation of an unnoticed set of events which are at odds with the accepted beliefs about hazards and the norms of their avoidance" during which things go wrong, Edmondson and colleagues talk of the *recovery window.* They describe this as the "period between a threat and a major accident (or prevented accident) in which constructive collective action may be feasible".[95] The first may be seen as being a pessimistic approach and the second as an optimistic one. They do however both, I would argue, cover the same period.

Edmondson et al. state that the "recovery window in the Columbia case began two days into the mission (when the organization members discovered a visible foam chunk had struck the orbiter during *Columbia*'s launch". I would question this assertion. Here I give three reasons. The first is based on their own definition. They say the *recovery window* is the "period between a threat and a major accident". What the organisation members discovered, which happened two days after the launch, was not the threat; if anything, it was the strike on the day of the launch. My second reason for questioning their assertion is that the inquiry report did not start even at the point of launch. The inquiry team saw that "constructive collective action may be feasible" far earlier in this project; their recommendations where far ranging when looking at what needed to be done to prevent the accident. As well as the thermal protection system, they encompassed many other issues including scheduling, training and organisation.[96] My final reason for questioning their assertion is their reliance on *hindsight* to make their

---

95 Edmondson et al. (2005:220)
96 CAIB (2003:225–227)

case. After the crash there was a well-defined problem. It was clear that the tile damage was the pressing issue. Before the crash NASA was not unaware of the problem but it was only one of 4,222 issues that, at that time, classified as critical.[97] For the purpose of their paper (espousing the value of an *exploratory response*) these issues may not have been pertinent. If they had limited their term to *crisis management* then these criticisms may not be valid. However, in terms of generating *foresight*, these flaws cannot be ignored. The threat to Columbia originated in the threat and the inadequacy of the associated *precautionary norms* and hence is why I see the construct covering the same period.

In summary, systems and process should therefore not be seen as being a homogeneous whole. They need to be assessed in order to determine where the key zones of vulnerability lie (whether they are at the *micro*, *mezzo*, *macro* or *mega level*) so that resources (whether this is materiel, manpower or simply mental alertness) can be escalated to match the prevailing circumstances.

ORGANISATIONAL OSCILLATION

James Reason has produced a helpful model that illustrates what he described as the "lifespan of a hypothetical organization through the production–protection space".[98] Reason's model can be taken to illustrate the need to balance production against protection. It can be seen that if too much emphasis is placed on production then one type of unwanted event, a catastrophic accident, is likely to occur. If, however, too much emphasis is placed on protection then another type of unwanted event is likely to occur, the organisation will be bankrupted. To Reason's original model, I have added the idea of *Type 1* and *Type 2 errors*. In his work on repeated failures in the management of high-risk technologies, Larry Heimann states that "organizations are often in the position to commit two types of errors: (1) implementation of the wrong policy, an error of commission; and (2) failure to act when action is warranted, an error of omission".[99] Later in the paper he says that, "Type 2 errors often lead to missed opportunities and wasted resources". The logical extension of this is that, if too many opportunities are missed and too much resource is wasted, then the organisation will be bankrupted and that this would be as unwanted as would any catastrophic accident. The revised model (see Figure 2.1) illustrates that organisations face two types of unwanted events that are diametrically opposed. On one side are *Type 1 errors* such as the catastrophic accidents.

---

97   Dunbar and Garud (2005:209)
98   Reason (1997:4–5)
99   Heimann (2005:107)

On the other side are *Type 2 errors*; these include events such as lost opportunities, unnecessary delays, inefficiency or, worse, bankruptcy.

When we think of the idea of oscillation we might be tempted to see a nice symmetrical wave of regular height and length. In terms of *foresight*, however, the wave is much more likely to be *chaotic* as illustrated in the diagram. This will be the result of many different threats, each having its own wave form, interacting. These waves will not only vary in height and length but will also vary between the rounded forms to the squared form created by the notion of tipping point. In the squared forms the speed of transformation from one state or mode to another is at its greatest. In this case we see oscillation when, in attempting to protect the organisation from *Type 1 errors*, it induces movement towards potential *Type 2 errors*. This would suggest that management requires good judgement and, in turn, good judgement needs room to manoeuvre or flex. Where this flexibility is too constrained, this can lead to unintended adverse consequences.

Within the boundaries created by *Type 1* and *Type 2 errors* there lies the permissible operational zone. While Figure 2.1 may be an exaggerated form of reality, it is designed to show the way organisations may oscillate between the two extremes and to point to some of the factors that prompt these oscillations. Diane Vaughan[100] introduces us to the idea of the *liability of newness*: Paul Slovic[101] includes the idea of newness as one of the factors to be considered in his risk rating scale. Vaughan goes on to extend the original idea. In its original form the idea suggests induced temporary weaknesses and inefficiency within an organisation due to the necessity of generating and learning new roles and skills, the absence of standard routines and other forms of stabilities. Vaughan expands the original concept, applying it "to analogical circumstances at other levels of analysis, explaining why new programs, products, or services by individual organizations get into trouble".[102] This source of risk may induce a risk averse culture to be overcautious and therefore to overspend on protective measures. In turn this may hit profitability, which then produces internal political pressure from stakeholders to make the organisation more efficient. Now protective measures are reduced and in time the organisation takes more risks until some near miss causes them to start to implement new protective measures. Over time the protective measure may fall into disuse; this is typical of what is referred to as *safety drift*. This *drift* may also end in some form of warning ("wake-up call") which results in another tightening of protective measures and so the oscillations continue.

---

100 Vaughan (1996:123, 125 and 140)
101 Slovic (2000:87)
102 Vaughan (1999:275)

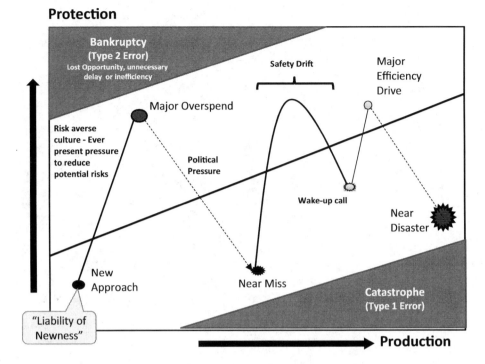

Figure 2.1   Organisational oscillation

It can be seen that organisations do not maintain an even course but, in fact, normally oscillate within boundaries that are acceptable to the organisation. These oscillations may, however, exceed the boundaries of what is acceptable which may end in a major disaster or bankruptcy.

BOUNDARY OF ACCEPTABLE PERFORMANCE

From James Reason's work we might perceive that there are lines that should not be crossed. Unfortunately it is not that simple or clear. Jens Rasmussen has provided us with a richer understanding of this issue in his work that examined the "boundary of acceptable performance".[103] He explains how neither organisations nor individuals tend to "play it safe", how they exhibit the tendency to see how far we can go before imminent apparent disaster stops us going any further. (Other research shows that as a member of a group we, as individuals, are prepared to take greater risks than we would

---

103 Rasmussen (1997:190)

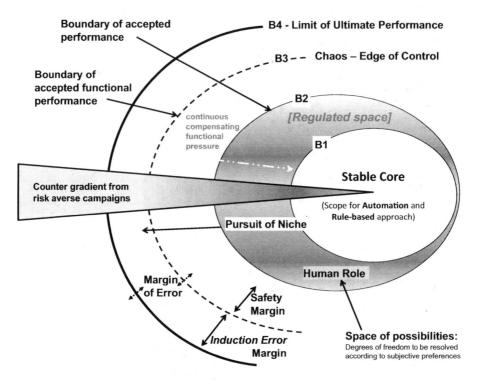

Figure 2.2   Performance boundaries

do as a single individual; this tendency has been labelled *risky shift.*[104]) We use metaphors such as "pushing the envelope" to describe these situations. The key boundaries I see are illustrated in Figure 2.2.

At the core of all systems is an area of stability where the context can be clearly identified and articulated. This enables rules to be set, whether through regulation or not, for the ways the activities are to be conducted; this area is bounded by B1 in the diagram. This provides scope for ensuring consistent performance and the potential for automating these processes. The second boundary (B2) is one of *accepted performance*. This boundary is the limit of performance deemed satisfactory within a recognised level of risk taking. The third boundary (B3) is that of the *accepted functional performance*; that is, the point before which the system, be it a machine or an organisation, will not break down given a specific set of circumstances. The final boundary (B4) marks the point at which the system will breakdown: this is labelled the *limit of ultimate performance*. In between each set of adjacent boundaries is a zone or gap.

---

104 Stoner (1968)

These gaps provide three sources of ambiguity when trying to manage these boundaries. The first ambiguity comes because experience shows that few organisations are aware of where these boundaries actually lie. The best that can be done is to consider the range of possible values which may include the actual boundary. This range is known as the *margin of error*. The second source of ambiguity is that the distance between the boundaries is also probably not known. The third source of ambiguity is labelled the *safety margin*. We see the margin of safety interpreted in similar ways between different disciplines. In medicine it is the difference between the amount of a therapeutic agent that causes the therapeutic effect and the amount that is toxic. In finance it is the difference between the intrinsic value of a stock and its market price. In accountancy it is the difference between the breakeven point and current output. The application of this construct to military logistics will become of relevance later in the book! The *safety margin* is therefore a "safety factor" built into a system that creates space or a margin between the force that the system can withstand and the force to which it may conceivably be subjected. However, when establishing a *safety margin* it is important to consider the ambiguous nature of the boundary in question. The *safety margin* therefore needs to take that particular boundary's *margin of error* into account as the worst case may be some distance from the position set by the most likely case. Therefore, in terms of pure safety, the *safety margin* should be set from the worst-case position, however this may not always be practicable.

In between the boundaries are zones of activities. I will start from the outside and work in towards the core of the system. The first zone is the one between the *limit of ultimate performance* and the boundary of *accepted functional performance*. I have given this zone the label the *induction error margin*. This zone needs to be considered alongside the *margin of error* and *safety margin*. The danger in this zone is that those involved may (repeatedly) see their system not breaking down although accepting that they may be pushing the boundary of *accepted functional performance*. The danger is that those operating the system then assume falsely that it is safe to push performance to this new point in the future. This is a false perception of safety and is the result of what is referred to as the *problem of induction* or Hume's problem.[105] Hence I have labelled it the *induction error margin*. Any activity that takes the system into this zone should be considered to be extremely high risk. The fact that it is possible for even a technologically sophisticated organisation such as NASA to confuse the roles of these three margins was highlighted by the Nobel Laureate, Richard Feynman, in his contribution (Annex F of the Presidential Commission) to the report into the destruction of the NASA shuttle Challenger.

---

105 Taleb (2007:45)

The next zone, between the boundary of *accepted functional performance* and boundary of *accepted performance* is a zone of high-risk activity. This is the zone between what the system is able to do safely and what it is allowed to do by regulation or public convention. This zone may be considered to be a societally accepted *safety margin*. While to society this is seen as the acceptable *safety margin*, to others (the operators of the system), it is a zone containing inefficiencies and therefore opportunities. They see underutilised capacity (a *Type 2 error*). Within this zone the vulnerabilities may be created by both technical limitation and organisational tempo. As stated earlier, tempo can be categorised as normal, *high tempo* and emergency modes. Normal is the day-to-day operation, *high tempo* is sustainable for a limited time before the organisation is stressed to the point of *crisis* and emergency is when the organisation is pushing itself to the threshold of *crisis*. The question for management is how far to push the boundaries and how hard to push the organisation. Some pushing may be needed to test the organisation's limits and can be done safely if done with care. However, how far and how hard to push any system is an issue of how much risk the organisation is willing to take (*risk appetite*). Again this is a judgement call for management as any centrally based rule on *risk appetite* will tend to be risk averse and therefore will tend to induce *Type 2 errors*. The process of adjustment will, in *hindsight*, always look *chaotic*. Where these boundaries lie and how hard to push the organisation are two of the key, but often hidden, assumptions which drive an organisation.

The third zone I have labelled the *regulated space*. This is a zone of relatively low risk taking as it is within what is permitted by regulation or public convention. It is however outside the stable core of the system. Within this zone there is a role for human judgment with all the attendant risk this brings. This is where humans experiment with their system in order to make themselves more efficient and productive. However, here we also see the pursuit of an expertise and therefore a market niche (for example a deep-water drilling expertise sold by TransOcean to BP in the Gulf of Mexico) and *production pressure* competing with safety considerations (labelled "continuous compensating functional pressure" in the diagram) pushing the organisation to take risks greater than those deemed acceptable by regulation or public convention.

Finally we return to the core. Here we see regulation and public convention as a strong force, powered by risk aversion, trying to drive activity so that it focuses such activity in the stable core. This area may be considered to contain low-risk activities but this may also be just an *illusion of control*. Research that considered whether *verbatim compliance*[106] was possible found that often

---

106 Hirschhorn (1993:139)

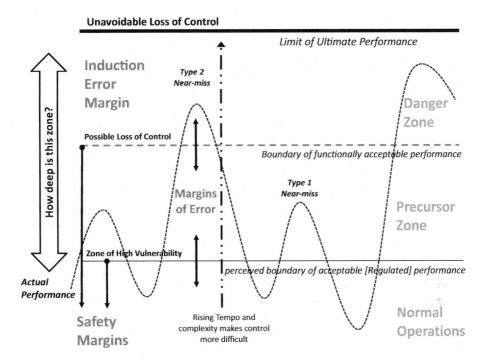

Figure 2.3   Performance oscillation

it was not. Small differences between the situation that confronted them and the context implicit within the regulation meant that workers were not able to apply the rule as written. The process required a mechanism to adjust the rules to suit the prevailing circumstances; this adjustment process provided new risks to any time-sensitive process.

We can see, therefore, that systems contain many forms of ambiguity and that judgement as to where a boundary lies is more an act of faith than a scientific judgement. We see margins misunderstood and therefore misused. We see social convention driven by risk aversion compete against an organisation's need to find a niche and to be efficient. This all leads to a system that, in reality, is highly interactively *complex*. In turn this leads to activities generating *chaotic* (that is "apparently random") outcomes. Karl Wieck suggests that "what is distinctive about units that strive for failure-free performance is that they expect interruptions ... and develop broader capabilities for recovery";[107] therefore it is the expectation of disorder (apparent *chaos*) rather than order that is the key to failure-free performance.

---

107 Weick (2011:23)

If we take the boundaries of performance (see Figure 2.2) then map on to it the oscillations described in Figure 2.1, we come up with Figure 2.3. In Figure 2.3 we see the boundaries and the margins described earlier. In addition to notation used previously, we now also have *Type 1* and *Type 2 near-misses*. A *Type 1 near-miss* is where there is still a barrier in place that stops the accident. However the performance is inside the *safety margin*. A *Type 2 near-miss* is where an accident is prevented just by good "luck". A *Type 2 near-miss* occurs within the *induction error margin* and so the accident could take place but did not due to good fortune: this idea of luck is akin to Charles Perrow's *Union Carbide Factor*.[108] A *Type 1 near-miss* provides early warning of potential disaster. It would be a mistake to classify a *Type 2 near-miss* as an early warning; these need to be recognised as a lucky escape!

CHAOS THEORY

In the conclusion to his book on fundamental surprises, Zvi Lanir says,

> *These findings suggest that chaotic situations are much more common and systematic than we ordinarily think ... systems move between an ordinary and a chaotic mode as the result of indistinguishable situational changes ... chaos is not necessarily degeneration, but rather a stage in how systems cope with changes in their environment that are beyond their existing ... capabilities.*[109]

This conclusion was partly based on his observation that,

> *chaotic phenomena have been found even in very deterministic physical systems, such as simple electrical circuits, dynamos, and pendulums. Even pendulums, often thought of as the epitome of regularity, have been found to behave chaotically ... minute changes in their driving frequency ... produces unpredictable changes in their motion ... even the most detailed data do not allow predicting when the sudden shift from order to chaos will take place, or what will be the system's next motion, once it passes out of the chaotic mode.*[110]

This would suggest that *chaos* may be a normal part of all systems. As far back as 1994, Tony Burlando introduced the idea of *chaos* alongside *risk management*.[111] He saw this new science having a direct application to *risk management* and being

---

108 Perrow (1999:356–2588)
109 Lanir (1983:119)
110 Lanir (1983:118)
111 Burlando (1994)

> *based on the simple principle that order can be found in disorder ...*
> *it is not concerned with rules and order, but rather with rules of*
> *disorder and events that appear random ... (and that) risk managers*
> *must realize that there is an inescapable link between small,*
> *seemingly innocuous events and large catastrophic results.*

In this, whether consciously or not, he was linking *chaos* theory with *interactive complexity*, which is part of the idea of *normal accidents*.[112] In his article he describes how five concepts from *chaos* theory apply to risk management (see Table 2.2).

Table 2.2   Chaos and risk management

Concept	Link to Risk Management
1) *Universal* risk and scale	• "Chaos theory ... declar(es) that certain predictable patterns do exist in systems otherwise perceived as totally random" suggests that commonality exists between "otherwise divergent observable phenomena within certain predictable boundaries, different systems of risk should be identical to each other ... able to gain insight ... by studying parallel systems". • That it is "important to recognise the limitations of the chosen scale" and hence the use of the *micro* to *mega* layers suggested earlier in this book. • That "the nature of risk is universal, only the scale changes". • He see risk management that "suffers from a crisis of increasing specialization ... with specialization comes isolation". He sees the need for risk management specialists to step outside of their own expertise in order to appreciate the interconnectedness of the issues at hand.
2) Sensitive dependence on initial *conditions*	• He quotes the "butterfly effect" and "for want of a nail ... the kingdom is lost!" in order to highlight the issue that small events can have large consequences. • He presses home the "inescapable link between small, seemingly innocuous events and large catastrophic results". • He sees that without a basic awareness of the principles of *chaos* theory and sensitive dependence, the significance of small changes may be overlooked as being unimportant or irrelevant.
3) Strange attractors in phase space	• He says that the danger of those managing risk "deal with seemingly isolated or random events: but over time (proper scale), certain patterns being to emerge". • These patterns form around certain "basins of attraction" or that "regions with changeable boundaries begin to appear". In other words, what was once thought of as *chaotic* would appear to conform to a pattern.

112 Perrow (1984)

Table 2.2   Continued

Concept	Link to Risk Management
4) Basin boundaries and "fuzzy borders"	• He says "contrary to the classical sciences, chaos is not concerned with describing a final stable behaviour of a system. It is this preoccupation with predictability that has made the traditional sciences nearly worthless for most risk management applications".
	• He sees that "in risk as in chaos, the ultimate (stable) position is indeterminable" and therefore one should look for ways of managing *chaos* rather than trying to resolve it. He sees "small (seemingly inconsequential) behaviors are deterministic (and that) they define the boundaries of possible outcomes".
	• He goes on to say that before managers can comprehend risk, they "must understand the basin boundary in which it 'rolls' – this means (that they need to understand) the *complex* network of forces and external influences that shape the set of all possible outcomes" or, in other words, the range of outcomes possible.
5) Connectedness	• "The ability to see through the obvious and make connections to the implausible requires both insight and intuition. Risk Managers must wean themselves away from an overreliance on traditional math and science in favour of new ways of looking at (for) risks". The two examples they provide both illustrate *unintended consequences* of some conventional risk management methods; both transferred the risk to other stakeholders in ways that had not been foreseen.

"Chaos theory is about limitations on predictability in classical physics, stemming from the fact that almost all classical systems are inherently unstable."[113] Whether *chaos* theory can be applied to the social sciences, in its purest form, is still open to question. Whether fractals can be used to transfer ideas between the *mega* to *micro* layers still has to be proved. However the basis of *chaos* theory, that *chaos* is normal and order is transitory, does provide a useful catalyst to thinking about the management of *complex* systems. As a way of breaking up rigid thought patterns, it has a function to serve.

Conclusion

While complexity does diminish the scope for prevention, it does not diminish the role of *foresight*, the *anticipation* of what might happen. *Foresight* does, however, require those addressing the issue to approach the task in a particular way. The fundamental to this approach is the requirement to have an open mind and to embrace rather than diminish the complexity. In embracing this complexity, those involved have to accept the limits on what

---

113 Mainelli (2005:179)

they can actually control. They have to accept that the world is not ordered and that the order only occasionally breaks down; they have to accept that the world is *chaotic*. That is, that they cannot see all the factors that may have influence on them and their plans or even the path ahead that they may wish to take. They must expect that seemingly normal interactions will have outcomes that they never expected; they need to expect to *muddle through* as factors emerge around us. They have to accept that their actual *span of control* is more limited than they may like. While this situation may be uncomfortable, it is thought to be preferable to being cocooned within an *illusion of control*. They must therefore expect the unexpected and so be ready and prepared to act accordingly. To close this chapter I offer a metaphor to describe the work of *foresight* as I see it.

"MISTY PATH" METAPHOR

The worldview that comes across from a reading of many inquiry reports is that the future is ordered and foreseeable. For this to be the case then one has to envisage the world as being linear and therefore predictable. Choosing to take *chaos theory* as the new paradigm, we take on a view that "sees the world as (being) made up of complex systems that are nonlinear, dynamic, unstable and unpredictable".[114] This requires a new metaphor to help us explore these ideas. The metaphor to be used is based on the construct of a path over a narrow winding causeway where you have to try to navigate the path in a dense mist. The metaphor alludes to trying to negotiate a path, of known construction but unknown state (Boundary 1), which you cannot see and whose course you do not know. It also alludes to a number of unknown hazards if you stray from the path or stay on it. If you stray from the path you do not know where the edge of the path (Boundary 2) is, you do not know where the top edge of the causeway (Boundary 3) is or where the bottom of the causeway (Boundary 4) is either. The mist also covers the scale of the hazard, this is, the size and the nature of the drop between each boundary. The mist also covers the route of the path, the type and condition of the surface and the presence of any hazards in the roadway. Given all these unknowns, this metaphor is seen as representing most organisations and *conditions* under which they are required to operate. It suggests that those taking the path have to choose, given the degree of urgency they perceive, both the direction and speed of travel, and the measures they will need to take in order to determine a safe course. I have labelled this metaphor the "misty path" and see it as representing the unseen patterns and order that is inherent in *normal chaos*.

---

114 Goldoff (2000:2019)

Chapter 3
Issues for Foresight

Introduction

At the heart of the *foresight* problem is what Turner labelled the *incubation period*. As previously stated, Turner sees that during this period a dislocation evolves between existing beliefs and the precautions taken and the actual situation that the organisation faces: as the gap between the two increases, so does the likelihood of a *crisis*. This is the period where the norms are eroded and factors emerge that lead (directly or indirectly) to the subsequent events. This is the period during which the normal morphs into the abnormal and new hazards emerge in unexpected ways. This period is critical to the avoidance of *failures of foresight*.

Karlene Roberts and her colleagues expand Turner's ideas and see that this stage represents a period:

> … *during which minor failures persist or accumulate. The incubation period is characterised by a series of events that are at odds with the existing organisational norms and beliefs but that go unnoticed or unheard. These discrepant events represent opportunities for organisational members to recognize the inadequacy of their models and representation of the world. Vigilant organisations could take advantage of such discrepant events to bring their worldview into closer alignment with reality. However, Turner observes that in organisations headed for disaster these events go completely unnoticed, are noticed but not understood, or are noticed and understood but not adequately responded to.*[1]

To put this problem another way, as a system adapts to the changing environment, gaps are created, providing opportunities for unwanted events to occur and therefore for management to catch the problem and resolve it

---

1   Roberts, Madsen and Desai (2005:83)

before this happens. Also, as we have already seen, other researchers have identified the same stage but have approached it from a different perspective, thereby offering us the ideas of *precursor zones* or *recovery windows*.

At the heart of the *foresight* problem is the issue of why management fails to catch these problems as they emerge. This can be summarised as being because they do not see the signals of danger, they do not appreciate what they are being told or they do not act appropriately. Time and again we see that management were in possession of the vital piece of information but due to *structural secrecy* they fail to see or appreciate the importance of the information to hand. There are many research papers that talk about the types and the nature of the signals that are missed but they fail to explain convincingly why this happens. Even Turner just attributes these failures to "sloppy management".[2] In contrast, I once heard experts described as "knowing what is not there that should be"; the premise is that if you do not know what to look for, you will never see the deficiency. I refer to these items as *issues of interest*. Therefore, in this chapter, I will be concentrating on the potential *failure to see* and will suggest what people might look for during the *incubation period*.

In this chapter I will examine these *issues of interest*. I will first examine what these issues might be and how they may be articulated. I will point out the necessity of stratifying these issues in order to avoid confusion between those issues that can be resolved and those that must be continuously managed. I will then test these redefined *issues of interest* to see whether these issues appeared within the three data sets already used. I will separate this discussion out into the first four Turner stages. I will also look at the use of metaphor as a catalyst to *foresight*. In constructing his theory, Turner uses the term *incubation* to describe the period in which the unwanted develops and then manifests. I would suggest that the term *incubation* should be seen as a metaphor rather than an accurate description of what happens. While I shall continue to use the term in order to remain consistent with Turner's construct, I would not want the term to limit its catalytic power.

---

2   Turner (1994)

Issues of Interest

WHAT TO LOOK FOR

In Turner's original work he identified his own *issues of interest*. These are

- rigidity of perception and beliefs;
- decoy phenomena;
- information difficulties;
- *organisational exclusivity* (neglect of outside complaints);
- exacerbation of the hazards by strangers;
- failure to comply with regulations;
- the tendency to minimise emergent danger.

Since Turner penned his ideas in 1976, there has been much more work done that tries to identify the causes of failure. As part of my original research,[3] I identified over 200 issues within this subsequent work and collated them into a number of main themes: this resulted in "20 questions". In addition to the identification of single issues, others have taken Turner's lead and have produced their own lists. The totality of this subsequent work can be used to enrich the picture created by Turner's work. In this section I will examine three issues. First I will suggest a way to differentiate between those *issues of interest* that can be resolved and those that can only be managed. I will acknowledge previous efforts to identify the factors that may precipitate a *crisis* and explain why I see the need for another! The final issue is to explain the factors that I would suggest be used to stimulate *risk discourse*.

STRATIFICATION OF CAUSATION

Earlier in this book I have already introduced the *fallacy of homogeneity*. This fallacy can also be seen in work that does not stratify causation. James Reason offers a way to resolve this fallacy when it comes to pursuing *foresight*. Here we see that there may be scope for unintended adverse consequences to be created by trying to resolve an issue that can only be managed or managing an issue that needs to be resolved. While I have used the word "may" in this context, it may be more accurate to presume that, given the laws of large numbers, unintended adverse consequences are inevitable if we fail to resolve issues that should be resolved and vice versa. To assist us in this task James Reason

---

3   Lauder (2011)

differentiates between *Universals, Conditions* and *Causes* and sees the linkages between them as being:

- *Universals*: the ever-present tension between production and protection create –
- *Conditions*: latent factors that collectively produce defensive weaknesses that lead to –
- *Causes*: permit the chance conjunctions of local triggers and active failures to breach all the barriers and safeguards.[4]

Let us look at each in some more detail.

Universals

Reason describes *universals* as "the ever-present tension between production and protection". This is consistent with his view of *organisational oscillation* where there is an ever-present tension between production (a *Type 1 error*) and protection (a *Type 2 error*). These "ever-present tensions" can also be seen in the tensions between the two most fundamental business benefits (these are the need "to make money" and "to save money") and the "failure to comply with regulations"; "to make money" when described in the negative has also been referred to as *production pressure*. While these have been cited within inquiry reports as being the cause of an unwanted event, these *universal dilemmas*[5] should have been recognised as just being "ever-present tension" that needs to be carefully managed (see Table 3.1).

Table 3.1   *Universal dilemmas*

Small organisations v. Large organisations
Short-termism v. Long-termism
Empowerment v. Command and control
Devolution v. Centralisation
Individualism v. Team play

Universal dilemmas have been described as "issues that cannot be resolved but must be managed". Trompenaar and Hampden-Turner listed five such *universal dilemmas* (see Table 3.1). These dilemmas can be seen elsewhere. For example,

---

4   Reason (2008:137–138)
5   Trompenaar and Hampden-Turner (1999)

we see them in the writings of those who discuss *high reliability organisations* where there is a debate between the role of centralisation and decentralisation[6] within specific functions. We also need to be aware of how this idea may encompass similar issues debated under different labels such as specialisation verses intergradation or aggregation verses disaggregation. The key issue for those who wish to design or redesign systems is to identify those issues that cannot be resolved but can only be managed. It would be a fundamental error to confuse the two.

Universals can be seen in other areas as well. The key one of these is the availability of warnings of danger. A common thread in inquiry reports is that warnings of danger were present before the unwanted event occurred. The people offering these warnings have been labelled both as *whistle blowers* (for example, Roger Boisjoly in the case of the Challenger disaster[7]) or, using a more classical reference, as a *Cassandra*. Great weight is given to these warnings with the benefit of *hindsight*. However, this may be an oversimplification of the situation. While we may regret the warning missed, we need also to be aware of the flood of false warnings (by those, in *hindsight*, who can be seen to be *crying-wolf*) that may blind decision-makers to the reality of their situation. Therefore, to truly understand such events, we also have to recognise all the cases where decision-makers have been warned of pending disaster, where they have ignored these warnings and have been proven to be correct. Military history is full of examples of this phenomenon and the successful commander is just seen to be a bold leader. In 1944 Eisenhower was warned by his senior air force advisor that the US airborne force faced a disaster which would result in 85 per cent casualties; Eisenhower overruled his advisor, sent in the two US airborne divisions who, despite heavy losses, successfully achieved their missions. Whether the decision was bold or reckless I will leave others to debate. The weighing of warnings both for and against a proposition is a *universal dilemma*.

The false nature of this dilemma is demonstrated by a simple example of deception. It is possible for a fraudster to show that they have had perfect *foresight* by providing independent testimony that they perfectly predicted a sequence of events, for example a sequence of dice rolls. As is often cited, this can be done by giving different sequences to different people and then only providing the testimony of those to whom the correct sequence was provided. While not accusing those who cite *whistle blower* testimony of deliberate fraud, it is to suggest that the data they provide is only part of the full picture, it is

---

6   Weick and Sutcliffe (2007)
7   Vaughan (1996)

incomplete and therefore provides a false picture of the events in question. Warnings of failure are *universal*. In his book *The Psychology of Intelligence Analysis*[8] Richard Heuer therefore asks not for more data but for better analysis. Managers are likely to be faced by warning of dangers. Their issue is to determine which warning to take seriously and then to take action. For if they heeded every warning their organisation is likely to suffer a *Type 2* rather than *Type 1* failure.

Universal issues are phenomena that cannot be resolved. It is a mistake to think that they can. If organisations are to avoid preventable failures they need to be clear about the issues that will require constant and diligent supervision and adjustment.

Conditions

While the term *incubation* may offer positive images (eggs turning into fluffy chicks), the picture created in this context is more likely to be one of an infectious disease developing unseen within an organism. The image is made more specific in the work of Professor James Reason when he evokes the construct of *latent factors* or *pathogens*. Reason equates *latent failures* to *resident pathogens* in the human body. He describes *conditions* as "latent factors that collectively produce defensive weaknesses". Another way of looking at *conditions* is that while they may exist within an organisation, they are not in themselves the immediate cause of an unwanted event. Alluding to his *Swiss cheese theory* of disaster causation, Reason says that the "holes due to active failures are likely to be relatively short-lived, while those arising from latent *conditions* may lie dormant for many years until they are revealed … by incidents and accidents".[9] The question this raises is what these factors may be. Examples of such pathogens are poor leadership, poor communications, poor coordination, poor training or the dislocation between established procedures and what is actually required. These failures are therefore decisions or actions that may lead to the defeat of an organisation's defences but that happens sometime before any recognisable accident sequence begins.

Ron Westum provides us with indicators that may alert us that these *conditions* are arising. He offers us a continuum of how organisations may react to warning of pending harm. Westrum gives the continuum as:

---

8   Heuer (1999:vii)
9   Reason (1998:296)

- **Suppression** – harming or stopping the person bringing the anomaly to light: "shooting the messenger".
- **Encapsulation** – isolating the messenger so that the message is not heard.
- **Public relations** – putting the message "in context" to minimise its impact.
- **Local fix** – responding to the presenting case, but ignoring the possibility of others elsewhere.
- **Global fix** – an attempt to respond to the problem wherever it exists. Common in aviation, when a single problem will direct attention to ones elsewhere.
- **Inquiry** – attempting to get at the "root causes" of the problem.[10]

To be useful these indicators and all examinations of *conditions* rely on candid *risk discourse* where there is a thorough reflexive evaluation of the organisation's activities. This scale enables those engaged in a *foresight* exercise to identify whether they are honestly evaluating the data available to them.

Causes

Reason describes causes as those factors that "permit the chance conjunction of local triggers and active failures to breach all the barriers and safeguards". Here we see causes as the last final action that enabled flaws to align as they need to in order to create a *crisis*. Here we are generally looking at such phenomena as *slips, errors, mistakes, violations, folly* and *negligence*. Reason sees *slips* as being failures of attention such as intrusions, omissions, reversals, mis-ordering, or mis-timing. He sees *lapses* as being memory failures such as omitting planned items, losing your place or forgetting intentions and *mistakes* as being the misapplication of knowledge or rules.[11] Reason sees *violations* as the "deliberate ... deviations from those practices deemed necessary ... to maintain the safe operation of the potentially hazardous system".[12] *Folly* on the other hand, is defined by Barbra Tuchman as when a "perverse persistence in a policy (that is) demonstrably unworkable or counterproductive";[13] this is when people knowingly take decisions that they know to be wrong due to bureaucratic pressure. *Negligence* is seen to be failure to take "proper care" however that may be defined. In the end, however, in all of these factors we see immediacy between causes and the resultant harm produced.

---

10 Westrum (2004)
11 Reason (1990:207)
12 Reason (1990:195)
13 Tuchman (1984:29)

In terms of *foresight* there is a role for the stratification of causation between *universals*, *conditions* and *causes*. This stratification will enable those involved in *risk discourse* to start thinking about differentiating between those issues that have to be managed rather than be resolved, those issues that may sit dormant within the system for many years and those issues that are likely to be the immediate cause of a *crisis* or a disaster. When considering how *universals*, *conditions* and *causes* interact to precipitate a *crisis* we can see a *chaotic* rather than linear relationship at work. We can now start to understand what Charles Perrow meant by the *Union Carbide Factor* when he said, "it takes just the right combination of circumstance to produce a catastrophe".[14] When we use James Reason's *Swiss cheese*[15] metaphor, we see why the holes in the cheese might only align occasionally giving us, what Dennis Smith called, the *pathways of vulnerability*.[16] I have always thought of the defensive barriers, as represented by the slices of cheese, as being too static. I see these flawed barriers as being on a variable crank shaft so that, as they move, sometimes the holes align but at other times they do not. This means that the precipitating act has to occur at just the wrong time (when all the holes align) for there to be a *crisis* or a disaster. This explains why the same act, at another time, does not precipitate a *crisis*. If we refer back to Figure 2.2 and Figure 2.3 it helps to explain why we have such difficultly in knowing precisely where our performance boundaries lie.

REFINED *ISSUES OF INTEREST*

Turner originally identified seven *issues of interest*. I have collated over 200 such issues identified in the years that followed. The question for this book is, how many of these issues should be highlighted by this proposed catalytic framework? In my original work I consolidated the issues under 20 headings that became my 20 core questions for *risk governance*. Subsequent conversations suggested that this was still too many for people new to the idea of *risk discourse*. The danger of highlighting too many issues was seen to be that they would be used in a mindless way as a checklist rather than encouraging those involved to engage in "talking, digging, comparing, refining, and focusing". The key was to focus on what was critical. When considering what is critical, I go back to John Rockart's[17] description of *critical success factors* as "the few key areas where things must go right". Using Miller's *Magical number 7 (plus or minus 2)* provides a justification to limit Rockart's "few" to about seven. Having revisited the original issues and how they were distilled down to 20 groupings,

---

14   Perrow (1999:356–358)
15   Reason (2008:97–99)
16   Smith (2005:313–315)
17   Rockart (1979)

I then took this process a stage further and consolidated them under seven headings. The issue selection was therefore based on these groupings being higher-level (overarching) phenomena that encompass the original 200 plus as these were deemed appropriate by the practitioners consulted for discussion at the executive level.

The areas selected centre on a number of issues that are perceived to be key. The first of these covers the changing perspectives of stakeholders and is labelled *"who cares?"* The second is based on the proposition that disciplined team work is required to be successful and that the failure to prepare your team properly will lead to unwanted outcomes: this is given the label *failure to launch*. The third area covers the decoupling of practice from the official, documented routines; this is given the label *practical drift*. The fourth area covers the organisational factors that affect effective communications: this is given the label *structural secrecy*. The fifth area covers the *erroneous assumptions* that result from not seeing or appreciating the data available and adjusting one's beliefs as circumstances change. The sixth covers mechanisms that affect how the natural impetus of organisational efforts may prevent more appropriate action being taken: this is given the label *dysfunctional momentum*. The final area covers how, even when individual decisions are sound and logical, they may combine to lead the organisation in an unintended direction or may even generate unintended adverse consequences: this is given the label the *Plowman Effect*. As will be shown below, each of these terms has a specific technical meaning. However, for the purpose of this work, these terms are used as a label to cover a richer view of these issues.

The label *"who cares (about what)?"* derives from the idea that a risk or benefit perceived by one person or group may not be viewed in the same way by others. Where I have looked at the many ways the term *risk* is used,[18] I summarised my understanding of the term as being an "unwanted occurrence about which you care". Implicit within this definition is the potential for there to be different views taken about the same series of potential events. In some cases the individual or group may view the potential for jeopardy as being serious while others may not have the same concern. In other cases the positions may be reversed. Both situations may affect the emergence of some adverse occurrences. Tony Jaques[19] provides two such examples: the first being Shell's Brent Spar and the second Monsanto's attempts to use certain types of biotechnology within Europe. Both organisations faced a *crisis* when their worldview about hazards and the

---

18 Lauder (2011:16)
19 Jaques (2010:476–477)

associated *precautionary norms* crashed against the belief and norms of other significant stakeholders. Crises may incubate where there is a power gradient between those who perceive the risk to be significant and those who do not; in *hindsight* the latter are often labelled as *whistle blowers* whose warnings go unheeded. Alternatively, within a board, two members may just have subtly different priorities and the pursuit of each may generate unnecessary friction and dysfunctional interaction; these circumstances might have been avoided through the realisation that they actually had only minor differences. For the purpose of this work the term *who cares (about what)* needs to be associated with the potential changes of stakeholders or their beliefs. This label should prompt senior managers and executives to consider whether their worldview is held consistently by other stakeholders and where differing views may be the genesis of a future dysfunctional behaviour or even *crisis*.

The term *failure to launch* was inspired by Scott Snook. In the conclusion to his case study, Snook spoke of a "weak launch" and how "an underdeveloped team ... confused authority and diffuse responsibilities led to inaction. Inaction led to tragedy".[20] Snook goes on to say that research has shown "how critical a good launch and crew-member stability is to team development and performance"; the reverse of a good launch has therefore been labelled a *failure to launch*. Much of Snook's analysis of this issue is based on Katzenbach and Smith's work on *real teams* where a real team is a "small number of people with complementary skills who are equally committed to a common purpose, goals, and working approach for which they hold themselves mutually accountable".[21] This work links to a wider variety of constructs such as theories around *high reliability organisations* to circumstances where a team's *failure to launch* because they are "talking past each other" or due to *new group syndrome*.[22] Boin et al. go on to explain that "during the first, and often critical, stages of an acute crisis, group members are uncertain about their roles and status and thus are concerned about the possibility of being made a scapegoat". This idea of the "new creating problems" is also encapsulated in the term *liability of newness*; Diane Vaughan took an original idea by Stinchcombe and stated that "his concept also may apply to analogical circumstances at other levels of analysis, explaining why new programs, products, or services by individual organizations get into trouble".[23] This construct can be seen to include Turner's issue of "involvement of strangers" as this concerns the interaction of individuals with a system and how the individual will affect the overall

20   Snook (2000:208)
21   Katzenbach and Smith (1993:92)
22   Boin, Hart, Stern and Sundelius (2005:46–47)
23   Vaughan (1999:275)

outcome but whose role is ambiguous (and thereby adding another element of *chaos* into the system). From this body of research we can see why organisations may fail to work together effectively and how important the launch is. For the purpose of this work the term *failure to launch* needs to be associated with the planning, training, briefing and management of teams as they go about their allotted tasks. This label should prompt senior managers and executives to consider whether the teams working for them are ready to launch properly.

Practical drift is another term coined by Snook. Snook used the term to mean "the slow steady uncoupling of local practice from written procedure"[24] where "locally efficient procedures acquired through practice gain legitimacy through unremarkable repetition".[25] *Drift* can be seen as one of the mechanisms that leads to what Turner labelled as the "failure to comply with existing regulations" as it also concerns how practice may start to deviate from the formally established routine. Snook is not the only person to talk of *drift*. Johnson and Scholes talk of *strategic drift*[26] and Farjourn talks of *safety drift*.[27] *Drift* can be seen in other phenomena. Two examples of this are Vaughan's *normalisation of deviance* and Wohlstetter's *slow pearl harbour*. When discussing *normalisation of deviance*, Vaughan talks about "how signals of potential danger can be normalized"[28] and how deviance can subsequently be reinterpreted as being within normal or acceptable limits;[29] here we see *drift* away from a standard to one that was originally considered to be dangerous. Wohlstetter defines *slow pearl harbour* as when "the change at any given time seems innocent enough", but, over time, "the changes add up and can ultimately spell disaster";[30] here we see *drift* as an unconscious change over time. This subject can be investigated in greater depth in several directions. One such direction might be to look at the various types of signals of potential danger already utilised; an initial list might include signals that have been classified as routine, *messy*, mixed, strong, misinterpreted, missed or *decoy*. While specialists may need to be aware of the material at this depth, the majority of executives are more likely to be deterred by this level of detail.[31] For this reason, the mechanisms that drive *drift*, such as the *problem of induction*, are not listed either. Therefore, for the purpose of this work, the term *practical drift* is used to stimulate the idea that accepted practice changes over time. While this change may provide some advantages to the organisation, such

---

24 Snook (2000:24)
25 Snook (2000:184)
26 Johnson and Scholes (1997)
27 Farjourn (2005:60–78)
28 Vaughan (1996:xiv)
29 Vaughan (1996:65)
30 Wohlstetter (1979)
31 Lauder (2011)

as adaptive flexibility, it may also have unintended adverse consequences. The idea of *drift* should make those engaged consider the potential danger of the decoupling of formal and informal organisational routines and to be aware of where this might be happening within their organisation.

Diane Vaughan's work also provides us with the term *structural secrecy*. Vaughan describes it as "the way that patterns of information, organizational structure, processes, and transactions, and the structure of regulatory relations systematically undermine the attempt to know and interpret situations in all organizations". I see this term as encompassing what Turner referred to as *information difficulties* and decoy phenomena as these consume the resource that might otherwise overcome *structural secrecy*. Turner also says, "Rigid hierarchies can further inhibit the flow of information and contribute to the typical range of problems which build up during an accident incubation period".[32] Work, such as that done by Bella, shows how organisations distort information as it flows through the system or how senior managers might think that "because I do not know about it: it cannot be happening", what Westrum called the *fallacy of centrality*[33] and Snook referred to as "the commander's delusion".[34] Again while there has been a great deal of research done in this area, for the purpose of this work, the term *structural secrecy* is used to encompass the many ways that the organisation's structure might inhibit rather than enhance internal communications. This might mean that those who may be later accused of having caused a *failure of foresight*, might not have seen, appreciated or acted on the data available to them. The purpose of this label is to remind senior management or executives that, rather than assuming that their structure will ensure that the necessary data is delivered to where it is required, they should be aware constantly of how their structure might prevent them receiving that last critical piece of data. Linked closely to *structural secrecy* is the result that this might have throughout the system. This resulting phenomenon is discussed next.

The term *erroneous assumptions* is used to cover a wide variety of issues. It includes instances where any perception, belief or assumption proves to be false which may have been induced by decoy phenomena. This term is seen to include Turner's issue of "Rigidities in perception and beliefs" and "minimizing emergent danger". While the first may seem an obvious inclusion, the second may not. The reason that I have included "minimizing emergent danger" is

---

32   Turner (1994:216)
33   Westrum (1982:393)
34   Snook (2000:177)

that it is the frequently held cultural beliefs that insist that "it could never happen here" that mean that signals of pending danger are ignored. *Erroneous assumptions* also link *fundamental surprise* with *cosmological episodes*[35] and the like. Weick defined a *cosmological episode* as a "sudden loss of meaning ... (due to) fundamental surprise ... A cosmological episode occurs when people suddenly and deeply feel that the universe is no longer a rational order system". His point is that these episodes can happen to anyone in any walk of life. It is not that these issues concern "failure in gathering, analyzing or distributing information", which might be labelled *situational surprise*, it is that they "reveal a mind-set that ceased to be relevant"[36] that leads to them no longer being able to make sense of the world around them. While *erroneous assumptions* are very closely linked to *structural secrecy*, where one may be seen to cause the other, it is considered that they are worth separating out as the second is the mechanism and the first is the result. Mitigating the second may be about refining a process, while the first is concerned with changing the understanding of individuals. The methods required to mitigate each are quite different and therefore need to be considered individually. For example, within this subject there is the fundamental issue of whether you trust the data presented to you. John Adams[37] unwittingly has provided a useful categorisation that helps me to think about this problem. He talks of three categories of risk. These are those risks we: 1) perceived directly, 2) perceived through science (measurable by instruments) and 3) what he called "virtual risks" (which we may not understand but accept as an act of faith; the example he gives is global warming whether we rely on expert opinion when forming our own judgement). From this categorisation I have evolved a method I use when I receive new data. I start by questioning: 1) whether I believe my own sense, 2) whether I believe the instrument from which I am reading the data or 3) whether I believe the person or source of the data. As assumptions will be built on whether I believe (trust) the data, this device is my starting point for a more thorough analysis of the data. The purpose of this label is to remind executives of the need to check the validity of all critical beliefs and assumptions associated with the system in question and to question the sources of the data on which these assumptions are based.

The term *dysfunctional momentum* comes from Barton and Sutcliffe, who say it is "when individuals or teams continue to engage in a course of failing action".[38] *Dysfunctional momentum* occurs when people continue to

---

35 Weick (1993)
36 http://www.articlesbase.com/economics-articles/fundamental-surprise-israeli-lessons-2784076.html, accessed 8 December 2014
37 Adams (2007:38)
38 Barton and Sutcliffe (2009:1331)

work towards an original goal without pausing to recalibrate or re-examine their processes or their goals, even in the face of cues that suggest they should change course. Charles Perrow also identified a kind of *dysfunctional momentum*. He refers to *error-inducing systems*.[39] These are systems that prompt behaviours which are contrary to the system's overall purpose. One example would be a safety system that makes it difficult for those involved to conform to the prescribed rules or even encourages them to break the rules. In contrast to *dysfunctional momentum*, Sydow et al. talk of *organisational path dependence* which examines "how organizations can lose their flexibility and become inert or even locked in".[40] Barton and Sutcliffe look at the forces that promote or work against the *mental interruptions* (what Klein et al. called *frame-breakers*[41]) needed to make people re-evaluate their actions. While Barton and Sutcliffe list some of the factors (such as "voicing concern", "scepticism of expertise", "situated humility" and "seeking disparate views"), they miss a number of others already identified within academic literature. In addition to Turner's list are such phenomena as the *escalation of commitment*,[42] *unresponsive bystander*,[43] the *unrocked boat*,[44] the *fallacy of social redundancy*,[45] *learned helplessness*[46] and *social shirking*.[47] These ideas of why people may not act need to be linked to why people may not see the problems facing them. Klein talks of the *garden path scenario* which "documents the knowledge shields that people use to explain away discrepancies that signal that they are mistaken in the way they are framing the situation".[48] He goes on to speculate "that the more explaining away people do to preserve their frame, the more resistant they will be to a framebreaker". The purpose of this label is to remind senior management or executives that, rather than assuming that their decision-making process will ensure that the data is appreciated and the appropriate act will follow, they should be constantly aware that the momentum of their organisation might mean that it fails to change course when this is necessary.

The final grouping, labelled the *Plowman effect*, focuses on where a combination of decisions or actions, which are correct in isolation and on an individual basis, when combined may take the organisation in an unintended

39 Perrow (1999:172–173)
40 Sydow, Schreyogg and Kock (2009:689)
41 Klein, Pliske, Crandall and Woods (2005:20)
42 Keil, Depledge and Rai (2007)
43 Latané and Darley (1970)
44 Reason (1997)
45 Snook (2000:210)
46 Reason (2008)
47 Ghaffarzadegan (2008)
48 Klein, Pliske, Crandall and Woods (2005:20)

direction or may have unintended adverse consequences. This idea can be seen to be akin to *random walk theory* in statistic and *muddling through* that was mentioned earlier in this book. In their 2007 paper Plowman et al.[49] demonstrated how small changes can accumulate in such a way that they can, unintentionally, change the strategic direction of organisations. This change may be beneficial but it may also bring adverse consequences. Diane Vaughan states that "we are reminded of how repetition, seemingly small choices, and the banality of daily decisions in organizational life – indeed, in most social life – can camouflage from the participants a cumulative directionality".[50] Irwin gave us the idea of *compounded abstraction*[51] (where new data is added to old conclusions which lead us down a different path to the one we would have gone if we had added data to data): Klein's garden path scenario also talks of where "taking one step that seems very straightforward, and then another, and each step makes so much sense that you do not notice how far you are getting from the main road". All these ideas add up to an awareness that progress does not necessarily take us to where we thought we were going. From this we can derive the importance of appreciating that change with adverse consequences does not need a mistake or error to precipitate it. Charles Perrow warned that *normal accidents* are inevitable in systems that are *complex* and closely coupled. Even advocates for *high reliability organisations* recognise that they cannot ensure that accidents will not happen.[52] The purpose of this label is to remind senior management or executives that, rather than assuming that for things to go wrong, for crises to happen, an accident or mistake must occur, it may simply be the conjunction of normal events. People in those roles need to be constantly aware of the potential for adverse events within their organisations to emerge from routine activity. They therefore need to try to appreciate the potential *unintended consequences* that may lurk within the overarching direction of activity.

In my previous book[53] that looked at the constraints on inquiries and commissions to produce *active learning*, I pointed to the idea that those conducting investigations have an implicit *mental model* of how they expect the system under investigation to work. Within these *mental models* are embedded basic assumptions about how the system works. In the same way, the seven issues described above describe an implicit *mental model* for how crises may

---

49 Plowman, Baker, Beck, Kulkani, Solansky and Travis (2007)
50 Vaughan (1996:119)
51 Irwin (1977)
52 Bourrier (2005:95)
53 Lauder (2013)

emerge and therefore another way of viewing this *mental model* is as a basic working proposition. For clarity, my basic working proposition is as follows:

> *For a crisis to emerge there will be a misalignment between the issues that stakeholders care about and therefore their priorities for action (who cares (about what)?). There will be misalignment within the teams tasked to manage the issue and in them having the necessary resources, skill and authority to deliver the desired outcome (failure to launch). There will be a decoupling of the formal and informal routines used and necessary to perform their tasks (Practical drift). There will be failures in communication due to the organisation's structures working as a barrier rather than an enabler (structural secrecy). There will be the use of incorrect beliefs and assumptions within decision-making processes about the organisation, the issue and the context (erroneous assumptions). There will be factors that will prevent organisations seeing, appreciating and acting in new ways that would have been in their own best interest (dysfunctional momentum). There will be individual decisions that, while being valid and logical in isolation, will shape emergent organisational properties; these consequences may be beneficial but they might also be adverse (the Plowman effect).*

More detailed *mental models* of *crisis* emergence can be used. These might be based around the issues imbedded within my 20 questions[54] or they may be based around the formulation of recommendations produced by public inquiries and commissions.[55] These two models were designed for the more experienced risk practitioners whereas the model proposed in this book is designed for practitioners not so familiar with the subject of *risk governance*. In summary, distilling previous research carried out into the causes of crises and disaster suggests that the critical issues that should be used at the start of *risk discourse* are 1) *who cares (about what)*, 2) *failure to launch*, 3) *practical drift*, 4) *structural secrecy*, 5) *erroneous assumptions*, 6) *dysfunctional momentum*, 7) the *Plowman effect*.

GENERAL GUIDANCE

We can now compare my seven *issues of interest* with those offered by other authors. A number of authors have produced their own list of issues: I have taken six of those lists for the sake of this comparison. These offerings are detailed in Table 3.2.

---

54   Lauder (2011)
55   Lauder (2013)

Table 3.2   Other issue lists

Hollnagel, E. (1993) – five classic patterns

- Drift towards failure as defences erode in the face of production pressure.
- An organisation that takes past success as a reason for confidence instead of investing in anticipating the changing potential for failure.
- Fragmented distributed problem-solving process that clouds the big picture.
- Failure to revise assessments as new evidence accumulates.
- Breakdowns at the boundaries of organisational units that impedes communication and coordination.

Smith, D. (2002)

- The scale and severity of the event(s) (which may include the loss of life, damage to property, or reputation).
- The speed of escalation of the event and its impact upon the organisation as a whole.
- Failures in early warning processes and weak systems of controls.
- The lack of a precautionary approach, poor weak signal detection and impaired communication.
- The failure to recognise the validity of external warnings and concerns.
- The role of management in creating the conditions and climate within which errors may occur.
- The generation of changes to the culture of the organisation as a result of the event.

Smith, D. (2003) – indicators of crisis

- Role of assumptions and core beliefs.
- Poor weak signal detection.
- Failure to adhere to early warnings and disregarding complaints by outsiders.
- Erosion of systems of control.
- Lack of sense-making by management.
- Power gradients around technical and political elites.
- Constrained communications.
- Focus on contingency planning over softer issues.

Hale, A. and Heijer, T. (2006)

- Defences erode with production pressure.
- Past performance leads to complacency.
- No shared risk picture.
- Risk assessment not revised with new evidence.
- Boundary breakdown impedes communication.
- Not high enough devotion to safety.
- No flexible response to change.
- Safety not inherent enough in design of system.

Jaques, T. (2010) – areas for issue management

- Proactively addressing underlying systemic causes of potential crisis.
- Establishment of effective signal detection mechanisms.
- Properly identifying stakeholders and their perspectives.
- Learning and unlearning on an ongoing basis.

Table 3.2   Continued

Fischbacher, D. (2013) – latent and active errors

- Cultural constraints.
- Regulatory gap.
- Incubation process.
- Systems design.
- Failure of control.

In analysing these proposed factors we do see some direct connection between the factors in multiple lists. One example can be seen in the linkage between "failures in early warning processes and weak systems of controls", "failure to adhere to early warnings and disregarding complaints by outsiders" and the "establishment of effective signal detection mechanisms". Another is "failure to revise assessments as new evidence accumulates" and "risk assessment not revised with new evidence". However, overall correlation between the six lists can be seen to be very weak.

If, however, you take a broader view the correlations can be enhanced; at a raised level of abstraction we can see more of the factors correlate. For example "drift toward failure as defences erode in the face of production pressure", "erosion of systems of control", "defences erode with production pressure", "regulatory gap", "failure of control", and "focus on contingency planning over softer issues" can all be linked to *practical drift*. Another example is "role of assumptions and core beliefs", "an organization that takes past success as a reason for confidence instead of investing in anticipating the changing potential for failure" and "past performance leads to complacency" might all be associated with the generation of *erroneous assumptions*.

The third consideration is that, at this level of abstraction, we can see that not all the *issues of interest* that I have identified are embraced by the factors within these lists. There is no reference to anything like the *Plowman effect* in any of the existing lists. In addition only Jaques' list includes "properly identifying stakeholders and their perspectives", which comes anywhere near the question of "who cares". This would suggest that my revised list of *issues of interest* does enable the other lists of issues.

Finally, in terms of general *foresight* a number of the factors suggested within these lists do not really help as catalysts to *foresight*. Suggestions such as "proactively addressing underlying systemic causes of potential crisis" is more a direction that a causal factor. Therefore, based on this analysis I shall continue to use my seven revised *issues of interest* as my discourse catalysts using the re-imagined Turner's stages.

Stage I – *Notionally Normal Starting Point*

In this next section I will discuss how Stage 1 may be used in order to facilitate *foresight*. I will look at six aspects: 1) the nature of the problem, 2) boundaries issues, 3) our *point of entry* into the model, 4) reviewing the past, 5) the source of future crises and 6) what is a norm? I will start by examining the nature of the problem.

I have previously described the many different ways that people use the term risk.[56] These usages range from inputs to subsequence across five considerations. In this context the assumption is made that what matters to the executive is the consequence of any unwanted event rather than the event itself. Therefore, in this context, what the executive needs to consider when determining what is important to them is the potential consequences of non-delivery of a defined output, of any barrier to delivery, any unexpected occurrence, any unknowns and any other *unintended consequence* that may emerge from the delivery process. It is these consequences that will be judged as acceptable, controllable or manageable and will be set the priorities and resources allocated to avoiding or mitigating them. From *chaos theory* we understand that the selection of our starting point is important in determining the final outcome. Therefore we can presume that selecting the true nature of the problem we face is also critical to success. We therefore need to be clear how we look at the problem at hand, about the *mental model* that is fundamental to our view of the world; we need to be clear about the paradigm we are using.

In my previous work[57] I identified three distinct risk paradigms (see Table 3.3), each of which brings with it its own management assumptions. I labelled the paradigms *line, circle* and *dot*.

Lines are problems constructed over a linear scale: this scale is often time based such as in project management. *Circles* are generally problems that repeat in similar forms, such as are found in process management. *Dots* are one-off events such as a natural disaster or an industrial accident; while these are normal viewed looking backwards, by the very nature of *foresight*, the *dot*

---

56 Lauder (2011)
57 Lauder (2011:Ch3)

Table 3.3   *Line, circle* and *dot* paradigms

	Forward or Backward Looking	Desired or Unwanted Outcome	Chosen or Imposed Outcome	Variance or Invariance of Process	Unique or Recurring
Line	Forward	Desired	Chosen	Variance	Unique
Circle	Forward	Desired	Chosen	Invariance	Recurring
Dot	Backward	Unwanted	Imposed	Variance	Unique

paradigm also has to be made to look forward. While I recognise that these forms interact, it is still important to determine a common paradigm if general *cross-understanding* is to be achieved. Within the *line* and *dot* paradigms it is easier to identify a starting point than it is within the *circle* paradigm. Within these paradigms you know where you are now, what has gone before and what has not yet happened. However, when it comes to a process, *circles*, where to start becomes a classic chicken and egg problem. In order to differentiate the chicken from the eggs, we can next use the *seven dimensions of risk*.

Using a basic systems model we can map the way people use the term risk to things going wrong at each stage of the process. However, when trying to find a remedy for the particular problem, we need to be clear whether it is, for example, a faulty input, the result of the process or even just an unrealistic expectation. I describe each in Table 3.4 I describe how they may be used in later chapters.

Finally it is necessary to limit the boundaries of the specific case. Therefore the next part of the discussion needs to determine the boundaries that should be placed around our area of concern. Even where one's view is that the world is an open system, it must be recognised that this scope is too broad to enable any coherent analysis or narrative to be produced. At a minimum, three boundaries need to be set. The first is geographic. The second is organisational (set around the structures, people and prescribed outcomes). The final boundary is temporal. The basis of Turner's theory is that problems incubate over time. Therefore, in any study of this nature the temporal boundaries need to be considered just as carefully as the others. The temporal boundaries should be such that it goes back to when the organisation had last demonstrated that it was fully alert to the threats and hazards it faced and had demonstrated its capability to manage these threats. The purpose of this is to establish a baseline (benchmark) against which future drift can be judged. These ideas are pulled together and depicted in Figure 3.1.

Table 3.4   *Seven dimensions of risk*

Category of Risk	Explanation
RI – unwanted inputs	Any unwanted input to a process such as a failure of design, incorrect material or a failure to train the operators. For example, all that is required to design, build and operate an aircraft safely.
R2 – transformation risks	These risks include problems during the transformation process. These are either breakdowns within the system (such as operator errors) or where "normal" interaction produces unforeseen results. For example, the process the plane is involved with: flights.
R3 – unwanted results	The result is an initial outcome of the mechanism at play on an entity in creating the negative outcome. For example, if the mechanism at play is the continual flexing of a structure due to natural phenomena such as wind, the result of this may be that the structure becomes stressed.
R4 – unwanted effects	The effect is the end product of the result on the entity causing the negative outcome. Taking the stress structure example from above, the effect of the stress may be that it induces part of a structure to fail.
R5 – unwanted consequences	A consequence is the automatic effect (cascade effect) that will occur as the end product of the effect unless an intervention is made. Continuing the example from above, the consequence of part of the structure failing may be the total collapse of the structure.
R6 – unwanted subsequence	The term "subsequence" is therefore defined as "the consequence of a decision that follow an unwanted occurrence rather than being part of any cascade of events". An example of such a decision would be to ground the aircraft type following an accident with all the knock-on or ripple effects that this might have.

The term "impact" is reserved for an overarching term that embraces all negative outputs (R3, R4, R5 or R6) relevant to the matter in hand.

Category of Risk	Explanation
R7 – an expression of what is acceptable exposure to the unwanted	These are metrics that are used to control the system or process. The controls cover constructs such as risk tolerance, risk exposure or acceptable risks. From our example this may be the flight hours permitted for each airframe.

So where do we start? It might be assumed that we would start at one end of the model and work our way through it. I would suggest that this, in practice in not the case. In Karl Weick's[58] discussion of sense making, as it might be applied to the NASA's Columbia accident, he reminds us that "we do not begin at the

---

58 Weick (2005:162)

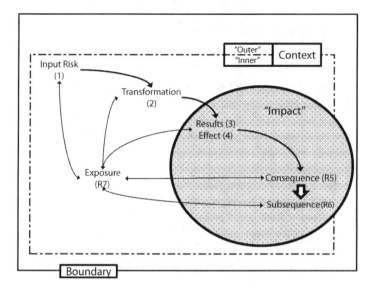

Figure 3.1   *Seven dimensions of risk*

beginning … Instead we always begin somewhere in the middle of everything".
Therefore when we join a new company, start a new task or establish a new
relationship we can be seen to be joining an ongoing conversation.[59] We do
not therefore start at the beginning. In each of these cases we can see that we
join the conversation somewhere within Stage 2, the *incubation period*. Our first
task is then to establish where we are. To do this we need to review that past
and look to the future; see Figure 3.2. From the past we look at both the good
and the bad, the wanted outcomes and the unwanted. We will examine the
organisation's legacy and its successes. We should look at past failures (and
what has been learnt from them), the hazards intrinsic to the organisation and
the normal precautions already in place. We also need to look at what the future
might hold for the organisation, both what is wanted and what is not. At this
point in the discourse there needs to be a discussion about how much time and
resource is expended in looking back compared to that expended in looking
forward. I would suggest that one of the reasons we fail to learn from past
failure (both endogenous and exogenous) is that we do not expend sufficient
resource looking back: the temptation is solely to look forward.

Part of this model forces us to look back in order to establish a *notionally
normal starting point*. While the story may be apocryphal, it still makes my point:
when a Chinese politician was asked whether the French revolution had been

---

59   Here I have to thank Professor Anne Huff for introducing me to this idea

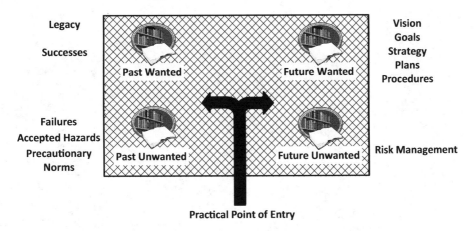

Figure 3.2   Entry point

a good thing, his reply was, "it is too early to tell". The point is, how far back do we need to go in order to establish an appropriate *notionally normal starting point*? We have seen this issue raised by the cases already used. We see that we need to look for either the last time the subject had been rigorously reviewed or where the last major planned change had taken place. While the selection of a suitable point may be very difficult, it has to be given careful thought for, as we are warned by *chaos theory*, minor changes in the starting point can change the outcome significantly. Therefore the selection of a *notionally normal starting point* is critically important to the process of *foresight* and needs careful attention.

In considering Stage 1 we again fall prey to the *fallacy of homogeneity*. In Figure 1.2 we see Stage 1 being depicted as a single entity. The complexity of Stage 1 is more accurately depicted in Figure 3.3 which shows many hazards and their associated *precautionary norms*. We see these overlap in ways that makes some more difficult to see. In this case theory reminds us that, given the right *conditions*, even apparently small problems can suddenly escalate into major crises. The significance of this is that the normal *risk assessment* tool that ranks risk by size and certainty may actually be distracting management from what is critical to the business. This reinforces the need for the executive to do their own top-down analysis in order to provide a different analytical perspective to the more conventional bottom-up *risk assessment* process.

In reviewing what we might consider to be the *notionally normal starting point* we have to reappraise where our norms might fall into the category of being *fantasy documents*. These are plans and policies created to cover bureaucratic gaps

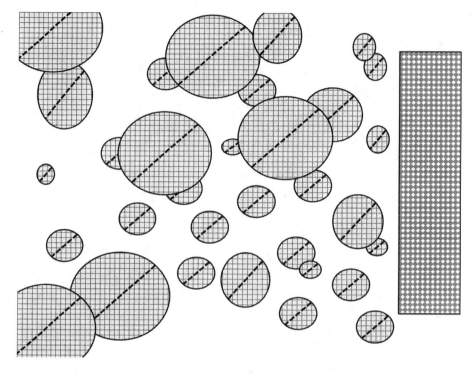

Figure 3.3   Hazards and norms

but, if scrutinised, would be seen as "unfit for purpose"[60] or, as Charles Perrow more colourfully describes them, "plans that are so fanciful that it's hard to take them seriously".[61] If *fantasy documents* are seen at the *micro level*, the same idea has been extended to the *mega level* in the construct of *hollow government*.[62] *Hollow government* is defined as "government that has been stripped of the resources, authority, and respect it needs in order to effectively protect public health, safety, and the environment".[63] In between these two layers we might also find the *hollow corporations* or *hollow departments*. When trying to prevent *failures of foresight*, self-critical reflection is required to ensure that organisational politics do not lean towards the production of *fantasy documents* and *hollow corporations*.

While I have been talking at length about *precautionary norms*, I have not clearly identified what they are. I see *precautionary norms* falling into one of two groups. The first concerns practice and the second concerns formal standards. In the first instance a *precautionary norm* may constitute an accepted practice

60   Clarke and Perrow (1996)
61   Perrow (1999:374)
62   Steinzor (2008)
63   Flournoy (2011)

or work routine whether it has been documented or not. These norms are therefore practices that have been accepted as normal. In the second instance these norms are formal standards, some backed by statute, which are espoused as being best practice. For those seeking to prevent a *failure of foresight* it is important to note that the first required a cultural change for it to be modified and the second is a piece of bureaucracy, fanciful or not, that then has to be put into practice. Confusing the two may just lead to the production of *fantasy documents* within *hollow departments*.

In the case studies taken from work done by Cohen and Gooch,[64] of which you will read more in the next two chapters, we can see examples of the failure to take the necessary *precautionary norms* at Pearl Harbour,[65] in the US anti-Uboat campaign during the Second World War[66] and where the Israelis thought that a 1:8 tank ratio was quite an acceptable norm.[67] In the case of the fall of France in 1940 they show how *risk assessments* were conducted, reviewed and still failed. They point to a review of a possible German route of attack taking place in 1927. They pointed to the fact that the French assessment was reviewed in 1934 by the future Marshall Petain and again in 1936 by the man who was the French Commander-in-Chief at the time of the French defeat by Germany in 1940 (Gamelin).[68] Unfortunately, as history shows, the resulting precautions taken proved to be inadequate. This reminds us not only of the need to see and appreciate that we have a problem but also to act appropriately.

Contrary to what might seem an obvious expectation, when using this model, *risk discourse* does not start with Stage 1. The *point of entry* into the model is somewhere in Stage 2, *the incubation period*. As part of the process of orientation those involved need to decide how much resource needs to be spent on learning from the past and the point at which they need to start their discourse. As we have seen there is potential for standard *risk assessment* tools to misalign the selection of the risks with potential critical failures. The top-down approach suggested here offers one way to correct these misalignments. Finally, those conducting *risk discourse* need to be clear amongst themselves about the types of *precautionary norms* available to them and how they are going to be used. Failure at this point means that while they may see and appreciate potential sources of failure they do not act appropriately and thus ensure that they become a *hollow organisation* that produces *fantasy documents*.

---

64 Cohen and Gooch (1990)
65 Cohen and Gooch (1990:49 and 57)
66 Cohen and Gooch (1990:66)
67 Cohen and Gooch (1990:106, 107 and 121)
68 Cohen and Gooch (1990:220)

Stage 2 – *Incubation Period*

Stage 2, the *incubation period*, is at the heart of using Turner's model as the basis of a tool to promote *foresight*. I see it as being important to accept that if we are not in *crisis* then we are in the *incubation period* of one. However, even if we are in a *crisis*, another even bigger *crisis* may still be haunting us. In these circumstances we need to be constantly aware how an apparently normally situation can be nurturing something far more malevolent. In this section I will address six issues. These are: 1) preventing or preparing, 2) instability in the system, 3) the iterative nature of the process, 4) span of control, 5) *critical success factors* and 6) *issues of interest*.

PREVENTING OR PREPARING

In terms of *risk governance* the key task for the executive is to decide what they need to *prevent* and for what they need to *prepare*. They need to decide on the unwanted events that will really damage their organisation that they must *prevent* and then how to *prepare* the organisation to manage the other unwanted events when they arise. It has to be accepted that organisations have finite resources and so it would not be feasible for them to ensure that they never were confronted by unwanted occurrences; any such expectation can only be a product of *hindsight* where a particular unwanted occurrence becomes well defined and so subsequently it is seen as being obvious. For *foresight* the issues of what to *prevent* and for what should they *prepare* are less clear cut. These issues need to considered carefully and stated clearly if they are to be managed properly. However, even with such careful consideration the issue should not be considered to be fixed as the system is actually more unstable than they might originally envisage.

INSTABILITY IN THE SYSTEM

Much of management practice would seem to be rooted in the idea of stable systems, such as a process, that are repeated faultlessly time and time again. This is based on the idea that *verbatim compliance* will ensure error free performance. However, this assumption of stability is an illusion and needs to be recognised as such. Plans, even when well thought through, have to be constantly adapted to respond to the circumstances that prevail at the time. The sources of instability are numerous but I have, for ease of reference, divided them into two categories. These are internal and external drivers of instability.

Internal drivers of instability may include factors such as: 1) the original design having faults that result in design changes, 2) organisational turbulence that means that new people are assigned to existing tasks, 3) operators' *slips*, lapses, *mistakes* and other types of errors that disrupt the process, 4) *interactive complexity* and close coupling that lead to unexpected outcomes from an apparently stable system, 5) efficiency drives that remove apparent waste from the system, which in the past has provided necessary operational slack or redundancy, that has unintended adverse consequences.

External drivers of instability may include factors such as: 1) a change of client who brings slightly different priorities, 2) changes in technology that necessitate changes in organisational structures and skill, 3) changes in the operational environment, which may be political, social or physical, that force the organisation to adapt, 4) finally, changes in the competitive environment that means that a once sound offering has to be adapted to a new market.

All these changes, whether they are large or small, mean that every system is in a state of constant flux where the pattern of change is unlikely to be fully *anticipated*. Rather than being ordered, these changes are likely to be perceived as *chaotic*. This means that the process also needs to be iterative if it is to remain fit for purpose.

ITERATIVE NATURE OF THE PROCESS

This instability in the system necessitates that the system be under constant review. This iterative process is embedded in ideas such as *organisational learning*. *Organisational learning* has essential features such as *double loop learning*. From the point of view of *foresight*, this suggests that Stage 1 and Stage 2 need to have a circular relationship. As the situation changes during the *incubation period* (whenever you are not in an identifiable *crisis*), there is a need to re-evaluate the *notionally normal starting point* and its associated *hazards* and *precautionary norms*. While a continual re-evaluation would be desirable, a periodic review may be the best that can be achieved. To ensure that these reviews are not allowed to slip, there should be strict criteria established for when such reviews are conducted. One model that suggests a method for this assessment is *Trigger Action Response Plans* (TARPS):[69] this might be thought of as a "rule of three". This method suggests that the organisation should select a number of criteria which indicate, in this case, significant change. Should one of the criteria manifest, the organisation could conduct a review; should two

---

69   Hopkins (2011:114)

emerge then a review might be considered to be highly desirable. When the third appears then a review is deemed to be mandatory. As it is the executive that would set up such a system for themselves, it would be up to them to ensure that the criteria warranted the effort of the subsequent review. The purpose of methods such as this is to ensure that the executive is not tempted into *minimising emergent danger* by just ignoring the warning signs.

This iterative process has also to be applied to the *prepare* component. As the situation changes so may the applicability of contingency plans. Reviews of inquiry reports often point out the inadequacy of contingency plans and how poorly they are executed. I accept that only in *hindsight* will it become clear which contingency plans should have been given the highest priority. This is therefore of little help when seeking *foresight*. This lack of clarity means that once again the board is faced by a resources priority issue. While others within the organisation may prepare and practise the various contingency plans, I would suggest that it is up to the board to give direction on *never events* and which contingencies should receive what level of preparation. While it may be tempting to try to tailor a contingency plan to a specific event (against something deemed possible by inquiry teams with their benefit of *hindsight*), events rarely occur in the form envisaged. Therefore consideration needs to be given to producing generic plans which are then tested against specific events in order to identify their weaknesses. Only once a range of scenarios has been tested should the plan be changed as altering it to match a specific event may (will probably) bring with it *unintended consequences*. As part of the purpose of *risk discourse* undertaken within the *incubation period* is for them to determine the best mix of capability, which will enable the organisation to regain the control that they need over the widest range of possible impending crises.

SPAN OF CONTROL

If systems are so unstable there must be questions about how much control we, as individuals or even as a group, can have. Some suggest that mechanisms that we put it place may only offer us an *illusion of control* rather than real control.[70] Langer defines *illusion of control* as "an expectancy of a personal success probability inappropriately higher than the objective probability would warrant".[71] Research has shown that this illusion influences the types of bias

---

70   Drummond (2011)
71   Langer (1975:313)

exhibited, the magnitude of errors they cause[72] and decrease the perception of risk.[73] In his personal annex to the Challenger accident report, Richard Feynman discusses this issue. In his opening paragraph he states:

> It appears that there are enormous differences of opinion as to the probability of a failure with loss of vehicle and of human life. The estimates range from roughly 1 in 100 to 1 in 100,000. The higher figures come from the working engineers, and the very low figures from management. What are the causes and consequences of this lack of agreement? Since 1 part in 100,000 would imply that one could put a Shuttle up each day for 300 years expecting to lose only one, we could properly ask "What is the cause of management's fantastic faith in the machinery?"[74]

I have labelled this *illusion of control*, that we have greater control than the probability would suggest, as *Feynman's numbers*. But why are we prone to this illusion? Research has shown that negative memories were found to trigger strong emotions, affecting sense-making and distorting reasoning.[75] It would seem that most of the human race is prone towards an *optimism bias*.[76] This may be because "decision makers actually perceive negative feedback as indicative of a problem and ... this influences (how) their decision(s) ... escalate"[77] or to misquote the film *A Few Good Men*, "we can't handle the truth"! This may result in one person interpreting data presented to them in a very different way to the way the person presenting the data expected.[78] If we have an illusion about what we can control then we are likely to act inappropriately. So the question becomes, over what do we have control, over what do we have influence, and where are we subject to random change due to external uncontrollable factors? What is our actual *span of control*?

While the *span of control* may vary in size, scope and duration, it may be more limited than we would like to think or realise. The term *span of control* brings with it hidden assumptions about responsibilities, levers, boundaries and the stability of the system. Research shows that control can be only temporary. *Control bubble*, a metaphor that alludes to how quickly the bubble of control can

---

72 Durand (2003)
73 Houghton, Simon, Aquino, and Goldberg (2000)
74 Appendix F to the Rogers Commission report
75 Cannon (1999)
76 Weinstein (1987)
77 Keil et al. (2007)
78 Dudezert and Leidner (2011)

disappear and this may help us to think about the transitory nature of control. Gene Rochlin describes the concept of "having *the bubble*".[79] Within his work the bubble is where a person who has the appropriate *seat of understanding* has a temporary comprehension of a *complex* and dynamic situation. The system expects the person to become fatigued or have lapses and, at that moment, they have to call "lost *the bubble*" and a deputy, who has been shadowing the situation, steps in. This example shows how an organisation that expects temporary loss of control designs a way to manage it. From Naval operations the metaphor can be raised a number of levels to move from the operational control room of one ship to the naval formation. A US carrier group tries to establish a bubble of several hundred miles around the group over which they exercise control: this is a definite space although the actual boundaries may be ambiguous and mobile. In the context of a nuclear power station or some other industrial site, the bubble may be bounded by the perimeter fence. In terms of an office manager the bubble may be the physical space within which they work or it may be the virtual space in which their knowledge exists. The size, shape, boundaries and external influences on control will vary from case to case and it is therefore up to the protagonists to define their own space realistically.

However the space is defined what is important in terms of *foresight* is that the control is real and necessary. When I say real I mean it must reflect reality; if the level is only of influence then the manager needs to act accordingly. If there are factors over which they recognise that they have no control, they need to prepare to react appropriately to counter any unwanted effects should they occur. When I say necessary, a great deal of resource, including time, is wasted attempting to exert full control when this is not possible. The debate about this subject is widespread within the literature on *high reliability organisations* and is characterised in terms of *centralisation* or *decentralisation*. Therefore once the *illusion of control* is being properly managed, the term *span of control* can be established.

CRITICAL SUCCESS FACTORS

In 1979 John Rockart started to expound the idea of *critical success factors*. His motivation for doing this work is important. The title of his first article on this subject was "Chief executives define their own data need". His concern was that executives were being swamped by the data available to them. He saw the need for a clear definition of the type of information that the executives required and for organisations to move away from the trap of building control systems based

---

79   Rochlin (1991:117)

on the data that is easiest to collect. His message was very simple: it was for organisations to concentrate on what was critical. Over the period he wrote on this subject his message remained consistent:

> Critical success factors ... are, for any business, the limited number of areas in which results, if they are satisfactory, will ensure successful competitive performance for the organization. They are the few key areas where "things must go right" for the business to flourish. If results in these areas are not adequate, the organization's efforts for the period will be less than desired.

> Critical success factors are the few key areas of activity in which favorable results are absolutely necessary for a particular manager to reach his goals.

As a result, the *critical success factors* are seen to be the areas of activity that should receive constant and careful attention from management. There is therefore still the need to define the idea of criticality. Accepting that *critical tasks* may be different at different organisational levels, the definition needs to hold true for each and every level. To come to my definition of *critical task* I have combined two ideas previously discussed. The first comes from *critical success factors*. This is the idea that they are "something that must go right" and the second is that the failure must cause harm that is not recoverable at the level it occurs; here I define harm as an unwanted outcome totally unacceptable to the organisation in that it is highly likely to produce the demise of that part of organisation or some people within it. Each of these criteria is now discussed in turn.

Something that must go right

The original idea for *critical success factors* is that they were "the few key areas where 'things must go right'". Here the "things" can be defined as processes or activities. In their book on "military misfortune", Cohen and Gooch identify military "doctrine" or "image of Future War" as being critical. This criterion for what is critical would exclude these two factors. However by focusing on the processes by which doctrine or image of future war are developed and adapted (rather than concentrating on the finished outcome, the final doctrine, for example) then they could meet this criterion. It is also legitimate to speculate that, as Cohen and Gooch labelled one side of their matrix critical "task", they also saw the process not the outcome as being critical.

Non-recoverable harm

The second criterion for being critical is that the failure must not be recoverable at the level it occurs. There are two aspects to this criterion. The first is whether it is possible to recover from or reverse the failure. The second is whether it is recoverable at the level the failure occurs or whether recovery would depend on action by a different command or hierarchical level. Looking at the first aspect, I use as my example the list of *never events* published by the UK's National Health Service. Included within this list of 25 events are four which are immediately reversible; these are: 1) misidentification of patients, 2) escape of a transferred prisoner, 3) entrapment in bedrails or 4) wrongly prepared high-risk injectable medication. While these are all highly undesirable, they can all be reversed before any harm is done. The other events listed would seem to fall into two other categories. There are those where damage is likely to occur but where the damage is likely to be recoverable, such as 1) the maladministration of Insulin or 2) wrong implant/prosthesis. The second is where non-recoverable damage occurs which may result in harm (such as an avoidable death or the removal of the wrong limb). In such cases the harm may befall a subordinate level of the hierarchy rather than to the overall system.

The second aspect of non-recoverable harm is whether the harm is limited to the level at which it occurs. We can use an example provided by Cohen and Gooch to illustrate this point. In the Korean War the Eighth Army was destroyed as a fighting force and was not able to recover its position from within its own resources. However, reserves available to higher levels of the hierarchy meant that a bad situation was recoverable overall. Therefore, the idea of harm needs to be defined as a graduated scale. One way these terms may be defined is:

> *Critical harm is an unwanted outcome totally unacceptable to the organisation in that it is highly likely to produce the demise of that organisation.*

> *Serious damage produces a crisis for the organisation but that level of the organisation is able to recover overall although not necessarily in the identical form. This may have caused critical harm to some sub-components or stakeholders within the system.*

> *Containable disruption has a significant effect on a level of the organisation but that sub-component of the system or stakeholder is able to recover and continue in their existing form. Again this may have caused critical harm to some sub-components or stakeholders within the system.*

> *Normal disruptions are the everyday failures within a sub-system*
> *where the sub-system is ready and able to manage these disruptions*
> *without any real damage being caused.*

Systems often do not have to be perfect to operate effectively. However, perfection may be demanded in *hindsight* by inquiry teams or the public however much of an *illusion of control* this may be. In describing the effective British anti-Uboat campaign, Cohen and Gooch acknowledge that the "British arrangements were far from perfect"[80] but they worked. In fast-moving *complex* situations "good" is often all that is required or achievable in the circumstance. The quest for perfection often becomes the enemy of the good because in the time it takes to perfect a response the situation may well have changed ("moved on"). The supposedly perfect response is then no longer applicable. However, in their report on BP's Deepwater Horizon accident (2010), the members of the Presidential Commission find against such an approach. They say:

> *BP's overall approach to the centralizer decision is perhaps best summed*
> *up in an e-mail from BP engineer Brett Cocales sent to Brian Morel on*
> *April 16. Cocales … concluded the e-mail by saying: "But, who cares,*
> *it's done, end of story, [we] will probably be fine and we'll get a good*
> *cement job. I would rather have to squeeze [remediate the cement job]*
> *than get stuck above the WH [wellhead]. So Guide is right on the risk/*
> *reward equation."*

While in *hindsight* one may judge this view to have been in error on this occasion, we cannot know how many times such a judgement had been made previously within other organisations and proved to be correct. Such value judgements are made every day within both civilian and military organisations. As postulated in the hypothesis of *normal chaos*, such judgements are seen as errors only in *hindsight*. Criticism of such judgements is characteristic of the *reverse fallacy*. While the Commission's criticism might be justified in this case in *hindsight*, there have to be questions as to whether, if the action perceived as being correct by the commission had been taken in every case where such judgements were required, it would have led to the *unintended consequences* of bankrupting the industries of oil using nations. Here we see the public desire (promoted by journalists who seek someone to blame and courts that expect unrealistic standards to be upheld) to maintain the fallacy of the world being a stable system where perfect outcomes are the norm. In this environment it becomes politically unacceptable to acknowledge that harm may result from

---

80   Cohen and Gooch (1990:79)

an activity and that this results in resources being wasted on unachieved goals. This inability to accept any harm (as unrealistic an aspiration as it may be) adds to difficulties for executives trying to determine what is actually critical and what must be avoided. Here we again see the desire for perfection having *unintended consequences*.

An issue with the way *critical success factors* have developed, and have been used, is that the ideas of criticality and identifying "the few key areas" seem to have been lost; there is now a tendency to include everything that needs to go as planned. To ensure this does not occur, the test for what is critical needs to be extreme. Once what is critical has been identified, degrees of sub-criticality can then be considered. In summary, that which is deemed critical must actually be critical to the success of an imperfect system. The temptation is to try to define a perfect system where everything becomes critical if the system is to stay perfect. When this happens, the system becomes swamped by the data required. The only conclusion to be drawn is that management is not about perfection but being good enough: perfection becomes an illusion when *chaos* is accepted as being normal.

ISSUES OF INTEREST

Finally I feel that I need to demonstrate the utility of the *issues of interest* identified above. To achieve this I look to show evidence from each of the data sets, as limited as they are, that the *issues of interest* (at whatever level they may occur) can be identified within each case.

Data set 1

Data set 1 provided a relatively simple and abbreviated scenario. Table 3.5 gives evidence of the *issues of interest* being present within the case.

Table 3.5   Evidence for issues within data set 1

Issue	Evidence
Who cares (about what)?	While the focus of the team was on the surgery being performed, the consequence of the action is due to the views of people external to the team.
Failure to launch	The ineffective team briefing at the start of the procedure.
Practical drift	The move away from using the prescribed WHO checklist.

Issue	Evidence
Structural secrecy	While one part of the surgery team knew the list order had changed, this was not known by everyone involved.
Erroneous assumptions	The surgeon did not know who the person was who was in front of them. Management's belief that the WHO check list was being used.
Dysfunctional momentum	Other members of the team will have heard the surgeon using the wrong name but it did not cause them a *mental interruption*.
The Plowman effect	Many of the decisions made on the day were not wrong but they did enable the final error to be made.

Data set 2

Data set 2 provides a rich stream of data in three layers within a single narrative. Table 3.6 gives evidence of the *issues of interest* being present within the case.

Table 3.6   Evidence for issues within data set 2

Issue	Evidence
Who cares (about what)?	There was a clear clash between the perception of the issue as seen from the foreign ministry and those in the defence ministry.
Failure to launch	While a number of working groups formed in order to manage this issue, at no stage did there seem to be a single clear allocation of authority and responsibility for handling this issue.
Practical drift	There was a major misalignment between practice and formal procedure when it came to the storage of the munitions. Many of the normal procedures were ignored in practice.
Structural secrecy	On 3 September 2010 the Director of the Diplomatic Office of the President of Cyprus was told by the Ambassador of Iran, that there were no longer any objections to the munitions being destroyed. After the Ministry of Defence raised serious concerns about the safe storage of the munitions on 7 February 2011, "The Minister of Foreign Policy insisted that the Republic of Cyprus was under pressure from Iran and Syria to return the cargo".
Erroneous assumptions	The belief by those outside the Ministry of Defence that the conditions in which the munitions were being stored were not a "real" issue.
Dysfunctional momentum	Despite the many opportunities for *mental interruption* being offered (warning from the Ministry of Defence for example), at no time did those involved seem to examine the basic assumptions that prevailed in this case.
The Plowman effect	There were many individual decisions taken in a number of organisations which, presumably, seem to be correct to those people taking them at the time they were taken. They did, however, lead to adverse consequences overall.

Data set 3

Data set 3 also provides a rich stream of data. Table 3.7 gives evidence of the *issues of interest* being present within the case.

Table 3.7   Evidence for issues within data set 3

Issue	Evidence
Who cares (about what)?	There was a difference in perspective about the risk of bushfires between those planning the *crisis* response: (1) the incoming population who failed to appreciate the dangers in their situations, and (2) the environmental lobby who worked to restrict the use of precautionary burning of scrubland.
Failure to launch	The conclusion that there was an "inadequate planning system" makes failure to launch inevitable.
Practical drift	The abandonment of prescribed controlled burnings for many years that resulted in high fuel loads; "hazard reduction burns seem not to have undertaken the required burns despite legislative requirements".
Structural secrecy	The Royal Commission also recommended improving the information and communication systems which suggest that information that was held in one part of the system did not get to where it was required in another part.
Erroneous assumptions	A "substantial discontinuity between the individual's risk beliefs and their level of preparation".
Dysfunctional momentum	The conclusion that decision-makers "seemingly staying with a plan that may no longer reflect the reality of events on the ground".
The Plowman effect	The author says "it is not easy to estimate the ripple and unintended effects arising from such a decision".

From these three data sets, as limited as they are, we can see that the *issues of interest* are present within each case. I would therefore suggest that we have firstly issues that are key (they are a high-level abstraction of a wider body of the research done on the origins of *crisis* to date) and secondly they are worthy of attention as part of a *foresight* discourse as they will provide a catalyst for the debate.

Empirical testing

The *issues of interest* have been tested in a more practical context. They were taken by Mark Baker and were tested by a number of the executive teams within the Pentland brands. At the time, Mark was the Head of Risk and Assurance at

Pentland Brands. He was also a fellow doctoral graduate who had a particular interest in management control systems. He used the questions as a way of stimulating discussion of risk as an adjunct to the management control system he developed during his award-winning doctoral research. He published the results of this piece of his research amongst his CIMA colleagues.[81] The aim of his research was to test the *issues of interest* for their *practical utility*. He went through an iterative process modifying the ideas as he progressed. The outcome of his research is presented in Table 3.8.

Table 3.8   Pentland modifications

Key Sources of Risk Incubation	Question	Questions for Risk "Discourse" – Talking about It *What Executives Should be Asking Themselves and Each Other*
Different perspectives on problems	*Who cares about what?*	What are the differences in views on potential unwanted occurrences?
Lack of preparedness and coordination within teams	*Ready to launch?*	Are our teams prepared, coordinated and aligned?
Routines becoming dislocated	*Practical drift?*	Where are there risks to plan delivery, caused by an unconscious *drift* over time from accepted practices?
Communication failures	*Structural secrecy?*	Are the organisational structures and processes preventing the delivery of critical pieces of data?
Validity of assumptions	Are *assumptions* valid?	Are we checking the validity of critical beliefs and assumptions?
Locked into a course of action when change is needed	Is there *dysfunctional momentum?*	Are we seeing and appreciating critical data and making necessary changes, which may be against the momentum of the organisation?
Decisions leading to adverse *unintended consequences*	*Unintended consequences?*	Are we keeping constantly aware for adverse *unintended consequences* emerging from routine and change activity?

The reasons for his modifications are worth noting. For a start, he changed three of the labels. He changed *failure to launch* to "ready to launch". He changed *erroneous assumptions* to "are assumptions valid?" and he changed *Plowman*

---

81 See *Financial Management*, December 2014, from the Chartered Institute of Management Accountants, pp.59–61

effect to *"unintended consequences"*. In the first two cases he argued that the executive found the tone of the labels to be too negative. The argument that the alternative negative lens was meant to enrich their analysis held no water; they did not like the implicit pessimism. Arguments about the danger of *optimism bias* were also rejected. The term *Plowman effect* was rejected because it did not mean anything to the audience. They preferred to use a term to which they could relate, *unintended consequences*, rather than a term intended to invoke the richer idea of the danger of correct, small, related ideas that might lead to *unintended consequences*.

Whilst I might argue that my ideas were theoretically purer, I cannot argue against Mark's version as they have proved to have *practical utility* within his context. What we agreed was that those facilitating the use of the questions need to understand their background and context if they were to derive the greatest utility from them. We also agreed that as people become more sophisticated users of this process then they may gravitate to a pure understanding of the ideas. However, as their purpose is to promote debate about the risks the organisation faces, the most important thing was that they got people talking constructively to each other about this difficult issue.

SUMMARY

In past debates we have heard about what people have done wrong based on the assumption that if they do not do that again, all will turn out satisfactorily in the end. As an alternative approach, I have used this section to suggest how they may approach the subject of *foresight* and what issues they might start by questioning. I have made a number of suggestions for where the focus should be during Stage 2 (the *incubation period*).

1.   The main tasks during this stage are preventing those unwanted events that you need to avoid or preparing your organisation to manage the others as they arise: the fundamental issue for the executive is to decide which is which.

2.   It is important when involved in this work to recognise that, whatever system you are involved with, it is unstable rather than stable; it is in constant change. You therefore can never be sure that what has been done successfully in the past will be so again in the future.

3.   The constant flux of the system means that the review process has to be iterative in nature. This means reviewing the assumptions arrived at in Stage 1 and the action that will be required in Stage 5.

4.   While we may wish and seek to have control over our situation, we need to recognise the real limits to our *span of control* and recognise the dangers created by having any illusion as to the extent of our actual control.

5.   We need to determine what is genuinely critical to success and plan our controls around those issues. We have to accept that the dilemma created by the reality of what we can control and the public's desire to maintain the illusion of a perfect world will be at odds and to manage the situation accordingly. The risks to brand and reputation need to be balanced against the risks created by accepting the public's illusional state.

6.   Finally, I have offered seven *issues of interest* as subjects to start the top-down search for potential sources of failure. I have provided evidence from the three data sets and previous research that the phenomena labelled *who cares (about what), failure to launch, practical drift, structural secrecy, dysfunctional momentum,* and the *Plowman effect* are ever-present dangers. However I would accept that the use of these labels is not essential as long as the facilitator in a particular case understands the underlying premises and that any labels are just used to start a constructive debate.

Stage 3 – *Onset*

I have one additional point to make about the transition from what is considered to be normal and what is recognised to be a *crisis* and this is the speed at which it happens. I have identified two distinct timescales. While some crises evolved over a prolonged period, others evolved more rapidly. The first, which is the conventional idea of a looming *crisis*, I label as *the critical days* and the second I label the *30-minute window*. I discuss the idea of *critical days* further in Chapter 6. Here I examine the *30-minute window*. During my previous analysis of inquiry reports, I was struck by how often how often the disaster unfolded in under 30 minutes. This is the time between a moment when those involved thought that they had everything under control and when the *crisis* overwhelmed them. I have chosen the examples in Table 3.9 because the reports provided enough detail to allow me to determine the transition time.

Table 3.9   Examples of a *30-minute window*

Event	Transition Time
Mann Gulch – 5 August 1949	26 minutes
Bradford Stadium fire – 11 May 1985	6 minutes
Chernobyl – 26 April 1986	39 seconds
Capsize of Spirit of Free Enterprise, Zeebrugge – 6 March 1987	23 minutes
USS Vincennes shoot down of Iran Air Flight 655 – 3 July 1988	7 minutes
Crash of Flight G-OBME at Kegworth – 8 January 1989	12 minutes
Hillsborough Disaster – 15 April 1989	<30 minutes
Iraq "friendly fire" – 14 April 1991	8 minutes
Explosion at BP Texas City – 23 March 2005	18 minutes
Crash of Flight AF 447 – On 31 May 2009	4½ minutes
Explosion on Deep Water Horizon – 20 April 2010	29 minutes
Flood of Fukushima nuclear power station – 11 March 2011	45 minutes*
Capsize Costa Concordia – 13 January 2012	30 minutes*

The cases of Fukushima and Costa Concordia are marked with an asterisk because it is not clear within these timeframes when those involved recognised that they had lost control. In the case of Fukushima, while the installation had a 45-minute window between the warning that an earthquake had happened and when the tsunami struck, the time between when they realised the *precautionary norms* (the seawards barrier) had failed and the site being inundated was a matter of seconds. We also have to question whether in this case anything else could have been done. In the case of the Costa Concordia the window of 30 minutes was between the time the ship left the authorised route to the time it struck a rock. The report does not say when the captain realised that his manoeuvre was not going as planned and that grounding became a likely probability (in other words the point at which he realised that he was losing control). I speculate that this was far less than 30 minutes. In the case of the Hillsborough disaster I see this point being reached somewhere between 20 and 15 minutes before the crush became apparent.

The importance of the 30 minutes is that this is not a long period of time to recognise that *normal chaos* is in the process of transition to becoming *abnormal chaos*. It is only with *hindsight* where the issues are clear does this period appears to give adequate time to those involved to take the appropriate action. In Chapter 2 I looked at the difficulties encountered when moving from one *operational mode* to another. Here we have the transition from Stage 2 to Stage 3 and this transition is equally difficult to recognise as it is occurring. Unless the organisation has clear markers of change (such as those developed through the *Trigger Action Response Plans* process) this transition is likely to be missed due to *dysfunctional momentum*.

The issue of recognising the transition from *normal chaos* (Stage 2) to *abnormal chaos* (Stage 3) is poorly understood. Developing appropriate markers is fraught with difficulties but those involved in *risk discourse* need to attempt to do so.

Catalytic Questions

In order to use the refined theoretical stages of Turner's *Disaster Incubation Theory* as a catalytic framework to generate *foresight*, statements need to be changed into questions that promote "talking, digging, comparing, refining, and focusing". Here I look to provide some initial questions, based on the preceding discussion, designed to stimulate a debate and to get people to ask questions about what the future might look like. This section sets out some of the initial questions that may be asked at each stage.

STAGE 1 – *NOTIONALLY NORMAL STARTING POINT*

The essence of Stage 1 is to determine where to start the debate and to establish the *precautionary norms* that are considered adequate, in those circumstances, to confront the hazards perceived. The key questions for Stage 1 are seen to be ones that test these basic assumptions and establish a baseline for the coming debate. Examples of such questions may be:

- What point in time do we choose to be our *notionally normal starting point* and why?
- What hazards do we perceive to exist at this time and how have we decided to handle them?
- How effective do we assess the *precautionary norms* to be at that time?
- How do we see the *precautionary norms* that are in place safeguarding against the emergence of new hazards?
- How much energy do we need to expend to learn from the past?
- On what core beliefs and assumptions do we base our plans?
- How do the beliefs and assumptions change through the different organisational layers?

STAGE 2 – *INCUBATION PERIOD*

The essence of Stage 2, like any *risk assessment* process, is to assess what has changed since the baseline was set and to determine where gaps have left the organisation vulnerable to emerging risks. The purpose of this stage is to determine how the original *precautionary norms*, with their inherent weakness, may mutate into a form somewhat less effective, whether this is through mechanisms of *drift* or by instability in the system. Any assumption of continuing effectiveness needs to be tested. Examples of appropriate questions for each of the *issues of interest* may be:

Who cares?:

- How might the beliefs and assumptions for each stakeholder or stakeholder groups within the system differ and what might be the consequences?
- What are the goals and priorities for each stakeholder or stakeholder group within the system and whether they may conflict?
- On what might each stakeholder or stakeholder group within the system not be prepared to compromise and what might be the consequences?

Failure to launch:

- Are the systems and processes in place to ensure the delivery of the required outcomes?
- Is the team involved clear about their tasks? Is each person clear about their role and responsibilities and who makes the decisions in any particular circumstance?
- How can we be sure that the nominated procedures work effectively and as planned?
- Who might get caught up in this problem and, by not knowing what to do, may exacerbate potential difficulties within the system?

Practical drift:

- Which regulations (or, if relevant, procedures) apply in this case?
- How do we ensure those who need to comply on our behalf are conversant with them (where are they listed)?
- Where are we failing to comply with existing regulations?
- Where may the regulations generate unintended adverse consequences?
- How has the context changed since the regulation been written that might make the regulation null and void?
- Where within our organisation do local practices differ from the formal procedure?

Structural secrecy:

- What data do we need and how do we know those who need it have it?
- Why might we underestimate our problems: from whom do we take warnings seriously and who do we ignore?
- What are the countervailing forces (*"decoys"*) that may distract the management from focusing on what is really important?

Erroneous assumptions:

- To counter the assumption that everyone is working towards the same end – what is the objective that the organisation is striving to achieve?
- To counter the assumption that the situation is receiving the appropriate resources – what priority is given to each and how does each relate to those few things that we deem critical?
- To counter the assumption that nothing has changed – what has changed since we last reviewed our systems and what is the natural oscillation rate for the issue (how quickly might the last experience be forgotten)?

Dysfunctional momentum:

- Where within the process is a natural point at which we can re-evaluate our beliefs and assumptions?
- What are the social and institutional pressures that may prevent us from acting appropriately as the situation evolves?
- What issues do we not, at present, have time to address? What danger does this pose: are these acceptable (*risk appetite*)? What might we be able to do about these issues in the interim (delegations)?

The Plowman effect:

- Do we have a clear picture of the overarching strategy and situation?
- How might we be seen to be *muddling through* and how might this take us off our expected course?
- What are our underlying assumptions about how our system works, the effect that individual actions might have and how do we know if these are valid?
- How do we scan the environment for the unintended adverse consequences created by individual decisions and actions?

STAGE 3 – *PRECIPITATING EVENT*

The essence of Stage 3 is to identify the potential sources of dramatic loss of control and the form in which they may appear. Examples of appropriate questions may be:

- What do we really not want to happen: what are our *never events*?
- What actually might go "bang"? ("Bang" = events getting out of control)
- For whom does this "bang" have consequences (need to define the victim groups) and how might this have consequences for us? (This is an issue of "blow-back".)

STAGE 4 – *ONSET*

The essence of Stage 4 is the potential for the events to escalate or morph into some quite different form. For example, within data set 2 the issue morphs at a superficial level from being one about the safe storage of munitions to a political/economic *crisis*. Examples of appropriate questions may be:

- If the "bang" happens, what may make the situation worse?
- How might the situation change or mutate?
- What forces might perpetuate or change the nature of the *crisis*?

STAGE 5 – *RESCUE AND SALVAGE*

As part of a *foresight* tool, the essence of Stage 5 is to envisage the resources and capabilities that will be required to counter the energies that seek to perpetuate the *crisis* or to turn it into a disaster. Here consideration needs to be given to two categories of resources. The first considers the resources that need to be put in place (prepared and rehearsed) before the event occurs. The second requires consideration of any additional resources that may be required but which can be organised and deployed post-Stage 3 or to counter developments that emerge from Stage 4; this would consist of a *force field analysis* that pits Stage 5 against the forces within Stage 4. Examples of appropriate questions may be:

- What contingency plans to we need to have in place?
- How do we know whether our plans will work or are they just *fantasy documents*?
- What additional resources might we need to call upon and from where will we find them?

This list of questions is not meant to be definitive. They are only meant to indicate the types of questions that may be asked. More importantly, these questions are meant to provide you with a clear understanding of the role I see for each stage so that you can devise your own questions more suited to your own context and situation.

Conclusion

In this chapter I have looked at issues in creating *foresight* when trying to prevent unwanted occurrences or when preparing to respond to those we do not prevent. In order to see a problem emerging we need to know what to look for and so I have provided guidance as to issues that might arise and, in due course, lead to a *crisis*. This is to present those engaged in *risk discourse* with issues to examine. I point out that these issues labelled as causation need to be stratified into *Universals*, *Conditions* and *Causes*. The importance of this stratification is that *Universals* cannot be resolved and therefore need to be managed. *Conditions* weaken defences created by *precautionary norms* and may be in place for a long time before their significance manifests itself. *Causes*, often labelled *sharp end* issues, are often the immediate trigger of a disaster however without the necessary *Universals* and *Conditions*, the triggers would not, in themselves, cause *crisis*. Misunderstanding the difference between these causations is likely to lead to misplaced and ineffectual efforts.

I have now elaborated on Figure 2.3 and developed a richer catalytic model. The re-imagined *Disaster Incubation Theory* is to be found Figure 3.4. We see that the entry point is somewhere in Stage 2 and this requires us to look back as well as looking forward. There is therefore a question over how much effort and resource is expended looking back and what will be missed if you do not, such as *failure to learn* the lesson produced by previous crises.

The next step was to look at the *foresight issues* for Stage 1. Here I looked at the importance of context, deciding what is critical and establishing the threat and the hazards they pose and the *precautionary norms* taken to manage them. During this stage there is the requirement to discuss how effective those norms might have been when they were devised and how.

This was followed by a similar discussion of Stage 2. Here six issues were addressed. These included the roles of prevention and preparation with its link forward to Stage 5, the inherent instability in any system, the iterative nature of the process and how it must continuously be linked back to Stage 1, the

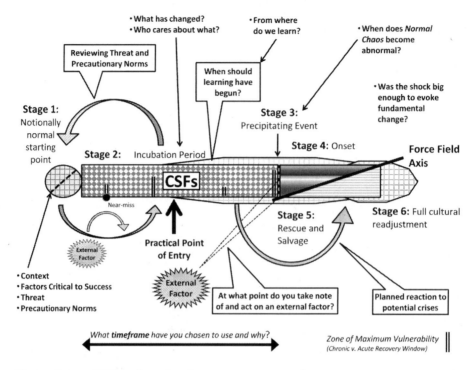

Figure 3.4   DIT re-imagined

real span of real control and the danger of being deluded, the identification of critical factors and discussion of the shape of potential *issues of interest*. As part of the debate about Stage 2, there was discussion of the issues of how and when we learn from the past. This learning starts by considering whether the *crisis* produces a shock large enough to stimulate change within the organisation. Where I differ from other models and their emphasis on learning at the end of the process is that, in order to use learning as part of *foresight*, it is more important to learn from the past rather than offering lessons to the future. This means that those involved need to ask themselves where the learning should begin.

For Stage 3 I point out the *30-minute window* that seems to typify the period during which transition from *normal chaos* (Stage 2) to *abnormal chaos* (Stage 3) occurs and I highlight the difficulties faced by those needing to recognise this change of mode. Finally, I provide a series of questions, covering Stages 1 to 5, which might provide a catalyst to debate but, more importantly, provides additional guidance on the role of each revised stage.

Chapter 4

Debate Framework

Introduction

So far in this book I have taken Turner's *Disaster Incubation Theory* model and re-imagined it as a tool designed to encourage *foresight*. In this section of the book, I concentrate on the issues which may precipitate unwanted events. In this chapter I am looking to provide a framework that would provide a structure for *risk discourse*. At this point, it is worthwhile reminding my reader that the basic premise behind my work is that the world we face is *complex* and even *chaotic*, it is full of uncertainty and ambiguity. Therefore, if we do not really understand an issue, the best thing to do is to discuss it with those around you in order to develop a clearer and more comprehensive understanding of the issues involved.

Developing a Catalytic Framework

In developing the framework that I propose, I have been greatly stimulated by a book written in 1990 by Eliot Cohen and John Gooch called *Military Misfortunes: The Anatomy of Failure in War*. Within the next two chapters I cite Cohen and Gooch extensively; therefore for ease of reference, I have put the page numbers in square brackets. It is important to note that I have used this work, not because I agree with it, but because it provides a rich stimulus to my thinking; in this case their ideas are my *postcard* against which I can make my comparison. I consider it important when trying to generate *foresight* to seek sources that stimulate debate rather than sources that bring agreement: the former helps open the mind to new ideas while the latter tends to close minds with the thought that an issue has been settled. I therefore accept that readers may disagree with the proposition that I offer within this book; this does not concern me if the reader then has a clearer idea of how they will go about generating *foresight* for themselves.

Cohen and Gooch explore why competent organisations might fail. To do this they use six case studies. These are: 1) the Japanese attack on Pearl Harbour in 1941, 2) the US anti-Uboat operation off the East coast of the USA in 1942, 3) the Yom Kippur War in 1973, 4) the Gallipoli campaign in 1915, 5) the Korean War in 1950 and 6) the fall of France in 1940. In this chapter I do not try to reanalyse these campaigns, what I do try to do is to look at the analytical method for its utility to *foresight*. I also try to show the similarities between these case studies and other work done within the *crisis* and disaster management area of study. It has to be acknowledged that Cohen and Gooch's book did provide an interesting perspective and, given the date it was written, it was of its time and it was probably well ahead of its time. Being of its time, the book explored the idea of "the organisational accidents"; being ahead of its time for, while the idea of multi-layer analysis is not original, this work does seem to be one of the first books to link it to disaster inquiry.

I did, however, find it difficult to come to any final judgement on their book as their purpose was ambiguous. The book starts with the question "Why do competent military organizations fail?"[p.vii]. However, many pages of the book are then devoted to examining incompetence: for example the Eighth Army in Korea (where they describe something akin to a *hollow corporation* [p.182] and therefore it could not be considered a *competent military organisation*) and General Stopford at Gallipoli whose serious "shortcomings" were recognised. For me the interesting issue here was why a *competent military organisation* would appoint someone so inappropriate to such a task; this remains a critical lesson as this issue still persists within organisations today. Instead of addressing such critical issues, the book seems to lose its way. In this case it blames Hamilton for not taking steps to compensate for deficiencies within his command [p.156]. This sentiment seems to be at odds with the spirit of their section that argues against blame [pp.6–8].

So, what was the purpose of the book? At the start of Chapter 1 it states that they are looking for "failure in battle (and) to explain how and why such failures occur" [p.1] but they say that in their selection of cases they rejected any argument of ineptitude [p.viii]. What the authors never made clear was how they defined incompetence and so did not clarify which failures constituted incompetence and which did not. This lack of clarity muddied their whole analysis. In the end their book seems to lead to the conclusion, which falls short of making recommendations [p.213], that what organisations need to do to avoid misfortune is to learn, *anticipate* and adapt. I concur with this sentiment; I have developed[1] a similar triptych. I use *see, appreciate, act* as a catalyst to *foresight* and so have no argument with this general idea. However, this remedy in itself would seem to be rather too abstract to offer any real remedy to military misfortune.

In this section I discuss three more detailed issues before looking at the framework itself. These issues are whether Cohen and Gooch's findings have more general utility than they give them. Secondly, I look at the issue of a *controlling mind* when considering counteracting movements within a *crisis* and, finally, I look at the utility of *hindsight* to developing *foresight*.

Generalisation

Cohen and Gooch provide a clear definition of what they mean by the term "misfortune". In this section I explore the parallels between military misfortune and its civilian counterpart. Here we do, however, have to heed the warning given by Tsoukas and Shepherd[2] about what they call "incommensurability". This is about whether it is impossible to define terms of one theory in the vocabulary of another. Our authors warn that "*disaster* is not a term that translates easily from the civil world to the military one". They explain that this is "because the military is a context where people are trained to function efficiently and effectively in an environment marked by danger and the imminent prospect of death". To support their case they quote Clausewitz who said, "No other human activity is so continuously or universally bound up in chance". I disagree. In this context I use Ed Smith's definition of "luck"[3] to encompass what Clausewitz meant by "chance"; this encompasses the recognition that there are forces that exist which are beyond our control. These forces exist for every person within every walk of life. (The habit of linking misfortune or bad luck to chance is common within human endeavours. I return to the ideas of *attribution errors* and the *illusion of control* later in this book.)

What I see in this division between civilian and military life is a case of *distancing through differencing*; this phenomenon occurs "when looking for events from which to learn, organisations ... discount relevant events because they find reasons to exclude them rather than relevant commonalities".[4] We also have to consider whether, as academics, Cohen and Gooch were only trying to compartmentalise their research into their own particular area of

---

1   Lauder (2011)
2   Tsoukas and Shepard (2004:51–53)
3   Smith (2013)
4   Woods (2005)

expertise irrespective of whether their findings were generalisable or not. As they accept the construct of *distancing through differencing* [p.234], we should also be careful before dismissing lessons from other sectors as well. Based on my experience, I think the commonalities are greater than the differences. For example, a civilian police officer in New York may feel in more danger of being shot than a soldier in the British Army. Medical staff treating victims of the Ebola virus in West Africa may consider themselves to be at great risk as there is for them an *imminent prospect of death* if they do not enact the *precautionary norms* effectively. Finally, firefighters are frequently put into contexts where they also face an *imminent prospect of death*. Decision-making within these latter three contexts can be as critical to survival and success as they are within the military. Cohen and Gooch actually undermine their own argument that the military are a special case. Failure to train these groups to face such difficulties would be a failure by their employer in their *duty of care*. In contrast, Cohen and Gooch state that "the Israeli Minister of Defence … suffered a collapse in confidence that rendered him ineffectual" for the rest of the critical period [p.33]. This would suggest that military personnel, despite being trained to deal with crises, may still be just as susceptible to having a *cosmological episode* as are those in other professions. In summary, when trying to understand how to forestall *crisis*, disaster or misfortune, there is little to be gained by seeing the civil and military problems as being fundamentally different; the only difference may be the context and, as every context is different, this may not provide a fundamental dividing line.

Intelligent Countermoves

Cohen and Gooch state that "the outcome of the battle depended on one commander reacting faster and more effectively than the other to the unexpected" [p.143]. Their book justifies the separation of civil and military disasters because "a fire will not 'react' to the actions of the men who are trying to put it out" [p.1]. Here the debate comes down to how you define the word "react" and whether there is a necessity for there to be a *controlling mind* that directs that reaction. It is clear that the authors conceptualise "react" as an intelligent, considered and appropriate countermove; my question would be how intelligent, considered and appropriate are most of these countermoves in reality. The reading of most military history leaves the impression (reinforced by *hindsight*) that commanders had very little real idea of what their enemy were actual doing or intended to do and the ones who succeeded were the ones who applied their force most effectively in a *chaotic* situation.

A reading of Robert McNamara's book *Argument without End*[5] makes it very clear that neither the American nor the North Vietnamese understood what the other side wanted to achieve or what their actions actually signified. In the case of the Vietnam War the countermoves made by both sides seem to have been no more intelligent or appropriate than those that can be seen in a forest fire. Cohen and Gooch provide their own examples of the same issue; I will take the case of the Korean War. A counter case to the one made by Cohen and Gooch is made in the book *Mao, the Unknown Story* by Jung Chang and Jon Halliday.[6] Chapter 34 is titled "Why Mao and Stalin started the Korean War". This chapter counters the idea that MacArthur's actions drew China into the war at the end of 1950 by threatening their borders. Chang and Halliday's proposition is that Mao started the war for his own purposes and that Mao was behind the original attacks carried out by North Korean troops. Chang and Halliday assert that Mao was gambling on the US wanting to keep that war limited to the Korean peninsula.[7] They argue his rationale was four-fold:

- He felt that he could not lose the war because he had "millions of expendable Chinese" at his disposal.
- He wanted to use Stalin to help him set up a national weapons manufacturing capability. He would do this by fighting a proxy war for the Soviets against the US in Korea.
- He wanted to bleed the US of men, materiel and prestige in a protracted war and he was prepared "to spend years consuming several hundred thousand American lives".
- He wanted to "consign former Nationalist troops to their death"; in effect, use the Americans to kill his internal enemies.

While Stalin manoeuvred to avoid transferring capability and technology to the Chinese, they did support Mao's war; as a consequence the Soviet failure to veto the UN resolution to deploy troops to Korea was no accident. The Soviets had their own aims for the war. These included: 1) the field testing of equipment, 2) acquiring intelligence on the US and their technology and 3) reducing the threat of US intervention when the Soviets tried to interfere in Western Europe. If the Chang and Halliday proposition holds true, then the UN in Korea were fighting a very different war to the one they perceived was facing them. In this respect Cohen and Gooch were correct to focus on the issue identified by Clausewitz, which is "to establish … the kind of war on which

5   McNamara (1999)
6   Chang and Halliday (2006)
7   Chang and Halliday (2006:375–378)

they were embarking". Rather than drawing the conclusions they did, I see the key lesson from this case as being more generalisable. At its heart, the problem is one about recognising the core issue. This holds true for all problem-solving. If you are not clear and accurate about the nature of the problem then the solution proposed (in this case the type of war to be fought) is less likely to be appropriate as the correlation between what each side thinks is happening and what actually may be happening might be purely coincidental.

Let us therefore return more directly to the issue of a *controlling mind* and our ability to *anticipate* countermoves. Cohen and Gooch would seem to equate the capability to react to human control. I would suggest that this is another form of *illusion of control* and a human vanity. In the case of a forest fire, it may actually be possible to predict the course of the fire as there are no forces deliberately trying to mislead you. Once we understand the laws of nature, how they interact with the topography and we have the ability to model them, then we can *anticipate* what will probably happen. We can then adapt our plans accordingly. However, even when the *controlling mind* is the laws of nature, what we do not know means that we are unlikely to predict what will happen but just *anticipate* what will probably happen. Weather forecasting is a constant reminder of man's inability to predict the course of nature. When we try to predict human activity, when there are forces that are trying to mislead, then prediction becomes even more difficult. While each side attempts to "get inside the head" of their opponent, and this may involve having sources (human or technical) that can accurately report what their opponent thinks and intends, I would suggest that any correlation between an opponent's intent and their final action may still be only coincidental. This is because the sequence necessary between intent and outcome is fraught with difficulties. Just because an opponent intended something to happen, does not mean that it will; if it does, it may just be the result of good fortune on their part. Here we can see that the *controlling mind* may still just be an *illusion of control*. We see therefore that what is judged to be an intelligence success may in fact just be an *attribution error*. In practice, the way a forest fire reacts may be more predictable than is a military opponent; it may be easier to get inside the *controlling mind* of a forest fire (by understanding the laws of nature) than it is to get inside the mind of a military opponent. In each case the pattern of activity and the relationships between the component parts of the problem may be just as unrecognisable or unforeseeable; in the language used earlier in this book, these relationships may be equally *chaotic*. To think we are able to predict what will happen requires us to understand how all the parts will interact. To believe we have that understanding may just be another illusion. Therefore within the re-envisaged *Disaster Incubation Theory* model we can see the forces that perpetuate "the existing course of action" being countered by the forces that look to resist that course of action. This proposition would seem to hold true whether the scenario is one where forces (heat, wind and terrain) perpetuate a forest fire while resisting the forces trying to extinguish it, as it does for events within a war. All we can do in both cases is to *anticipate* what might happen and adapt accordingly.

Foresight or Hindsight

The purpose of my work is to produce tools and frameworks that provide catalysts to *foresight*. As is often the case in work that examines failure, Cohen and Gooch try to reject the certainties produced by *hindsight* as being silly [p.41], but they do not go so far as offering a pathway to *foresight*. The furthest they go is to argue that organisations need to learn, *anticipate* and adapt [p.26] as a route to avoiding misfortune. There are however clear parallels between the outcomes required from *military intelligence* and *foresight*. Cohen and Gooch make the point that while we may be able to foresee [p.21], we cannot predict the future [p.42]. They say that as "the future is not predetermined, so intelligence cannot be the same as prophecy" [p.118]. They accept that avoiding the unexpected is difficult due to *interactive complexity*. They do not argue for prediction but against "inadequate or imperfect anticipation" [p.17] resulting in the "inability to foresee and take appropriate measures" [p.27]. I see all these sentiments applying to *foresight* as well.

Cohen and Gooch see the role of intelligence as "provid(ing) the bounds for strategic calculation, but (that) it is asking too much to expect it to look into the future" [p.43]. Similarly, the role of *foresight* is to envisage scenarios that are possible (given the existing context and capabilities) and to identify *unacceptable damage*. This, in turn, provides the basis of the setting and taking of those *precautionary norms* that are deemed reasonable. In this context, the greatest mistake that can be made is the "failure to think through the many dimensions of a changing strategic challenge" [p.130].

Cohen and Gooch attempt to avoid *hindsight* by looking at counterfactual arguments [p.45] in order to determine why they turn out as they did [p.46]. Their use of counterfactual analysis proved interesting but occasionally it was tainted by the use of facts that could only have been determined retrospectively. If we are to understand why people make the value judgements and decisions they do, we need to see the situation as they do. This must embrace the imperfect information and contradictory interpretations that face the person at the time they were required to make their decision. While the facts of the particular case may be questioned, the 2004 film *Ike: Countdown to D-Day*[8] provides an interesting study of the forthcoming "battle from the point of view of the commander … (showing the decisions he had to make based on) what he knew at the time" [p.36]. In this context one quote in the book stood out. In their Yom Kippur War case study, Cohen and Gooch revealed an important factor or constraint on *foresight*. After examining many of the possible sources of failure as to why the Israeli mobilisation of reserves did not happen in time, they quoted a senior intelligence staff officer as saying, "I knew that in any case no catastrophe could occur" [p.128]. This would seem to suggest that, despite the acres of articles and papers examining the precise timing of the mobilisation, the precise timing was not a major consideration for these decision-makers. This was because those tasked with the decision believed they already had the capability to manage any possible forthcoming *crisis*. If this is the case then the critical question becomes why they failed to keep an open mind to the possibility that the superiority gaps, which had been to their advantage, had closed.

Cohen and Gooch showed clear awareness of the dangers of using *hindsight* when trying to learn lessons for the future. They were clear that the purpose of their book was to examine pathways to misfortune, their method based on learn, *anticipate* and adapt, however, became their solution. In their *Afterword* they point to a *failure to learn* and *failure to anticipate* [p.250] in more recent military campaigns. It is interesting to note that they do not provide an illustration of *failure to adapt* in this section of their book. In this context I find it difficult to extract lessons from their method for developing *foresight*. This leaves me with the question of what to take from this book that will enable us to enhance our *foresight*. Their methodology is not clear. How we should use their framework and the triptych "learn … anticipate … adapt" is not clear. These issues will be explored in the next section of this chapter.

In summary, we can see that the way that Cohen and Gooch seek to separate military misfortune from other types of unwanted outcomes may not be as clear cut as they suggest. It is difficult to see the military as a special case based on their having to face the possibility of death and having to make decisions when highly stressed. Civilians also face such stresses. It is also difficult to accept that, in many instances, military opponents react to one another's moves in a way that is any more appropriate than a forest fire reacts to the activity

---

8   Directed by Robert Harmon and written by Lionel Chetwynd, it starred Tom Selleck as Eisenhower

of firefighters. While military commanders may think they are reacting to what is happening, they may in fact be reacting to what they perceive to be happening. This may have little correlation to what is actually happening and to the reasons why it is happening in the way that it is. Finally, their offering of "in lieu of remedies", the need to "learn ... anticipate ... adapt", while not used by them to generate *foresight*, might actually do so. As they suggest, their framework does provide a way forward.

Framework

Cohen and Gooch propose a framework as a way of establishing "pathways to misfortune", which they refer to as a "Matrix of Failure" [p.55]. The matrix consists of two dimensions (*critical task* and Command Levels) against which they map where there were failures of a *critical task* within particular Command Levels (a multi-layered approach). They are then able to illustrate the linkages between these failures to show the critical path. For Cohen and Gooch this was an exercise in *hindsight*. My challenge is to examine whether this tool could be used as a catalyst for *foresight*. To do this I will examine each part of their framework.

MULTI-LAYERED APPROACH

As I said earlier in this book, for an organisation to perform well, not every part needs to work well; for an organisation to fail, not every part of the organisation needs to fail. Therefore, analysis of systems must consider the action and interaction of sub-components. This does not always happen. One illustration of this practice is given by Cohen and Gooch. They call it the *55/95 problem*. This they say is the propensity a large part of a problem (55 per cent) as being near all it (95 per cent) [p.86]; this must be seen as being akin to another version the *80:20 rule*. They refer to the *fallacy of homogeneity* and agree that "failure is rarely if ever homogeneous" [p.43]. Therefore, we are in agreement that any examination of an organisation or system needs to provide a way of examining the effect that the organisation's structure might have on the problem. From this we can see that Cohen and Gooch's use of a multi-layered approach was well ahead of its use within safety science. For this advance their contribution needs to be acknowledged.

If you accept the *fallacy of homogeneity* then it would be a failure of logic to stop after solely constructing hierarchical (vertical) layers. Studies of organisations often highlight the problems created by *silo thinking*; in brief, this is when one vertically integrated section of an organisation (for example, a discipline such as marketing) forgets to coordinate their activities with another (for example, sales). The Cohen and Gooch model looks at the interaction between *critical tasks* at each hierarchical level, however they give little consideration to cross-silo interaction issues. This omission may be because, as I have found, representing the horizontal as well as the vertical layers is a difficult graphical challenge when the medium is two-dimensional as it is with paper or on a computer screen. Whatever the practical difficulties in the representation or articulation of these problems, it is essential that consideration of them is not omitted during the *risk discourse*.

Cohen and Gooch also recognise that "there is no formula for selecting the right level to examine" [p.52]; I agree. I have previously recommended[9] to people considering this issue that they may start by using the idea of *micro* to *mega levels* as an initial catalyst to their thinking. The purpose of this suggestion is to start the process of breaking down the organisation from being a homogeneous whole into the parts that interact. This last point is very important. I do not see this as a reductionist approach because I am still considering the organisation as a whole. I do not advise that the organisation is just broken down into smaller parts (the reductionist approach), I advise that it is the examination of how these parts interact in order to find the organisational fault lines that is the key issue. Experience shows that, once stimulated, those involved tend to identify the fault line within their organisation quite readily. The actual step size used between layers is not important as long as those involved consider them to accurately reflect the fault lines within their system.

What is important within this process is to set the boundaries of the debate. Again this concerns the clarification of basic assumptions and limitations around the specific *risk discourse*. Any such debate will have to be limited or it may expand beyond what is understandable or manageable. A key element would therefore be to identify the *control bubble* (a concept discussed in more detail in an earlier chapter) for the key stakeholder as it relates to the problem in hand. The logic is that while there may be many things we cannot control within our environment, it is often seen as our responsibility to take what steps we can where we can. In this context Cohen and Gooch admonished General Hamilton's conduct of the failed Gallipoli campaign in 1915 as he was in charge of the operation [p.156].

---

9   Lauder (2013:99–100)

Once this basic parameter of a *control bubble* has been set, this will provide some guidance as to the full scope of the system that needs to be embraced in any particular case and that *risk discourse* is the most effective way to establish the discussion layers.

CRITICAL TASKS

Cohen and Gooch use Clausewitz's idea of critical analysis (or *Kritik*) in order to discern the *critical tasks* within their framework [p.44]. The Clausewitzian idea of critical analysis has three steps. Step 1 is to discover the facts, Step 2 is to trace the effects to the causes and Step 3 is to investigate and evaluate means. This form of analysis, while very basic when compared to more recent analytical models, does include the idea of *double loop learning* ("that the end itself should be appraised"). I have no difficulty with the notion of the importance of determining what is critical; it is the practicalities that are the challenge. This idea has much in common with the construct of *performance indicators*. They both focus attention of specific areas. They are both looking to identify signals of potential failure. While indicators of failure are more commonly referred to as *key risk indicators* (*KRIs*), they are in essence the same of *key performance indicators* (*KPIs*) as I have explained elsewhere.[10] However, to catch failures before they occur requires examination of the process rather than the outcomes. For once we have the outcome it is too late. Therefore rather than starting with the idea of *Kritik*, my starting point would be the idea of *critical success factors* which, like *KRIs*, also focuses on areas where "things must go right".

Before we examine the *critical success factors* in these cases, we need to explore potential alternatives. Within literature on politics, security and strategy we see the *DIME* construct. In this context *DIME* stands for Diplomatic, Information, Military and Economic. Diplomatic covers negotiation between nations through official channels. Information covers knowledge gathered through non-official channels such as through their intelligence services or through news channels. Military covers the relative capabilities of potential protagonists to achieve their aims by force. Finally, Economics cover how the nation's wealth might be used to achieve its aims. Within business studies the parallel to *DIME* is *PESTLE*. *PESTLE* is meant to be a catalyst to managers to examine the political, economic, social, technological, legal and environmental factors that may affect the organisation's ability to achieve its goals. The weakness in using *DIME* or *PESTLE* as a dimension in any

---

10 Lauder (2011:Ch4)

framework is that they produce a rather coarse grain of analysis. I would suggest, however, that either or both of these could be used as a starting point for working towards an identification of what is critical.

Cohen and Gooch provide little guidance on determining what is critical. They say, "One way to find out the nature of *critical tasks* is to look at ways in which the defeated forces came close to achieving their objectives" [p.49]. I have three problems with this definition. The first problem is that this approach relies on *hindsight*. The second is that these tasks tend to be those closest to the point of failure. This encroaches on James Reason's *Sharp end – Blunt end* debate where those in close proximity to the failure are most often blamed for the failure. There is extensive debate that rejects this relationship. The final problem is the selection of the *critical tasks* within the six case studies matrixes.

The validity of the *critical tasks* for each case are not questioned, however the pattern they produce is. There are clear inconsistencies. For example, coordination is listed by itself, with control and with communications. From the book it is not clear how these tasks were identified, how they were selected nor is it clear how these phenomena relate to each other. (Here I refer back to the Clausewitzian notion of theory as something that helps develop our understanding of the relationship between phenomena.)

An issue with the way *critical success factors* have developed, and have been used, is that the ideas of criticality and identifying "the few key areas" seem to have been lost; there is now a tendency to include everything that needs to be performed as planned. To ensure this blurring of criticality does not occur, the test for what is critical needs to be extreme. Once what is critical has been identified, degrees of sub-criticality can then be considered. Within the matrixes produced by Cohen and Gooch there were hints that suggest they might accept this argument. They identify some partial, marginal and critical failures as well as some that are simply labelled "failures". As they do not define these categorisations, it is open to speculation about what they mean. I see a place for such categorisation based on the potential reversibility of the failure, the level of damage caused and the potential harm it may bring.

In summary, that which is deemed critical must actually be critical to the success of an imperfect system. The temptation is to try to define a perfect system where everything becomes critical if the system is to stay perfect. As no system is likely to be perfect, what happens is that the system becomes swamped by the data required; this returns us to John Rockart's starting point.

MAPPING PROCESS

The hierarchy and the *critical tasks* dimensions provide the building blocks for the next step in building on Cohen and Gooch's framework. The next step is to establish links between the building blocks. While it may be tempting to think of these links in terms of *cause and effect*, this would be a dangerously simplistic view. In an earlier chapter we discussed the non-linear relationships between components of *complex* systems. Therefore, these links need to be thought of as contingencies, designed to provide catalysts to the *risk discourse* necessary to test and understand the veracity and the resilience of these relationships. (In essence, this is a question of how likely these links are to be true or false under a given set of circumstances). This provides a graphical representation of the issue at hand. This kind of "mapping" is commonly used as a management tool. Examples can be found as *cause maps*,[11] *strategy mapping*[12] *success maps*[13] or the more intricate variants such as the causal maps used by Snook.[14] These are all forms of the schematic diagram map, the most well-known being the map of the London Underground rail network created by Henry Beck in 1931; in Beck's case the entities are the stations and the connections are made by the rail lines. These can all be seen as developments of the idea of *mental models*.[15] The *mental models* are our construct of "how things work". They are based on our view of the world, assumptions about how phenomena interact and are often constructed subconsciously. All these types of maps are used to articulate these subconscious ideas in order to facilitate *cross-understanding* between stakeholders. *Cross-understanding* refers to:

> the extent to which group members have an accurate understanding of one another's mental models. Such understanding can evolve through intermember communications ... members' factual knowledge, cause-effect beliefs, sensitivity to the relevance of particular issues, or preferences. Cross-understanding is a group-level, compositional construct.[16]

Cross-understanding should not to be confused with *common understanding*, which at its simplest, means what people understand in common.

---

11 Weick and Bougon (1986:102–135)
12 Kaplan and Norton (2004)
13 Bourne and Bourne (2011)
14 Snook (2000)
15 Senge, Kliener, Roberts, Ross and Smith (1994)
16 Huber and Lewis (2010:7)

Against this premise we see that Cohen and Gooch proposed the creation of a framework using the hierarchical and criticality axes. (It has to be noted that in their series of matrixes, the dimension *critical task* morphs into "function". This is neither explained nor justified.) There is then the need to identify what had to happen, where there were failures and the relationship between the tasks and the failures. For Cohen and Gooch the purpose of the framework is to facilitate *cross-understanding* on the pathways to misfortune. For their purpose they see the need to define the failures in each case. I see this as a weak part of their method. While, for the purpose of their book, their method may be adequate, for the purpose of generating *foresight*, it is not. For their book they required a failure in order to describe the pathway to it. The Cohen and Gooch book can be seen as one that describes a methodology rather than it being a forensic analysis of each case. Therefore the actual failures they use are not critical to their proposition. Whatever failures they use would still enable them to describe the different facets of their method. This limitation, however, needs to be addressed in order to develop their method into one that facilitates *foresight*.

This key problem in using their method can be seen in two of their ideas. The first idea is that the failure in the case of Pearl Harbour was the failure to take a sufficient toll of the Japanese planes to suggest an adequate defence [p.48]. Cohen and Gooch stated that it was this failure that caused the "shock"; they neither explain who was shocked nor do they seek to justify this claim. An alternative explanation of the shock might be the *unacceptable damage* inflicted on the nation by the attack under a specific circumstance; in the case of Pearl Harbour, the circumstance was that the attack took place on US home soil. It can be seen that similar shock was inflicted upon Israel by the Yom Kippur War because, although in the end they repulsed the attack, the cost of doing so was far higher than had been foreseen within their *precautionary norms*. The relationship between *cause and effect* is not clear in either case.

The second quote concerns the role played by the measurement of success of the US anti-Uboat campaign and whether the key measurement of their performance was the shipping lost or the Uboats sunk [p.68]. This is a standard debate within the *performance management* discipline. Here we see what a *circle paradigm* looks like in effect: the process is one of resupplying Europe and the disruption of this process is by Uboat activity. The debate is whether you measure means (sinking Uboats to reduce their ability to sink shipping) or ends (shipping sunk). This debate immediately raises a third possible measure and that is one that might consider measuring the tonnage of materiel delivered against the minimum critical requirement for survival. Within this means/end debate is the development of a model of how success might be achieved in order to plan and monitor progress.

In both of the instances quoted, the relationship between the components is not clear. In the case of the first quote the question becomes the relationship between the failure, the shock and people. In the case of the second we have an example of where we might use the *seven dimensions of risk* to bring structure to the debate. As described in a previous chapter, these dimensions are seen to be: unwanted inputs (R1), transformation risks (R2), unwanted results (R3), unwanted effects (R4), unwanted consequences (R5), unwanted subsequence (R6), and as an expression of what is acceptable exposure to the unwanted (R7). In the second quote a relationship can therefore be constructed between the Uboats (which I see in the R1 category), their impact (the sinking of shipping) (R5), what might be considered to be acceptable losses (R7) and any failure of anti-Uboat efforts (R2). I see the use of these categories as being a vehicle for the *risk discourse* that would enable those involved to delineate and then discuss the relationships between various parts of the issue at hand.

While the overall idea of mapping can be seen to provide a useful tool, Cohen and Gooch's methodology does seem to have flaws and it is described in too little detail to be useful. While Cohen and Gooch do not offer any suggestion on mapping cause to effect, I suggest that using the seven dimensions model is one way of articulating the sequences of risk produced within any *risk discourse* process.

FRAMEWORK REVISED AS A CUBE

In their final matrix [p.209], Cohen and Gooch underpin each of the three "*critical task*" or "function" columns by one of the three keys ideas from the book; that is learning, *anticipation* and adaption. Again this adaption of their matrix is neither explained nor justified. From this representation, it might be construed that these three constructs could be used as the labels for the three *critical tasks* in a potential catalytic framework. While this would still provide a two-dimensional framework, it fails to portray the true nature of this problem. It mixes critical operations tasks with issues related to *organisational learning*. When looking at the literature on the application of *chaos theory* to management we read: "Chaos theory highlights processes that are … unpredictable – apparently irrational – when mapped in two dimensions, but which reveal astonishing shape, order, and singularity when mapped in three dimensions".[17] Therefore, I would suggest that the Cohen and Gooch framework should be expanded using their three dimensions into a cube (see Figure 4.1) in order to enrich the catalytic process.

---

17 Goldoff (2000:2024)

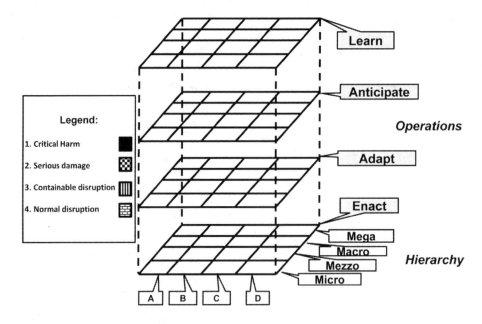

Critical Success Factors

Figure 4.1   Catalytic cube

The first dimension articulates the hierarchy. It describes the various structural layers that interact. Depending on how boundaries are set in framing the problem, the step size may be large or small. The number of layers of the hierarchy used in any particular case will depend on the nature of the issue being addressed. Cohen and Gooch use either four, five or six layers; Leveson used eight. However, it is suggested that a starting point for the framework may be just to give the dimension the labels *micro, mezzo, macro* and *mega* layers and then allow the hierarchy again to emerge through the course of the various iterations of *risk discourse*.

The second dimension lays out the *critical tasks* that need to take place. The process by which these *critical tasks* are defined will be a challenge to any organisation. Cohen and Gooch offer Clausewitz's *Kritik* as a way to determine what is critical. This approach is very broad brush and may not be considered to be too helpful. Rockart and his colleagues offer alternative and slightly more detailed methodologies.[18] Each organisation will need to select and perfect its own method. Whatever method is used, it will require deep reflection if an organisation is to be able to determine what critically needs

18   Bullen and Rockart (1981)

to be done in order to achieve and maintain a distinct competitive advantage over their potential contra-forces. However, as the Israelis discovered with their use of the concept prior to the Yom Kippur War, the construct of what is critical needs to be kept under continual scrutiny, review and adaption.

Finally, the third dimension needs to encompass how the organisation operates and learns. The *operations* label has been selected for its simplicity. A more accurate but clumsier label might be "the hierarchy as a *learning organisation*". This dimension is divided into four layers.

Enact layer

The bottom layer of this dimension would map or represent how the organisation currently plans to enact or does enact its *critical tasks* at each hierarchical level. This layer would be used to articulate where critical weaknesses exist or where failures may occur if the organisation does not learn, *anticipate* and adapt to the future. Critical weaknesses may include known flaws in existing arrangements or keys unknowns or uncertainties that would drive the learning process. Analysis provides something akin to what in the military is known as the commander's key information requirements. These drive their intelligence collection process, which I have labelled as *learn*.

Learn layer

Furthest away from the enactment layer is consideration of what the organisation needs to learn; by its very nature this learning would be from the past. Most obvious learning may come from past experience of the organisation or from similar organisations within the same sector but it should also encompass relevant experience from wherever it may exist. They also need to avoid missing useful experience by *distancing through differencing*. Even when looking to the future, typical of the *military intelligence* process considering contra-forces intent, it must be recognised that their intent would have been expressed in the past and so be subject to the same potential failure to enact or may simply have been changed since the intelligence was gathered. Therefore, drawing appropriate lessons from the past is a challenging task. The purpose of this layer is to identify where research, in all its guises, is required to extract lessons from the past and to shape that learning into practices for the future.

Anticipate layer

The layer under learning is one which encapsulates where the organisation needs to *anticipate* how the future may be different from what is currently expected. The purpose of this layer is to stimulate discussion about the critical differences between what the organisation may be expecting or preparing for and, what might actually happen. This would combine the product of the learn activities with, what Karl Weick called, *disciplined imagination;*[19] while great imagination is required it must be constrained and supported by a clear rationale. It is accepted that boundaries between what is imaginable and that which is unimaginable are difficult to define and manage. While *Black Swans*[20] are part of everyday risk management discussion, people find it hard to consider the absolute worst case. After the events at Waco in 1993, the agents debriefed by investigators told them "we are prepared for worst case scenarios but some events will invariably be even worse".[21] This is not helped by current risk management practice which recommends no action be taken on potential occurrences, no matter how harmful, that are very rare or improbable. Within the definition of critical being harmful to the organisation, executives should always consider taking action in order to prevent critical failures. Therefore the *anticipation layer* should provide a catalyst to the necessary discussion that then identifies where and how the organisation might need to adapt.

Adapt layer

The third layer down, and the one above the *enact layer*, should provoke discussion about how the organisation needs to adapt or should be prepared to adapt, and the operational implications of the transition. However the organisation looks to manage the change, during periods of change the organisation will be less effective and efficient as personnel learn to modify their work routines. A period of change will induce vulnerabilities and *chaos* into an organisation. The *chaos* (here defined as "the inability to see any pattern within an activity or series of events") is induced because no matter what routine is mandated by the organisation, until it is absorbed into the working culture, in a time of stress or *crisis* executives cannot be sure that those involved will not revert back to old routines with which they are more comfortable. The purpose of the *adapt layer* is therefore to provide a mechanism for executives to discuss the adaption process and any *unintended consequences* that it may induce, especially when these concern the *enact layer*.

---

19 Weick (1989)
20 Taleb (2007)
21 Goldoff (2000)

As with the Cohen and Gooch model, once the structure of the cube framework has been agreed, the stakeholders then need to identify where critical vulnerabilities exist or where critical failures may occur. In the six frameworks produced by Cohen and Gooch they not only identified "critical failures" but they also included some "partial failures", "marginal failures" and other "failures". The cube could be used to do something similar. I would look to use categories, defined above, such as 1) *critical harm*, 2) *serious damage*, 3) *containable disruption* and 4) normal disruption to identify the potential for harm to occur. Here the balance to be struck is one which articulates the critical issues but does not swamp the decision-makers with unnecessary detail.

The final step would be to articulate the links between the critical factors to show the assumed relationships between the factors. One of the key purposes of this is not to suggest that these links are fixed or static but to articulate the assumed linkages so that they can be continually challenged and assessed for their validity. Again the purpose of this step, like all the others, is to provide an architecture for the debate. The debate needs to be iterative and, ironically, should those involved ever consider the matter resolved then this should provide them a warning that complacency might be setting in!

In summary, each part of this *catalytic cube* is designed to articulate assumptions about what is important and to enable those involved to debate how these elements might interact. At every stage these assumptions, once articulated, should be seen as the starting point for discussions about these factors rather than them being seen as being resolved and fixed. The cube format also provides a clear link between learning and enactment.

Conclusion

In this chapter we have examined, for its ability to engender *foresight*, a framework produced by Cohen and Gooch for the purpose of understanding the roots of military misfortune. In their Afterword Cohen and Gooch stress that misfortune happens when a competent military fails to learn, *anticipate* or adapt [p.247]. While these ideas of learn, *anticipate* or adapt were not new, others had already discussed the need to learn (see for example Mitroff et al.[22]) and the need to act on such learning (see Weick[23]); the triptych does provide a neat and practical synthesis of these ideas.

---

22   Mitroff, Shrivastava and Udwadia (1987)
23   Weick (1988)

While it is not always clear how they arrived at the outcome they did, their framework did provide the stimulus that led to the *catalytic cube* structure. While they limited their proposition to military operations, it can be seen that such a device will have application in a wider field: I did not, however, find their delineation between military and civilian operations convincing. In fact, I would be concerned that what might be seen as *military intelligence* successes are in fact just another example of *attribution errors* where randomness and *chaos* have not been given sufficient weight.

Finally we return to Turner's point that only in *hindsight* does the problem we face appear well-structured. While Cohen and Gooch espouse the rejection of *hindsight* as being silly, their analysis was steeped in *hindsight*. While they offer the proposition that with learning, anticipating and adaption military misfortune may be avoided, this is not offered as their remedy. While they did not offer a tool for *foresight*, their work has been helpful in doing so.

Chapter 5
Lesson to be Learnt

Introduction

In the previous chapter I examined the framework provided by Cohen and Gooch for its utility to stimulate *foresight*. In this chapter I intend to use the same work but for a different purpose. As previously discussed, Cohen and Gooch saw the military as being a special case and being separated from their civilian counterparts to the point that lessons could not cross over between the two areas. Attributed to Eric Hollnagel is the sentiment that "What you look for is what you find; what you find is what you fix".[1] In this idea Hollnagel warns us that we often have to know that a problem exists before we will find evidence for it in any particular case. If this is true then this would suggest that we have to be open to ideas coming from others if we are to recognise the problem in our case. In the context of Turner's work, this phenomenon would be seen as being part of the issue of *organisational exclusivity*: disregard of non-members. Therefore, before I look at the lesson provided by Cohen and Gooch, I will go back to my point that, at their root, military and civilian failures have much in common.

To show this I will first look at the phenomena identified by Turner and draw evidence from Cohen and Gooch's book that suggests that the phenomena may well be present within military misfortune. I will then use my revised questions and again draw evidence from their book showing where each question may have been appropriate within their cases. My aim is to show that if you look for a failure factor you may find it in most cases whether they are set in a military or non-military context.

Finally, from within Cohen and Gooch's work, I will draw different and more generalisable lessons. I agree with Cohen and Gooch [p.233] that there is no single solution to such *complex* problems and therefore I see the lessons as being more subtle. I break these lessons into two groups. The first are lessons about what needs to be understood and the second are concerned with the way

---

1   Hollnagel (2008)

(the "how") those involved need to approach the subject of *foresight*. Under the heading "what", I examine three causes of which managers should be aware and under the heading "how", I examine the mental attitude appropriate to tackling *foresight* tasks.

Turner's Phenomena

One might criticise Cohen and Gooch for falling short of their own standards as they failed to learn from lessons already identified elsewhere. In their defence they do have a cursory look at disaster theory and give a passing reference to Barry Turner [p.17, note 37]. However, they do miss Turner's major contribution to disaster theory which was his 1978 book *Man-made Disaster*.[2] A reading of their book provides ample evidence that the critical phenomena identified by Turner are present in cases of military misfortune. Table 5.1 opposite only provides examples sufficient to justify my assertion that these factors are present within military operations: they are not intended to imply that these factors were the critical failures.

From these examples, it can be seen that the factors identified by Turner are likely to have been present within the military cases. One can only speculate how many more examples would be found if Cohen and Gooch's original primary source data was re-examined.

Revised Questions

Again to illustrate Eric Hollnagel's sentiment that "What you look for is what you find", I examined the Cohen and Gooch text for evidence of the factors central to my revised questions. While there is evidence for many of the more detailed factors of failure identified in previous research (for example the *fallacy of social redundancy*[3] in the quote "let George do it" [p.56]). There are, however, too many to list at this stage. As explained earlier in this book, I have taken Turner's original phenomena, combined them with the other relevant factors in the post-Turner literature and synthesised them into seven questions. I use the question format as it is more likely to provoke debate. My choice to use seven questions was based on the *critical success factor* principle of identifying

---

2   Turner (1978)
3   Snook (2000:210)

Table 5.1   Turner's phenomena

Rigidities in perception and beliefs	Examples of closed-minds are provided by Cohen and Gooch when they say several times that the strategic conception caused them to close their minds to other possibilities [p.123 and 126].
Decoy phenomena	Examples of distractions provided by Cohen and Gooch are: • Sometimes distractions were caused by internal issue such as logistic difficulties [p.87]. • Sometimes the *decoys* were created deliberately [p.117].
Organisational exclusivity	This links to the notion that "nobody understands us better than we do" which leads to a reluctance to take lessons from outsiders. Examples provided by Cohen and Gooch are: • In the US anti-Uboat campaign, US commanders thought they had little to learn from previous British experience [p.89]. • At Gallipoli the British commander thought he had little to learn from his ANZAC counterparts [p.159]. • Just before the Second World War the French forces were reluctant to take lessons from outsiders [p.213].
Information difficulties	Communications is recognised as a *critical task* within three of Cohen and Gooch's cases; these are Pearl Harbour, the US anti-Uboat campaign and the Korean War. Failures were identified in all three cases and in two of these cases (Pearl Harbour and the Korean War) the failure was seen as being critical.
Involvement of strangers	In military operations this concept is referred to as *collateral damage*; this issue therefore can be seen to be common to both the military and civilian cases.
Failure to comply with existing regulations	It is recognised that the military, as an organisation, places great store by the production of plans and regulations. "Failure to comply" with existing plans and regulation is often examined as part of military history. While this issue was not central to the Cohen and Gooch proposition, such failures are mentioned. • At Pearl Harbour the commander's surveillance plan was ignored [p.55]. Within this idea is also the question of whether the existing regulations were adequate. One example of the failure to provide appropriate regulation is: • At Pearl Harbour there was central command and control set up [p.51].
Minimising emergent danger	There are many ways that people find to underestimate emerging dangers. Two examples are provided by Cohen and Gooch. These are: • Just before the Yom Kippur War the Israeli military commanders (Dayan, Elazar and Zeira) *Forgot to be afraid* [p.114]. • Internal myth building was used to create as false sense of security [p.211].

"key area" and the use the "magical number seven, plus or minus two"[4] in order to provide a numerical guide to the number of questions. The questions and the evidence from Cohen and Gooch's work are set out in Table 5.2.

Table 5.2   Revised questions

Who cares about what?	*Who cares* examines the issue of conflicting priorities between key players. Where priorities conflict there is the vulnerability that key players expend valuable resources in order to "get their own way" and prop up their ego, rather than completing the main task. During the Korean War, the difference in what commanders cared about was demonstrated within the priorities they set for their logistical chain. While the Marines ensured that frontline forces had the materiel they needed to fight, every soldier in the Eighth Army were given a "Thanksgiving dinner of turkey and trimmings" [p.188]. In post-Saddam Iraq, the US-led governing structure was led by a civilian and a military commander who had a very difficult personal relationship [p.249]. These personal animosities are often seen to arise because one feels that the other is thwarting their plans. These conflicts are often simply cases of differing perspectives and priorities.
Are we *ready to launch?*	Here the question is whether the organisation is fully prepared for the upcoming task. An area that is not fully prepared provides a potential vulnerability. Examples from Cohen and Gooch are: • The US General Board of the Navy failed to review whether their forces and structure were fit for purpose [p.88]. This can be seen as failure to prepare the resources required. • The lack of direction and guidance given by the French commander Gamelin to his subordinates and also the distrust between Gamelin and the French premier [p.221] can be seen as a failure to give adequate direction. • The failure of coordination between Britain, France and Belgium until it was too late [p.224].
Is there *practical drift?*	The issue of *practical drift* is, in essence, one of failing to *adapt* appropriately to changing circumstances. The fact that "adapting" is a major theme of their book, in itself, shows this commonality between military and civilian cases. One example given was that the Israelis had adapted to the changing strategic realities in the years leading up to the Yom Kippur War [p.122].
Is there *structural secrecy?*	The label *structural secrecy* includes those cases where the data required by one part of the organisation is held by another which fails to communicate it effectively, for whatever reason. The category would therefore be those examples listed as "information difficulties" in Table 5.1 and the many other examples given throughout their book, such as when they make the point of the importance of efficient communications [p.159]. One clear example from Cohen and Gooch is that at Gallipoli, due to *structural secrecy*, "many junior officers found themselves leading attacks without knowing their objectives" [p.155].

---

4   Miller (1955)

Are our *assumptions valid?*	Throughout their book, Cohen and Gooch provide examples of *erroneous assumptions*. Examples are:

* "The attack (during the Gallipoli campaign) was based on two assumptions, both of which turned out to be unwise" [p.137].
* By 1939 French military doctrine and practice was dominated by the belief that the next war would be similar in critical way to the last one and would be dominated by strategies of defence [pp.14 and 213].

Is there *dysfunctional momentum?*	The question of *dysfunctional momentum* is designed to expose where the internal momentum, often characterised as "this is the way we do things", drives the organisation towards activities that hinder rather than support its key purpose. Examples from Cohen and Gooch might be seen to be:

* The "artillery fixation" at Gallipoli [p.150] meant that the natural momentum of the organisation planning process took them towards the structures and materiel more suited to trench warfare rather than the conflict that actually faced them.
* For the French Generals the experience of the previous war meant that they "sanctified the primacy of the defensive" [p.214], in turn this led at the start of the Second World War to the French promotion of tactics and materiel geared to defence.

In *hindsight* it might also be used as an excuse for failure:

* In France, May 1940, some saw the situational momentum "had stacked the cards too heavily against" them [p.198] and their country "was 'spinning at a giddy speed' down the fatal slope" [p.200].

Have we generated *unintended consequences?*	The question of *unintended consequences* examines times where positive outcomes for one part of the system have unwanted effects in another area of the same system. Cohen and Gooch are seen to accept the notion of *interactive complexity* [p.5] which inevitably must lead to *unintended consequences*.

Prior to the Japanese attack on Pearl Harbour, commanders perceived the risk of sabotage as being greater than other risks. However, the precautions they then took, which might have been successful in deterring sabotage on the aircraft, had an *unintended consequence*. As their aircraft were tightly parked this made them easier for the Japanese air attacks to destroy in larger numbers than might otherwise have been the case [p.52].

In 1916 Hamilton had local success at Suvla Bay. They capitalised on this success by consolidating their position [p.142]. The *unintended consequence* was that the Turkish forces had time to reinforce their inadequate defences. The parallels with the Anzio landing in January 1944 are striking.

Again, from these examples it can be seen that the factors key to each question are likely to have been present with the military cases. We can only speculate how many more examples could be found if Cohen and Gooch's original primary source data was re-examined. While others might argue over whether the examples may be more suited to an alternative question, I do not consider this to be important as all the questions are linked and the issues interact. In this context we can see that the questions might be equally appropriate as a catalyst to *risk discourse* in a military as well as a civilian context.

The "What"

In addition to their main point about "learn … anticipate … adapt", Cohen and Gooch's writings stimulated consideration of three more detailed issues. These three issues were selected because they centre on the idea of *chaos* and the crossover between civilian and military situations. The issues are how *normal chaos* plays in both contexts, how a single solution may not be suitable for all occurrences (labelled "horses for courses"), and that any judgement as to "lost opportunities" that looks at the instance from a single side shows analytical bias and a lack of appreciation of the effects of the contra-forces in creating the phenomenon perceived as "luck".

NORMAL CHAOS

Throughout Cohen and Gooch's book, reference is made to the breakdown within communication systems. This seems to lay emphasis on the communication itself rather than the purpose of communication as an enabler of coordination and control. This accepts that the coordination and control can be achieved through a number of alternative modes such as mutual adjustment, direction, plans or standards. The issues of communications, coordination and control are, however, of second order to the question of whether one side is able to gain and maintain the initiative over the contra-forces (whether these contra-forces consist of the fire against firefighters or military attacking forces against defenders). Therefore, in *chaotic* circumstances, the critical issue becomes whether one side is deluding itself over whether it does understand what is happening and whether it is within their powers to do anything about it; this delusion has been referred to earlier as the *"illusion of control"*.[5] The critical issue for any organisation, civilian or military, is whether they actually have control over what they think they control and how effectively that control can be and is being exerted. The answer to the issue of control will, by its very nature, encompass discussion of communications as one of the means of exerting control. The pattern of this relationship, however, might never be clear.

Due to its *complex* nature, combat will include many examples of *chaos*, random occurrences, unseen patterns and what is referred to as luck. To these I add the idea of *normal chaos*. In an earlier chapter I have explained the construct of *normal chaos*. The pattern of *normal chaos* can be seen in Cohen and Gooch's work such as where military tension heightened and then waned as evidence emerged and was then submerged below waves of alternative data. In this

---

5   Durand (2004:109–130)

chapter all I wish to do is to take the evidence provided by Cohen and Gooch to illustrate how *normal chaos* exhibited itself within their cases. I consider three aspects. The first is *signal saliency*, the second concerns *attribution error* and the third is the *edge of chaos*.

Cohen and Gooch extract from the appropriate social scientist literature the idea of "noise" [p.41]. This is, however, just one example of many types of signal that distracts or *decoys* those involved away from the critical data. It is therefore but one of the causes that may account for failure of intelligence (I would characterise failure of intelligence more generally just as another type of *failure of foresight*.) They go on to say "the problem was not ... that organisations had too little information ... but too much". This statement is supported by many post-disaster inquiry reports. These show that the required information is often available within the organisations. The problem is just that it is in the wrong place or is not given the priority that *hindsight* would indicate it deserved. Since Cohen and Gooch wrote this book, social scientists have done more work in this area. As well as having to consider *noise*, which Cohen and Gooch define as "the difficulty of sifting out correct and important from the irrelevant and false", social scientists now sub-divide the type of signals available. Diane Vaughan,[6] for example, talks of *strong signals, routine signals, weak signals, mixed signals, missing signals* and the *loss of salience* of signals. To these we can add Turner's *decoy*[7] *signals* and Sutcliffe's *messy signals*.[8] In addition, we need to consider possible false warning, where people are "crying wolf" [p.119 and 120] or data that is "true but useless"[9] and therefore irrelevant. All these types of signals adsorb capacity to filter and comprehend. All these types of irrelevant or misleading data help to confuse the true picture of the situation and thus perpetuate *chaos* as being normal.

The idea of *attribution errors* is well known; in essence an *attribution error* is one where success is attributed to one's own prowess whereas a failure is attributed to bad luck. Cohen and Gooch veer towards this error when they say, "Of course, intelligence has, on a number of occasions ... enabled one side to anticipate another's actions". Unless that side had direct access to the decisions made by the other side, then the intelligent assessment is likely to have been based on some final subjective judgement. In *hindsight* that judgement will be seen to be correct or be seen as an error. In reality the correlation between the judgement and the contra-forces intent may, in fact, just be random. We may

6   Vaughan (1996)
7   Turner and Pidgeon (1997)
8   Sutcliffe (2005)
9   Grint (2008)

wish to delude ourselves that we made the "right call on this occasion" when, in reality, it should have been attributed to random coincidence of outcome and judgement. The relationship between decision and intent was no more foreseeable than the role of a dice. Within *normal chaos* therefore we should always think of such judgements as being an educated guess (where some are more educated than others) rather than being a scientific judgement. This is to avoid building up any *illusion of control* as we are warned by the words of Rudyard Kipling's poem *If*. He talks of the necessity to meet "Triumph and Disaster and treat those two impostors just the same". (This may help to explain Macarthur's roller coaster career. His ability did not change, it was just that sometimes he made the correctly correlated call and sometimes he did not.)

Finally we shall look at what has been labelled the *edge of chaos*. I have selected two cases, Pearl Harbour and the Yom Kippur War, to illustrate my point. In the cases described we see that the path to war was not linear. In the case of Pearl Harbour, Cohen and Gooch point out that the possibility of a surprise attack had concerned the commander's resident in the area for some time [p.52]. What the authors do not do is to trace the ebbs and flows as tensions rose and abated during that year. They did not explore the false alarms and any related precautionary deployment (later to be seen as being unnecessary) that might have played a role in conditioning the local commander's state of mind by the end of November 1941. Cohen and Gooch start their narrative on 27 November when both Kimmel and Short received warnings of war [p.53]. What they do not exclude is that some previous messages might also have raised the spectre of an imminent attack. The Report on the Pearl Harbour attack asked why the local commanders had failed to coordinate their activities during in the crucial days; that is between 27 November and 7 December 1941 [p.56]? From the perspective of *normal chaos*, the question becomes, how, without the benefit of *hindsight*, the commanders would have known that these were the "crucial days"? If they could not be certain that these days were crucial, this would have left them with the issue of how long they could have employed full precautionary measures and at what cost? What would have been the cost of fully manning the anti-aircraft guns or flying long-range patrol aircraft reconnaissance? This uncertainty may have been part of the reasoning for Kimmel ordering a variation on the normal alert protocols [p.53]: from this source we do not know. In the case of the Yom Kippur War, the conditioning of the Israelis had started a number of years before the attack. The conditioning took place during the War of Attrition which followed the 1967 Six-Day War. During this period tension rose and fell frequently, to greater or lesser extents. Examples of this are the expulsion of Soviet advisers in July 1972 or removal of the Egyptian Minister of War in January 1973 when this oscillating tension became normal. Therefore there was not a straight trajectory between peace and war; each peak of tension could have been one that went the next step and become a larger conflict; for example, in May of 1973 the Egyptians and Syrians increased the scale of their military activities on their borders, thereby raising tension, but no war had broken out unlike in October of that year [p.100]. As with Pearl Harbour, precautions come at a cost: the Israelis were very sensitive to the high social and economic cost associated with military mobilisation [pp.118–9]. Again, therefore, the question from a *normal chaos* perspective is, as tensions started to build again in September 1973, what made this period different from previous occasions? When considering issues of *foresight* the key issue for the *edge of chaos* is how those responsible know when they actually were entering the "crucial days".

As Turner states, *hindsight* provides a clearly defined problem. Those tackling problems that require *foresight* do not have this luxury. They suffer from "the inability to see any pattern within an activity or series of events": where they think they do see patterns these may just be personal constructs that have little correlation with reality. If we are not to beguile ourselves with *illusions of control* we need to accept events may be more random than we may like. We need to think of *chaos* as being the real norm.

"HORSES FOR COURSES"

As Cohen and Gooch point out, there is never likely to be a *universal* solution that suits all circumstances. In their paper on resilience within small teams, Furniss et al.[10] provide a clear example. They report:

> *Expert observers recognised two crews which were high performing across multiple scenarios. However, the different crews failed and excelled in two distinct scenarios. Crew A had a relatively novice shift supervisor (SS), an experienced team, and a very collaborative and reflective style. They excelled in Scenario X, where there was hidden complexity that was not obvious at the outset, but failed in Scenario Y that required fast and decisive action. In contrast, Crew B had an experienced and confident SS, a relatively inexperienced team, and a less collaborative style that centred around the decisiveness of the SS. Crew B failed in Scenario X and excelled in Scenario Y.*

---

10 Furniss, Back, Blandford, Hildebrandt and Broberg (2011)

The point is that what is effective within one context may fail within another. The Korean War case provides two examples. The first is General MacArthur and the second is the application of air power.

> *The case outlines MacArthur's chequered career. Being an extreme character, it is not surprising that his career had its low points as well as great achievements. This shows that, for whatever the reasons, MacArthur as a highly acclaimed leader did not provide a panacea to all issues of leadership in all circumstances. One has to question whether he was more suited to scenario X rather than Y and which categories each of his tasks would have been classified as.*

> *The case also looks at the application of airpower. The case does not however define what it means by air power and, in this, it contradicts itself. There is invariably some role for airpower in all cases. However strategic bombing, battlefield interdiction, close air support and tactical resupply are very different in the way they apply air power to a conflict. In the retreat from the Yalu River, the Eighth Army and the Marines used airpower quite differently. The Eighth Army was supported by an air force that was wedded to a doctrine of interdiction; on the other hand, the Marines had their own planes providing close air support. The latter was effective but the former was not. While this case considered strategic bombing, battlefield interdiction and close air support, these may be considered in terms of the application of force (in this case airpower) at the micro to mega levels: this demonstrate how the construct may be used more generally.*

When considering the issue of "horses for courses", or the potential for *universal* solutions, we again are faced by the *fallacy of homogeneity*. In this case the homogeneity may be a single person (MacArthur) or a single capability (airpower). The fallacy is they are not multi-faceted with each facet having its own strengths and it weaknesses. The general lessons from this are applicable to both the military and civilian situation. These lessons are that context is critical and the solution must be adapted accordingly. Whenever a solution is proposed, time needs to be taken to evaluate why the solution proposed is applicable to the prevailing circumstances and how it might provide the effect required. The use of *micro* to *mega* layers may help this analysis to produce a richer and more useful picture.

LOST OPPORTUNITIES

When one side sees a lost opportunity (or Manstein's "lost victory" [p.2]), the other may see a narrow escape. We should contrast the seven pages [pp.139–146] written by Cohen and Gooch on the lost opportunity at Suvla Bay (part of the Gallipoli campaign in 1915) and the six lines on the Japanese failure to destroy four and a half million barrels of oil at Pearl Harbour that prolonged the war by a couple of years [p.48] or the one line on the opportunity lost to Syria in 1973 [p.110]. The Syrians failed to regain the pre-1967 borders in the Golan Heights when only a minimal force stood in their way. In contrast, at the same time the Syrians were failing, the Egyptians were successfully dissipating Israeli Air Force (IAF) air attacks and counterattacks by Israeli tank formations showing that Arab forces had the capability to win this exchange. Cohen and Gooch discuss neither the reasons why the Syrians failed to learn the lessons that their allies the Egyptians had learnt nor the role played at Suvla Bay by the "energetic" local Turkish commander Mustafa Kemel (later known as Kemel Ataturk) in the first case [p.144].

In order to truly understand the relationship between the phenomena of success and failure, the analyst needs to look at both sides of the *force field analysis*. In military terms, a commander is trying to take the initiative by "getting inside the opposing commanders decision cycle". Outside military circles this same idea is encapsulated in the phrase (cliché) "getting ahead of the game". The idea is the same; it is about gaining control of events by taking the initiative; by bringing into action the forces available to one side more quickly than the other side can react (whether this reaction has a *controlling mind* or is just apparently the random forces of nature).

In summary, we see clear evidence supporting Hollnagel's warning that "What you look for is what you find". In looking for evidence of Turner's phenomena and for evidence that my questions would have raised issues, we can see that these campaigns were not immune from these types of problems that my questions address. This would also suggest that, unless investigators know what to look for, they may miss key issues that could have led to the failure. We also see that any sector of human activity that thinks it is different from more general human activities may be missing critical opportunities to learn; while I have applied the idea more widely than Turner, he did foresee this issue in what he labelled *organisational exclusivity*. The lesson this suggests is that if an organisation assumes that the general patterns of failure do not apply to them, this assumption may be erroneous. Finally, we see the pattern of *normal chaos* in military operations. We see that solutions may not be *universal* even if the perceived solution is a great military commander. We see that if we consider failure only from the perspective of those who are perceived to have "failed", this bias may prevent our fuller understanding of the events that happened. For *foresight* the lesson is both sides of any *force field* need to be examined with equal diligence and scepticism.

The "How"

As well as the "what" to look for, we also need to look at the "how": that is, we need to be aware of how we might approach the task of generating *foresight*. Again we can see similarities between the approach needed by both civilian and military personnel. I have selected from accident and *crisis* literature four examples of the required behaviours and show, by use of examples extracted from Cohen and Gooch's book, that those behaviours are equally applicable to the military. The behaviours I use are those of being *open-minded*, flexible, being proactive and knowing your own capabilities and weaknesses; I shall address them in that order.

OPEN-MINDED

Being *open-minded* concerns the readiness to consider possibilities that are at odds with one's own worldview and belief system. In contrast to Eisenhower, who Cohen and Gooch praised for being *open-minded* [p.236], they criticised Israeli politicians and commanders for being close-minded when they noted "the dogmatism with which they clung to the concept" [p.123–4]; the concept here being their strategic defence doctrine. In the defence of France in 1940, the French had the same problem with their commander-in-chief, Gamelin [p.218]. They failed and France fell to the Germans. These failures provided a warning to all executives and military commanders of the necessity to remain *open-minded* and to challenge your own beliefs to ensure that they remain valid.

FLEXIBLE

The second issue is closely related to the first. While the term *open-minded* is used to refer to the elasticity of thought, flexibility is more about the action you are prepared to take. Cohen and Gooch provide examples of inflexibility such as the failure of the US troops in Korea to find alternative forms of communications, such as by using runners, when their field phone wires were cut [p.194]. Cohen and Gooch also provided evidence of flexibility by the Chinese during the same campaign where they used a material weakness, a lack of mechanisation, to their advantage to minimise the US airpower advantage. The Chinese used more flexible means of movement and camouflage [p.180]. The requirement for flexibility is accepted by the British armed forces. It is amongst their principles of war. Within British doctrine, "Flexibility is the ability to change readily to meet new circumstances; it comprises agility, responsiveness, resilience, acuity and adaptability".[11] This requirement for flexibility has clear parallels within the academic literature on the concept of *resilience* and so should be seen as being required by both civilian executives and military commanders to enable the capabilities that exist to be used most effectively against emerging threats.

PROACTIVE

The third issue is the necessity to be proactive. The purpose of being proactive, as discussed earlier, is to gain the initiative over the contra-forces, be they human or otherwise. During the Gallipoli campaign the British forces became passive when they looked to consolidate their position around Suvla Bay. Conversely, a Turkish commander facing the British troops was proactive and so gained the initiative; "Kemal, reinforced by troops who had carried out an exhausting forced march, attacked first. Seizing the heights" [p.146]. The subsequent British attack was easily defeated. The Turkish forces had been proactive and had gained the initiative. Passivity can, however, come in many forms. After pointing to the Israeli failure to question basic assumptions, Cohen and Gooch state that "Intellectual docility is, among statesmen and generals, a grievous failing" [p.123]. At the other end of the scale, Cohen and Gooch point to an example of passivity in resolving a basic need. Again the example comes from the Gallipoli campaign. Cohen and Gooch point to the fact that a shortage of water is often cited as one of the reasons for the failure of the campaign against the Turks. They then point out that it was only the British troops who suffered water shortages because they waited for water to be brought to them; on the other hand, the Australian and New Zealand troops were proactive and showed "that with a little effort water could be found" [p.149]. Again, to be proactive is amongst British armed forces' principles of war. Within British doctrine it is referred to as *offensive action* which is defined as "the practical way in which a commander seeks to gain advantage, sustain momentum and seize the initiative". To be proactive is a requirement of any group, civilian or military, if they want to try to seize the initiative in any set of circumstances and so drive the shaping of the situation thus making it more easily predictable.

---

11 https://www.gov.uk/government/publications/jdp-0-01-fourth-edition-british-defence-doctrine, accessed 28 October 2014 – JDP0–01 has a publication date of November 2011

"KNOW YOURSELF"

After examining a wide variety of intelligence failures, Cohen and Gooch come to the conclusion that "military organizations must seek out the most difficult kind of intelligence – knowledge of themselves" [p.195]. Throughout his work on *fundamental surprise*, Lanir[12] also emphasises the need to learn about ourself, the need to develop self-awareness and our ability to exploit fundamental thinking, if we are to avoid surprise and particularly *fundamental surprise*. He acknowledges that this can be a painful process. Here I will address three aspects of *knowing yourself*. These are: 1) your worldview, 2) your strengths and 3) your weaknesses.

The issue of worldview is linked to the idea of *mental models* and is formed by a person's perspective of the world. In his book on the perception of risk, Paul Slovic says, "Worldviews are general social, cultural and political attitudes that appear to have an influence over people's judgements about complex issues".[13] A person's worldview is therefore central to their beliefs and biases. If we wish to decrease the likelihood of misunderstanding data presented to us, we need to truly know ourselves; we need to understand our own forms of bias. While understanding one's own bias is a major part of academic training, it does not receive the same attention within other professional spheres. Many people find this sort of refection a difficult task. This can be seen to leave critical gaps in their analytical capability.

The second part of *knowing yourself* is knowing our own strengths. In her work analysing the causes of the NASA Challenger disaster, Diane Vaughan provides the phrase "seat of understanding".[14] I defined[15] this phrase to mean having the training, knowledge, experience and current data required to make the appropriate judgements. Expertise has been described as "knowing what is not there that should be". Wrapped up in these ideas is whether those involved in decision-making at every level really understand the implications of proposed courses of action and can thereby avoid generating *unintended consequences*. In the end this links back to knowledge of oneself and, therefore, while recognising our own strengths and expertise, we also need to recognise our weaknesses. Once we have identified these we can seek advice and support. In theoretical terms this issue of "knowing yourself" links to the argument within the study of *high reliability organisations* of whether decision-making should be centralised or decentralised depending on where the appropriate expertise lies.

---

12 Lanir (1983)
13 Slovic (2000)
14 Vaughan (1996:261 and 363)
15 based on work by Klein et al. (2005)

This brings me to my final point, that perfection is difficult to achieve! It is therefore likely that every person and every collection of people will have their own weaknesses. Within cybernetics there is the argument for *requisite variety*.[16] This concept argues "only variety can control variety"; this idea has been extended to include the sentiment that it takes complexity to control complexity that, in turn, has led to the belief that managing *complex* situations needs a variety of talents. This ensures that multiple *seats of understanding* are available that can buttress each other's efforts. From the point of view of knowing yourself, the key point is to know the limitation of both yourself and your group. The law of *requisite variety* suggests that the greater the diversity within the group (thereby increasing both the types of expertise and the number of perspectives), then the less likely it is to be trapped by tunnel vision such as *groupthink*. It is within this context that a number of the recommendations of the Agranat Commission's should be seen [p.115].

Cohen and Gooch point out that knowing yourself is a most difficult task, however it is possible, as they illustrate. They provided the example that the Egyptians, prior to the Yom Kippur War, demonstrated the appropriate level of reflection on their own capabilities [p.101] (as did the Chinese in the Korean campaign) and thereby turned their weaknesses into strengths. I would suggest that if we do not understand how we view the world, what we really understand and those areas where we are not an expert, then we are more likely to misunderstand the data that assails us.

In summary, again Cohen and Gooch's case that the military are a special case can be seen to be suspect. The need to be *open-minded*, flexible, proactive and to know yourself would seem to be *universal* requirements in the pursuit of *foresight*. This cannot be a surprise as much of the early research on *high reliability organisations* was conducted by academics on US Naval aircraft carriers[17] and submarines.[18] This reinforces my belief of the similarity between civilian and military operations in this area of study.

Conclusions

In conclusion, we see clear similarities between civilian and military operations in this area of study. Hollnagel's warning that "What you look for is what

---

16 Ashby (1956)
17 Roberts and Rousseau (1989); Roberts and Bea (2001)
18 Bierly and Spender (1995)

you find" seems to hold true. We see evidence of Turner's phenomena and evidence of the issues that my catalytic questions raise. It is, therefore, not too big a stretch to assume that military campaigns are also not immune from these types of problems. From the point of view of promoting *foresight* this would lead to the suggestion that those seeking *foresight* need to know what they are looking for. If they do not, or if they are not fully aware of the wider variety of reasons for which organisations of their type might fail, they may miss key warnings that these issues are present within their sphere. We also see how sectors of human activity can fail to learn from others because of the *erroneous assumption* that they are different. Turner recognised this problem in the issue he labelled *organisational exclusivity*. In examining the work of Cohen and Gooch from a different perspective, we see the pattern of *normal chaos* in military operations, we see that solutions may not be *universal* and we see how a single side bias may prevent our full understanding of what is happening around us. For *foresight* the lesson is both sides of any *force field* need to be examined with equal diligence and scepticism.

Re-examining Cohen and Gooch's work from another perspective suggests that, in this subject area, the military should not be considered to be a special case. The military also need to demonstrate open-mindedness, flexibility, proactivity and to know themselves as these would seem to be *universal* requirements in the pursuit of *foresight*. This argument extends to other organisations in that, if the military (with all their differences to civilian operations) are not a special case, then it might be assumed that it is unlikely that other organisations will prove to be exempt from the lessons set out here as having general utility.

Chapter 6

Pursuing Foresight

Introduction

In this final chapter I plan to pull together all the threads laid out in this book with the aid of my final case study. Again I focus on the Yom Kippur War. In this instance, the story is told by Frank Stech and the words are taken from a paper he wrote in 1979.[1] This paper was chosen because it is one of the original studies to use Turner's framework. I have to note that the aim of his work differs from mine. He states his purpose as being:

> ... to determine how intelligence specialists and policymakers estimate the intentions of a foreign nation ... how they make mistakes in doing so (and) to compare the tasks and processes of intention estimation to research on related cognitive social, and organizational behavior.

Given his aim it is understandable that the section that covers Turner's work and the Yom Kippur War are only a small part of the whole. I have therefore had to supplement his work with details provided by Zvi Lanir in his paper on *fundamental surprise*. This paper also used the Yom Kippur War as its case study. The Lanir work was first produced in Hebrew in 1983 and first translated into English in 1999.[2] I have generally tried to use their words for it is they, not I, who are the authorities on the case material. I am very grateful to them both for allowing me to use their work in the way I have. Their generosity is greatly appreciated. In order to make the text easier to read I have removed the references they quote in the original texts. Quotes from Frank Stech's work are annotated "[1]" and quotes from Zvi Lanir are annotated "[2]".

As in previous chapters, I again use the data supplied to illustrate the analytical method based on my re-imagining of *Disaster Incubation Theory*. I also look to illustrate the use of a *catalytic cube* as a way of identifying gaps

---

1   Stech (1979)
2   Lanir (1983:119)

within a specific analytical process and the use of my seven *issues of interest* that have been developed from the over 200 factors that academics and others have identified as having caused crises. It is also important to note that this process does not produce a neat narrative of events for that is not produced by *foresight*. What we do see is ambiguity, overlap and contradiction. Life is not simple when *complex* systems interact. In my terms, *chaos* should be considered to be normal and so we need tools to help us cope. We have to work hard if we are to develop *foresight*.

I am also not looking to produce succinct explanation of the Yom Kippur War. I do not suggest that I have re-examined the case itself and therefore the points made here should be taken as being no more than an illustration. I accept that if I did a full review using this method I might well come to a different conclusion about this case than the illustration here might suggest. I also recognise that pure historians may think that I have taken liberties with the facts: if this is the case I apologise but would ask them to recognise the facts are only being used to tell a story that illustrates my method.

While this case study may be based on *macro level* issues, this should not be taken to mean that my framework and the factors are only applicable at this level. By contrast we can look at the case of producing this book and there is no more of a micro issue than that! As part of this process I encountered two issues relevant here. The first is one of ambiguous boundaries and the other concerns error-inducing organisations. The ambiguous boundary encountered was one that concerns copyright. It was the issue of "fair usage"; that is how much of another author's work can be quoted for analytical purposes before that author's copyright is infringed. This boundary is not set down and so it is for each publisher to decide the point at which the line has been crossed. This is not a simple issue when you quote many authors. A great deal of time would need to be spent on checking every quote in every case, and so decisions have to be made on when I perceive the line may have been crossed and when it has not, as some publishers have a very generous interpretation and others do not. Arguments become embroiled in semantics about what is a quote or just a discussion about a word used. If such *micro* tasks can be bogged down in such minutiae, it does not take much imagination to see how progress at the *macro* and *mega levels* can be derailed by *micro* events within their environment. Related to the first issue is a *universal dilemma* which pits good scholarship against copyright. As the advocate for my argument, at many points, I would have liked to make my case clearer by quoting exactly what someone else had said. In some instances, however, copyright issues meant that I literally could not afford to do so. Good scholarship had to be sacrificed for expediency due on this issue. In terms used by Perrow, we have here an *error-inducing system* where what is best in one area is compromised due to considerations in another. Again we can see a simple illustration at the *micro level* where it does not need much imagination to see the effect such issues might have in a higher-level system. While in this chapter I am illustrating a *macro level* issue, it is easy to see how the same process might be applied at other levels and that this is akin to the idea of fractals in *chaos* theory. Therefore, I would suggest that the same method could be illustrated by a case at any of the four levels; it is just that I have selected a case that focuses on a *macro* issue.

NATURE OF THE CASE

The case under examination here looks at the prevention of a military disaster. It is a case where international tension led to war as it has in so many other times and in so many other places. In this case it involved Israel and their Arab neighbours and is set in the earlier 1970s at the height of the Cold War. The war that came was but one in a series of wars in that region as the level of tension between the neighbours oscillated. When it came, seen from an Israeli perspective, it produced an initial failure at the *mezzo level* that turns into a success at the *macro level*. Finally, however, it might be seen to have been a failure at the *mega level*. I have chosen this case for two reasons. The first is that the war proved to be a significant milestone in the history of that region. Israel's bubble of invincibility was burst and this changed the paradigm in the region. The second reason is more prosaic; the papers by Stech and Lanir provided me with suitable base data. Based on their data, I have chosen to look at the events from the Israeli perspective. I would suggest that the basic analytical paradigm is *dot* (see earlier chapter). This means that we will be using *foresight* to look forward to a specific unwanted *macro level* outcome imposed by others, where we have an opinion on the way we might prevent or prepare for this unique problem. Other issues about the true nature of the problem being faced will be addressed as they arise.

POINT OF ENTRY

When it comes to developing *foresight*, the *point of entry* is not something you select. It is today. It is the moment you decide you need to address the issue of *foresight*. However, in order to illustrate my method we need to go back in time so we can review events as they unfold both before and after our chosen point. The *point of entry* in this case could therefore lie anywhere between the end of the Six–Day War on 10 June 1967 and the start of the Yom Kippur War on 6 October 1973. In the next section I will explain my reasons for going back no further than the end of the Six-Day War. The period described contains an episode called the War of Attrition that officially lasted from 8 March 1969 until the 7 August 1970; another key event occurred in this month and that was the death of President Nasser of Egypt. Such a significant change might seem to warrant the conduct of a major review to evaluate what might change in Egypt under a new President. For the purpose of this illustration, the *point of entry* that I have chosen is a day in September 1970; therefore, when reading the "looking forward" section, the reader has to remind themselves that they have to look at events as if today was a day September 1970. (As such this chapter is written in a normative style rather than the descriptive style used in the previous chapters.) That means that all events prior to this date have happened and those after this date have not. While this may seem obvious, it is a point often missed by those reviewing past events where each are afforded the same level of certainty. Therefore, in this case, I will only use our current knowledge of the outcomes after this point to question whether what the Israelis did was adequate while accepting that they only had the uncertainties of *foresight* rather than the clarity of *hindsight*.

The first issue we need to address is the more detailed nature of the problem. I see this as being the defence of Israel from external enemies. If we placed ourselves of the Israelis at that time, at this point we might have assumed that the aim was clear to all for we had a history of success in this area and we had a well-refined doctrine. If we were not familiar with the idea of *chaos*, *drift* and the way this might produce *fantasy documents*, we might have thought no more about the accuracy with which we could articulate the event or outcome we were trying to avoid. We may have just allowed *organisational momentum* to carry us forward, doing what we have done in the past.

Having just joined the conversation about the defence requirement, we now know that we would have joined it somewhere in the middle. There was history and there would be a future. I know therefore that I must look back in order to learn from the past and to re-examine critical legacy issues. This examination should focus on where past success may distort our view of the potential for success in the future as well as looking at what we might learn from past failures. The examination would also need to identify the issues that threaten successful defence in the future and the precautions that have been put in place to prevent such failures. Having examined the past then it is time to look to the future. When looking to the future we need to examine how the tools for planning such things as visions, goals, strategies, plans and procedures may induce instability and change that unintentionally weakens our existing *precautionary norms* and allows new or mutated threats to emerge. Finally, when looking forward, we need to consider how we will approach the management of these risks. A key point for *foresight* is to decide how much of the resource available should be spent on looking back rather than looking forward. While the temptation is to prioritise resources to look forward, past *failures of hindsight* (the *failure to learn* from the past), would suggest that insufficient resource is spent on this issue and that this failure, in itself, presents a distinct danger to the organisation. Therefore, I will first look back and then I will look forward.

Looking Back

In looking back we are trying to prevent *failure of hindsight*. However, it is not solely about such learning. It is also about understanding why we are thinking the way we do and it is about understanding what has shaped our beliefs and biases. Lanir's work on *fundamental surprise* is based on the premise that we have the greatest difficulty in understanding situation change when our fundamental understanding of the world is challenged by the data we see before us. This makes *fundamental surprise* akin to having a *cosmological episode*. Therefore to forestall *fundamental surprise* we need to understand ourselves and our belief systems. When looking back, the first task is therefore to establish what has formed our beliefs and biases, and why we believe what we do. We then need to establish a point at which to start our analysis. Turner referred to this as the *notional normal starting point*. An alternative description may be a *start somewhere point*. Having established our starting point we can then determine the threats we perceive and the precautions taken to mitigate them (Stage 1). This is followed by looking at what has changed between then and now which should lead us to understand where there may currently be gaps in our defences that must be addressed (Stage 2).

WHY DO WE BELIEVE WHAT WE DO?

In the case of the Israeli military, Lanir lays out in some detail why they believed what they did. He starts with their,

> *vivid memory of the Holocaust and the imminent fear of an Arab attack aimed at eliminating the young and fragile state … Israel's doctrine confronts a wide range of questions regarding how the society viewed itself in relation to its hostile environment … (and it) contains the following assumptions: The Israeli–Arab conflict is unique in its intensity, since the goal of the Arabs is to eliminate the State of Israel … The myth of the undefeatable Israel Army … the realization that Israel*

> *cannot afford a large regular army ... (that) The army was built and trained to move the battle quickly to the enemy's territory, maneuver, and concentrate forces in the critical battles.*

Lanir then confirms that "Israel's doctrine had direct implications on the structure of the Israeli army. Intelligence, the air force, and the armored corps were given priority (and it) assumes political goals that do not contradict or limit the full, swift expenditure of force in war".

There is one other factor that Lanir highlights and that is that "Israel's doctrines relied on the willingness of commanders at all levels to be personally responsible and dedicated in fulfilling their missions with self-reliance and self-initiative". He continues,

> *Israel's doctrine is seen to have two main structural advantages: simplicity and a high degree of internal coherence. In it, no basic contradictions exist between political goals and military objectives from the top of the political pyramid in the prime minister's office, through the ministry of defence, to the general staff and the army. The goal of decisive victory subordinated political considerations to military necessities.[2]3*

Within these quotes we develop a clear understanding of the fundamental issue that lies at the heart of Israeli doctrine and the sense of the deep distrust of their neighbours that underlined their thinking. As the nation was formed in conflict and as the people had a history of being persecuted such a mindset may be understandable. They could also see their own weaknesses (such as not being able to afford a large regular army) which would have helped to form their state of mind. The question for *foresight* is that while this state of mind may be understandable, might it also generate blind spots and other unintended adverse consequences. While self-reliance and self-initiative brings advantages they also bring potential problems as they create issues for control and stability in the system. For a full *foresight* exercise each of these key elements would need to be tracked and monitored for *drift*. For the purpose of illustration I have selected to follow only a few main issues.

---

3   Quotes from Frank Stech's work are annotated "[1]" and quotes from Zvi Lanir are annotated "[2]"

START SOMEWHERE POINT

The question of picking a starting point is to work out how far back in history we need to go. There is general agreement amongst writers on this subject that (although you may not use the word) Israel entered a new paradigm at the end of the Six-Day War. Lanir says: "Following the 1967 'Six-Day War' the Israeli army took up its new boundaries position on the Suez canal". The pre and post-war boundaries of Israel were very different as were the disposition of forces. Stech also says that "Following the 1967 Israeli victory over the Arabs certain assumptions formed the core of the Israeli defense concept". As a result both military tactics and strategy would change as the new boundaries gave Israel the opportunity to trade ground for time in a future conflict. This was something that they had not had before. The Israelis used the end of the Six-Day War as a fundamental opportunity to learn and they identified lessons about the conduct of that war and about its relationship with its neighbours.

Therefore, at a *macro level* of analysis, I have selected the end of the Six-Day War as my *start somewhere point*. It has to be noted however that while at a *macro level* this may be valid, there is a danger of *compounded abstraction* if this line is held too rigidly at the *micro level*. While the *start somewhere point* provides a general guideline, where an individual factor can be traced back prior to this nominal point there may be a need to do so. This is because the partial information available prior to this point may lead to one set of deductions, whereas when new data is added to the original data it may change the deductions completely and so to add new data to incorrect conclusions would not provide a new one that is valid either. The *start somewhere point* should therefore be used flexibly and with reflexivity.

STAGE I

Having decided that my *start somewhere point* is the end of the Six-Day War, I would now start to examine what I might learn from both past successes and failures. For the purpose of this illustration I will only look at the main lessons that come out of the Six-Day War as explained by Lanir. If this was an actual *foresight* exercise, I would be far more rigorous in the examination of my starting point.

Past success

At this point we look at what we learnt from past successes. In this case we would be looking at what went well during the Six-Day War that has driven the way we have acted since then. For the purpose of this illustration I will limit the lessons to three areas of success. The first success is that of the Israeli air force. The second is that of armoured formations and manoeuvre warfare and the third success is the capture of territory.

In looking at the past we see how victories in the air during the Six-Day War and the War of Attrition had created the myth of "the invincible Israeli Air Forces" (IAF).

> The overall success of the IAF in the War of Attrition and several dogfight victories ... reinforced the collective impression that the IAF could not be defeated, that Israel would have air superiority over the captured territories, and that Israeli counterattacks on the ground would have full air support.[1]

During the Six-Day War the Israelis had achieved incredible success through the use of "all-tank tactics". Stech says,

> The overwhelming success in the 1967 War produced an Israeli commitment to the doctrine of "all-tank" tactics: high armored mobility and rapid, shifting engagement ... The Israelis assumed that because fighting would be fast-paced and wide-ranging, Arab infantry would not keep up or would coordinate poorly and would pose little threat to the Israeli all-tank formations.[1]

We can also see that the success in capturing territory changed the defence paradigm for,

> until the Six-Day War, the issue of warning was a key component of IDF's (Israeli Defence Force) security doctrine ... Following that war, however, Israel's strategic depth increased and its sensitivity to the danger of a surprise attack concomitantly diminished.[2]

Lanir explains,

> The term "safe Borders" was coined by the Israeli Government after the Six-Day War to explain how the new borders were going to strengthen Israel's security ... Until the Six-Day War, Israelis lived in constant fear of the country being bisected by an offensive surprise attack. Within the new borders, it was doubtful that the Arab countries had the military power to capture its main population centers, even with a successful surprise attack.[2]

Israel considered the War of Attrition a victory. If the Six-Day War proved Israel's superiority in a general war, the War of Attrition demonstrated that even in static, partial, and defensive war (this reinforced their belief that) the Arabs had no hope to win against Israel.[2]

So here we can see why, based on this past success "the air force, and the armored corps were given priority"[2] and were developed in favour to other capabilities.

Past failure

We can see now how both the Israelis and the Arabs have learnt from past failures. I will illustrate this by looking at the Israeli Navy and the Egyptian Armed Forces overall. I take neither of these threads any further than using them as illustrations of learning from past failure. In terms of illustrating this particular case, I have to accept that these examples stray past simply looking backwards as per the section heading, however I do not feel that this detracts from my overall case.

During the Wars of Attrition the Israeli Navy had its successes and failures. If we were looking back from 1970 we would see their most notable success came in July 1967 when the Israeli Navy destroyer (INS Eilat) and two torpedo boats sank two Egyptian torpedo boats off the Rumani coast. Conversely in October of the same year the Egyptians sank the INS Eilat killing 47 Israelis. "After the 1967 war (the navy) was completely rearmed with Gabriel cruise missiles mounted on Saar-class and Reshef-class fast attack boats and its tactics were revamped to deal with the Soviet supplied Osa- and Komar-class missile boats in the Syrian and Egyptian navies".[1] This revamping included *Operation Noa* which was executed between 24 and 31 December 1969 in which the Navy "liberated" five Sa'ar class boats from the French in Cherbourg which allowed the Israeli Navy to adapt to meet it future needs.

Stech says that "in so many other respects the story of precautionary failures does not apply to the Israeli Navy". When war came in 1973 the Israeli Navy appeared to be ready: they were put on a war footing on 1 October and ordered to battle stations at 05:00 hrs on 6 October. "The IN was totally successful in dealing with the enemy's tactics and equipment in the October War, destroying 19 Arab vessels including 10 missile boats without suffering a single loss … Only the Navy seems to have stuck to its pre-war plans and tactics".[1] For the sake of space in the chapter I will not therefore consider the activity of the Israeli Navy any further as part of this narrative.

At the end of the Six-Day War the Egyptians also seem to have learnt at all levels from past failures. At the *mega level* they accepted that they were unlikely to be able to obliterate Israel.

> *Before the Six-Day War, Egypt's objective was "freeing the conquered lands", which actually meant annihilation of the State of Israel. After the Six-Day War, it was rephrased as "annulling the results of aggression", which meant returning the occupied territories. (However) even this more moderate goal was not perceived by the Egyptian leadership as feasible by purely military means … Nasser … formulated the concept of a "military solution", … as a necessary component of a "political solution". [This would not be a new idea to students of Clausewitz's work.] Nasser interpreted the United States and Israel policy of status quo as an unwillingness to return occupied Egyptian land … his belief (was) that the only way to convince the Americans and the Israelis to change … was by demonstrating that it was a dangerous, unstable situation. In this context the meaning of "military solution" was to undermine the status quo and not to conduct a total war. This set of conceptions was published at the time in numerous articles appearing in the Egyptian and foreign press and even in an Israel military publication[2] (such as the one produced by Haykal in 1968).*

> *Nasser declared in a public address … (March 27, 1969) that the Egyptian plan was comprised of four stages: the first stage was to bombard the Bar-Lev Line with artillery fire; in the second, Egyptian commandos would cross the canal and attack Israel strongholds near the canal; in the third, the Egyptians would intensify their raids on the Bar-Lev Line, increase penetration of the heart of Sinai, and attack Israel units and installations there; in the fourth and final stage, Egyptian forces would cross the canal in an extensive campaign and seize territory on its east bank, thus breaking the political freeze.[2]*

The change in the type of war to be fought was then reflected down through the other layers of the "military solution". The lessons learnt were practised and refined by the Egyptians during the War of Attrition.

Threat and precautionary norms

At this point of the illustration we are still in Stage 1 of the analysis. We are still concerned with our basic perception of the threats and their associated precautions at our starting point, which is at the end of the Six-Day War.

To enrich our understanding of the threats we may use the *DIME* and *PESTLE* acronyms discussed in earlier chapters as a further catalyst to our analysis and discourse. However, for the purpose of this illustration I will restrict my analysis to the top-level issues.

From my reading of Stech and Lanir's work the key threat that drove doctrine was an Arab attack designed to annihilate of the State of Israel. The main precaution taken to prevent the annihilation of the State of Israel was to mobilise full military power within 48 hours. This would be done by the use of air power to deliver pre-emptive strikes and all-tank formations on the ground employed in manoeuvre-based warfare. The military looked to inflict disproportionately high cost on the attacking nations.

Starting assumptions

Embedded within the perceived threats and their associated precautions are a number of key assumptions. I would summarise these as:

- The nature of the war to be fought if the Arabs attacked. The assumption was that they would seek a total military victory and the Syrians would only attack jointly with the Egyptians.
- The Israelis would receive at least a 48-hour warning of an impending Arab attack.
- The Israeli Air Force would be able to dominate the air space above the battlefield and would be able to deliver a decisive pre-emptive strike.
- The all-tank ground force formation would use speed of manoeuvre to dominate the land battle.

These statements now give us a starting point for our *risk discourse* and so we can move to Stage 2.

STAGE 2

Within Stage 2 we can now examine what has changed since the *precautionary norms* were set down (at the end of the Six-Day War in June 1967) and now (September 1970). We now need to examine what has changed both internally and externally that might have eroded the effectiveness of our precautions. Again for the purpose of this illustration I will restrict my analysis to three considerations. These remain: 1) the kind of the war to be fought, 2) the likelihood of having air superiority and 3) all-tank tactics.

The kind of the war to be fought

It is not clear from the two texts that I have used whether the Israelis have, when establishing their *precautionary norms,* placed much emphasis on Clausewitz's point about the necessity to establish the kind of war for which you are planning. In these texts we see a clear inconsistency within the Israeli establishment on this issue.

Lanir tells us that "the environment had changed considerably ... The fundamental changes after the Six-Day War were of a political ... nature" and he suggests that these were not noticed. The evidence for this is that at a doctrine level the assumption remained that the Arab's objective for the next war would be an "all-out" victory. This is despite that fact that during the period in question there was growing evidence to the contrary. The key examples cited are the 1968 article by Mohammed Haykal and the speech by President Nasser in 1969.

When looking back from 1970 we would have been able to see evidence of change in the kind of war that Egypt was looking to fight. At the same time we should have been able to see evidence of *practical drift* on the Israeli side where doctrine remained the same yet there were shifts in practice causing a misalignment between the two.

Air superiority

During the War of Attrition the Israelis lost around 25 aircraft, mainly to anti-aircraft missiles. The threat to Israeli airpower from these missiles was well recognised. During the War of Attrition the Israelis were, however, always able to find and exploit holes in the missile coverage. This changed in July 1970, when a cease-fire was agreed. "Immediately ..., Nasser ordered Egyptian anti-air missile batteries to advance to the canal region, contravening the agreement under cover of the cease-fire. This was a most important and influential move, which enabled Egypt to engage in the fourth phase: the Yom Kippur War".[2] Lanir comments that,

> At the time, most of the Israel leadership did not comprehend the significance of this event. The increased supply of American planes to Israel and the provision of an excuse for retreat from negotiations over the Rogers Plan were, at the time, perceived as appropriate compensation for Israel's acceptance of Egypt's cease-fire violations and the existence of missile batteries near the Suez Canal.[2]

In this you can see that the Israelis saw the events but did not appreciate them for their significance; the decoy effect of the "excuse for retreat from negotiations" was enough to distract them from this real threat. On the other hand, Ezer Weizman (commander of the Israeli Air Force who was later to become Minister of Defence and who was later elected President in 1993,) summed up the importance of this Egyptian move when he said: "The October 1973 war began in August 1970".[2]

All-tank tactics

Again in looking backward in Stage 2 we look to the War of Attrition to seek evidence of the potential vulnerability of all-tank formations. Despite the evidence of success provided by the Six-Day War, military orthodoxy recommends an all-arms coordinated battle rather the reliance on a specific capability. May I offer here an anecdote from my past? During my studies for a Business Masters our economics lecturer was an expert on what were then known as the Asian Tiger economies. In his lecturing to us he expounded the virtues of economic theory (orthodoxies) while telling us that the Asian Tigers were being successful by breaking all these rules. When pressed to explain why, he could not; in due course the Asian Tiger economies collapsed. Orthodoxy in any area of expertise is rooted in experience. In terms of the 80/20 rule, orthodoxies are likely to be correct 80 per cent of the time; that is also to say that they are not always right. The point is, however, if you are breaking orthodoxy you have to be aware that it is more likely to bring failure than success in the future; having said that, it may still work. I would therefore suggest that, in terms of *foresight*, if one of your planning assumptions breaks orthodoxy, that assumption needs to be monitored very carefully.

> *After the Six-Day War, the Egyptians sought to reduce the superiority of Israel armored troops in the Sinai Campaign and the Six-Day war. The Sager missiles were their solution. During the late 1960s and early 1970s, the Egyptians and Syrians stocked up on large quantities of these personal anti-tank missiles. During the War of Attrition, the new tactics were tested against Israel armored vehicles. The IDF (Israeli Defence Force) Intelligence Branch followed this development closely and warned of the existence of these missiles. Technical data were accumulated, operating methods studied, and a detailed report distributed among IDF units, including not only technical information but also tactical operational procedures.[2]*

In terms of the Israeli use of the type of war to be fought, airpower and all-tank tactics, we see by 1970 significant changes in the operational environment that provided indications of gaps opening up between established *precautionary norms* and the circumstances they were expected to mitigate. The question for Stage 2 looking forward is how we might recognise the significance of these gaps and the action that might be taken to close them.

BASIC FRAMEWORK

Therefore, from evidence obtained from examining the past, we can start to construct our analytical framework, our *catalytic cube*. We would need to start by deciding at what level of analysis we would focus. We would then decide on the initial division of hierarchical layers to be used and finally we would decide on the *critical tasks*. We would have to accept that any of these categories may be changed as a result of the initial *risk discourse* with the other stakeholders.

Level of analysis

The level of analysis in this instance is the *macro level*; that is the level where the effective defence of Israel as a whole is seen from the military point of view. While after the Yom Kippur War events morphed into a political *crisis* which, in the end, led to the Prime Minster Golda Meir resigning on 11 April 1974, this is not the story being told here. We are still back in September 1970, we are situated in the Ministry of Defence and we see the problem as the future defence of the nation. A ceasefire has ended the War of Attrition and Egyptian President Nasser has just died. Internal and external instabilities are changing the problems we face and this leads to questions about whether we need to change anything that we already have in place.

Layers

In this case the hierarchical layers that will initially be used are:

- *Mega* – political and diplomatic
- *Macro* – military strategic
- *Mezzo* – military operational
- *Micro* – military tactical.

Critical tasks

> *The Agranat Commission Report (the official Israeli post-mortem of*
> *the Yom Kippur War) highlighted the key assumptions that formed the*
> *basis for what they called "the conception". These assumptions were:*
> *(1) if the Arabs attacked they would seek a total military victory, (2)*
> *without air superiority over Israel, Egypt would not attack unless it*
> *could paralyze the IAF by air attacks deep in Israel, and (3) Syria would*
> *attack only jointly with Egypt.*[1]

However, from the perspective of our method, we need to look at what "needs to go right".

We label what "needs to go right" as our *critical task* or *critical success factors*. Earlier in this book it was stated that the purpose of *foresight* is either to *prevent* or to *prepare* for some unwanted event. In this illustration I would say that it is not for the military to prevent the next conflict: it is for the military to *prepare* to prevent the enemy achieving their objectives by military means and so deter them from taking action. Therefore the question becomes, "What can we do to *prepare* to prevent the enemy achieving their objectives by military means?" To be consistent with my previous illustrations these tasks are seen as being: 1) providing a 48-hour warning of any attack (including those attempting to destroy the nation) in order to enable our reserve force to mobilise, 2) using our airpower to dominate the battle space, including the use of pre-emptive strikes to disable enemy capabilities, 3) using the extra territory won in the Six-Day War, to add geographical resilience to the nation State of Israel and 4) using all-tank formations to dominate the land battle in manoeuvre warfare. Within these *critical tasks* is the genesis of an if-then *hypothesis for success*. This would read:

> *If our intelligence services provide 48-hour warning of any attack*
> *(including attempts to destroy the state) then we would have time to*
> *mobilise and deploy our reserve forces; these are sufficient to defeat*
> *any threat we may face. If our airpower is to dominate the battle space*
> *(which it is capable of doing) then it must use pre-emptive strikes to*
> *disable enemy capabilities at the outset of the campaign. If the extra*
> *territory won in the Six-Day War is to enhance the resilience to the*
> *nation state of Israel, then we must be able to trade it for time while we*
> *organise our defensive capability. If we are to dominate the land battle*
> *then we must use the mobility and firepower of all-tank formations in*
> *manoeuvre warfare to disrupt then destroy enemy ground forces.*

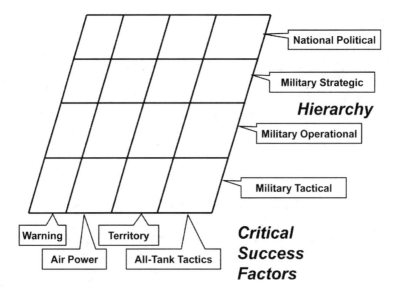

Figure 6.1   Basic analytical framework

This type of explicit hypothesis needs to link the outcome, the method (the how) and the resources required into a realistic and realisable whole. This is seen to be useful in a number of ways. It makes implicit assumptions explicit: this makes them easier to discuss. It provides assumptions that can be tested for their validity and veracity. It enables the connection between each statement to be explored and verified. These ideas can then be modelled in the form of a *mental model* or mind-map as described earlier in this book. The first layer of the *catalytic cube* is depicted in Figure 6.1.

Testing criticality

The first test of criticality is that it covers something, an activity, which must go as planned. The test is that it must be an activity. In this case the *critical tasks* all pass this test. The second test is the degree of harm inflicted and the level at which this is recoverable. In a previous chapter we have discussed four categories. These were *critical harm*, *serious damage*, *containable disruption* and normal disruptions.

In this case, and at the level of analysis we are talking about, *critical harm* (that is "an unwanted outcome totally unacceptable to the organisation in that it is highly likely to produce the demise of that organisation") might be seen to be defined as annihilation of Israel. If we take *critical harm* to be the annihilation of Israel then what they actually faced was *serious damage*. Here *serious damage* would mean that level of the organisation affected is able to recover overall although not necessarily in the identical form and it may have caused *critical harm* to some sub-components or stakeholders within the system. The notion of harm, however, does depend on what people care about, therefore when it comes to issues that are critical, the changing attitudes of the stakeholders, including in this case those within the nation, need to be kept under review as this may change priorities.

As part of previous research, the value of visceral reaction by managers to a stimulus was recognised; this was labelled the *squirm test*. This comes from experience that provides a warning that something is not right even if initially you do not know what. Another version is the metaphorical bet. One extreme modification to the test is the question, "Would you bet your life on the decision you are making?" A less extreme version uses a sum of cash. Each of these tests is based on the decision-maker accepting some personnel jeopardy for their decision and is a test of how much they think they are putting at stake. These tests can all be used to test what really is critical.

To some this may just seem to be a debate about semantics. I would say it is not for two reasons. The first is that if this debate generates any disagreements then you have identified that, on this critical issue, there are different views. If these differences are not addressed and resolved then they may cause the team to become dysfunctional. The second reason is that they are not "just semantics". They provide two very different starting points for the problem and, according to *chaos theory*, this will lead to very different outcomes. If we jump ahead to the end of the Yom Kippur War we can see the result of this discrepancy existing in that they had to fight a very different war from the one they planned and, in the end, they lost as much of the territory as they had won during the Six-Day War.

The test for criticality should make those involved identify and address the central point as to what is really important.

INSTABILITY AND REVIEWS

Finally, before looking forward we need to discuss and decide when reviews are required due to the instabilities inherent in the system. Within this final section of looking back we first look for sources of instability in the system and then decide when it might therefore be appropriate to review our analysis.

Sources of instability

Within the scenario being illustrated here, we need to look for sources of internal and external instability. These issues, however, were not discussed as such in either of the papers and so it is only possible to speculate as to what these may be from the narrative provided. Within Israel, internal sources of instability that may induce change may be such issues as the fluctuating strength of the national economy, new military capabilities and changes in political leadership, all of which may also signify changes in public expectations and sensitivities. External to Israel, sources of instability in the eco-system might be changes of key foreign leaders, changes in geopolitical factors or changes in specific military capabilities. All these factors and many more may undermine the premise on which *precautionary norms* are based and so as they arise these norms should be reviewed.

Review points

Once we accept that all systems are in a constant state of flux then we have to accept the need for review. We must also see that systems that do not conduct such reviews are a danger to themselves and this will inevitably be subjected to a *crisis*. We also need to accept that too many reviews will also lead to paralysis. We therefore need to consider our review point carefully. Review points need to be used to disrupt dysfunctional *organisational momentum* and to act as a *frame-breaker* at critical moments. These review points should initiate full reviews at potentially paradigm changing moments and they should be on top of or supplement any ongoing *risk assessment*. One of the purposes of these reviews being done in this way is to avoid the *Plowman effect* that is part of *muddling through*.

As well as not discussing sources of instabilities, the papers used do not discuss the need to establish review points so we cannot assess what was done. We can, however, see generic issues that might have provided a catalyst for this activity. We see changes in technology and capability, such as Israeli losses of tanks to the Arab guided weapons as early as July 1967 or the addition of specific weapons (the 4 barrelled 23 mm tracked self-propelled gun called the ZSU-23/4, and SA-6 Track mounted anti-aircraft missile and shoulder launched SA-7 anti-aircraft missiles) in late 1972 and early 1973. A review may have been initiated after the changes of key personnel.

> *The Israeli assumption of "all-out" Arab intentions was based on authoritative intelligence reflecting the thinking of Egyptian War*

Minister Sadeq and his military chiefs. When Sadat fired Sadeq in November 1972 (because, it was learned after the 1973 War, he opposed Sadat's limited war strategy), a major basis for the Israeli assumption was removed but the assumption was not re-examined when Sadeq was replaced by Ismail.[11]

Finally such reviews may be triggered by events such as the end of the Six-Day War, the end of the war of Attrition or mobilisation in May 1973. What is important is that such review points are the categories of events rather than the act of trying to predict a particular event. Examination of this case would offer the introduction of new capabilities, a change in key personnel on either side or the conclusion of a particular operational phase as the moment when such a review may be deemed necessary.

In summary, there is much to be gained from looking backwards and by learning from the past. By setting our thinking as if it were September 1970, we would have had evidence from the Six-Day War and the War of Attrition on which to base our judgement of future Arab intent and capabilities against which we could judge our existing *precautionary norms*. We would also have had evidence from the political and diplomatic arenas from which we may be able to deduce any changes in the threat whether due to changes in intent or capability. The problem, however, is often not to find useful information but it is to winnow what is available down to a quantity that is digestible. This is another reason for focusing on what is actually critical.

Looking Forward

If we go back to Figure 3.2, by looking back we have tried to establish "where we are". By looking forward we need to test whether we are actually where we think we are and, more importantly, we need to reaffirm where we need to be. By doing this we are trying to prevent a *failure of foresight*. In structural terms, looking forward is divided into the remaining stages (2 to 6) of *Disaster Incubation Theory*. This is now a question of what it might be possible to *anticipate*. Can you *anticipate* how you will slide into *crisis* (Stage 2)? Can you *anticipate* what *crisis* will befall you (Stage 3)? Can you *anticipate* how the *crisis* will develop (Stage 4)? Can you *anticipate* how you will salvage the *crisis* (Stage 5)? Can you *anticipate* how you will how you will learn from the *crisis* (Stage 6)?

As the date set for this illustration is September 1970, we do not know how events after this date unfold. However, with the tensions in the regions, we can be sure that there will be another war: it is only a matter of when. Sometimes even the best informed and most experienced can make errors of judgement.

> *On September 10, 1973, at an election meeting in Beer Sheba, Dayan (the Defence Minister at the time) expressed his confidence that: "Six years have already passed since the Six-Day War and we are talking now of another period of four years. We are used to having every ten years a war for six days".*[2]

In this section we are trying to identify what you might see. We are trying to see what is shaping the way decision-makers looked at the problem and recognise that what they will be looking at will affect what they actually see. We have therefore set ourselves a very difficult task. Where we prove to be right it may be as much by good luck (where there is a correlation between forecast and actual events aligning), as it is seen as bad luck when they do not. What we should be trying to avoid is overconfidence in our own abilities and the hubris that comes with it. Again we should see an overriding of orthodoxy; the part that says that you should never underestimate your enemy for, according to both texts, this is what the Israelis clearly did. Stech says, "Foremost ... was the overwhelming Israeli belief in Arab inferiority in all things military, and conversely, what (was) euphemistically labelled the Israelis' 'proneness to excessive self-assurance'".[1]

"Immediately after the (Yom Kippur) war, Israelis were accused of being surprised on many issues. However, closer examination of these issues shows that Israel had advance knowledge of most factors, in some cases with tremendous accuracy".[2] Lanir provides an example: "On October 6, at 11:00 a.m., the final war plans were presented to the Defense Minister ... the Chief of the Intelligence Branch ... describing its evaluation of the Egyptian war plans ... this was an accurate description of what indeed occurred several hours later". So what when wrong?

STAGE 2

In looking back we have established the threat we perceive and the precautions we have put in place. In looking forward it is time to review each critical factor for what may change in the future and how this may create gaps in our existing defences. Since I am only providing an illustration of the method, I will again limit the number of issues that I address. However, before analysing the critical factors, a moment of reflexivity is required. We first have to analyse our analytical method. The critical factors we would review are: 1) type of war,

2) utility of airpower, 3) viability of "all-tank" tactics and 4) the *universal* issue of communications. I will also consider the possibility of the failure of *active learning* and the final *zone of high vulnerability* that here I have labelled "*the critical days*".

Analytical reflexivity

The first issue for any *foresight* process is to analyse the analytical process itself. I will first describe the analytical method proposed and then will apply it to this illustration.

The analytical process can be broken down into two steps. In the first step I would use the *issues of interest* as prompts to examine whether any of the issues can be identified within a particular concern. As before these issues are: 1) *who cares*, 2) *failure to launch* (this includes a lack of accepted standards and precautions as they never existed or were deficient from the start), 3) *practical drift* (this is the exposed deficiency in standards and precautions as their effectiveness becomes reduced over time), 4) *structural secrecy*, 5) *erroneous assumptions* and 6) the *Plowman effect*.

The second step is to categorise the issues identified as possible *crisis* causation. These categories start with issues which are the ever-present tension between production and protection; they are labelled *universals*. In this illustration they include issues such as constant tension between utilisation of national resources to grow the economy or to strengthen the defence capability. The second are factors that lie as latent within the system that collectively produce defensive weaknesses; these are labelled *conditions*. In this illustration they include such issues as weakness within the communication system, the *failure to adapt* revised procedures universally (such as the tactic for using antitank guided weapons (ATGW)) and the misreading of the environment. The final category encompasses the local triggers and active failures that breach all the barriers and safeguards; these are labelled *causes*. In this illustration they include such issues as the dysfunctional interaction between key personnel and existence of closed minds and hubris.

The third step is to put the necessary changes into operation. At this point we need to refer back to Figure 4.1 the *catalytic cube*, which has a third dimension labelled *operations*; others might be more comfortable to see this as an *active learning* process. This dimension: 1) maps how we identified a gap in the enactment layers, 2) identifies what we need to learn, 3) *anticipates* where we might need to utilise that learning, 4) examines how we adopt the new ways and returns back to 5) the enact layer where the changes required are adapted as practice. This now produces the *catalytic cube* at Figure 6.2.

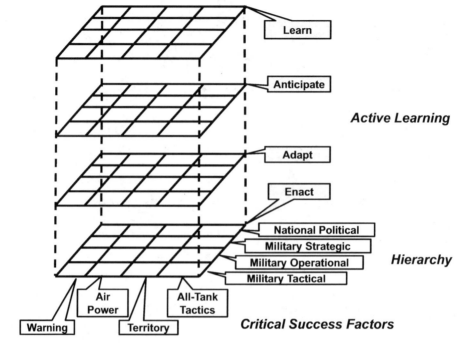

Figure 6.2   Yom Kippur War cube

With the fourth and final step we are returning to the questions of whether we believe the sources of our data and whether we value the analysis applied to it. We see an example of when outside advice is rejected. Stech says:

> *The Israeli Military Intelligence branch received many warnings from "outsiders" which it rejected. Within a month of Egypt's issuance in May 1973 of the plan for the October attack … the US CIA had obtained a copy and passed it to the Israelis. Both agencies concluded at the time that an attack was unlikely …*

> *The unusual military movements along the Canal in late September and early October led several junior intelligence officers in the Southern Command to predict war but these predictions were excised from the Southern Command report to the General Staff …*

> *Golda Meir noted the similarity between the departure of the soviet advisors and families on 4 October and a similar exodus prior to the 1967 War; the implication of her observations was generally ignored … Both lower … and higher echelon … warnings were ignored by the insiders in the Military Intelligence Branch.*

> *Nor were amateur warnings lacking: predictions of war in the*
> *autumn were made as early as May by Gabriel Cohen and Yair Evron,*
> *commentators on Israel's international relations.*

> *The CIA, DIA and NSA (these are the US Central Intelligence*
> *Agency, the Defence intelligence Agency and the National Security*
> *Agency) have collected enough evidence (on 26 September) to indicate*
> *the possibility of a combined Syrian-Egyptian attack on Israel ... The*
> *Israeli Intelligence chiefs rejected this warning however and attributed*
> *the activity to exercises.*

The Agranat Commission suggest that the foremost problem was the monopoly on intelligence evaluation of the Military Intelligence Branch, and its role as sole guardian of intelligence received both from abroad and from other Israeli intelligence-gathering agencies. This created a bottleneck in the flow of signals from below and outside of the Cabinet-level decision-maker, fostered the "conception" and reinforced it by self-censorship (*groupthink*). The Agranat Commission (concluded that):

> *... independent evaluation of political strategic, operational and tactical*
> *intelligence was prevented through centralization in one organization*
> *and under one authority on the one hand and the absence of a special*
> *intelligence advisor to the Prime Minister.*[1]

Perhaps a reflexive examination of the analytical process may have highlighted the lack of *requisite variety* within the system and how such a monopoly is likely to lead to the lack of challenge necessary within any such analytical system.

While we have issues here of *structural secrecy* we also have, in terms of analytical method, a question of what data we believe and what we reject. The analytical reflexivity exercise needs to identify and evaluate patterns of both the data that is accepted and that which is rejected to ensure both judgements are valid. As part of the testing process we might consider using *Westrum's Continuum* for openness. In this case we may see the excising of the junior officers comment from the Southern command report as a "red flag" that opens up a discussion about what other evidence had been suppressed and why this had happened. The question may then become whether, when collated, this evidence has more weight.

For this illustration we look at the potential issues that Stech and Lanir suggest might be present within the Israeli system. These are collated in Table 6.1.

Table 6.1   Issues in the Israeli analytical system

Who cares	"The Chief-of-Staff proposed … (a) preventive air strike on Syrian air force bases (and) … an immediate large-scale call-up of reserve forces. Prime Minister Golda Meir rejected both proposals on political grounds".[2] Here we see politicians and the military caring about different things. We also see on "October 6, a dispute arose between Defense Minister Moshe Dayan and Chief-of-Staff … regarding the extent of reserve mobilization demanded on the Northern front".This dispute demonstrates how the political and military focus of the two people can become a source of tension within the executive team.
Failure to launch	"Hareven's analysis of the personalities of the central actors provides additional, psychological reasons why Ze'ira's estimates were not challenged seriously until they were obviously wrong"[1] thus showing that the team of the top fell short of being a real team.
Practical drift	We see *practical drift* in the fact the defence doctrine espoused many ideas (such as total war and the use of pre-emptive strikes) that were no longer the case in practice.
Structural secrecy	The Intelligence "Branch had a reputation virtually unchallengeable by Israelis or their allies"[1] thus limiting the scope for constructive challenge.
Erroneous assumptions	Israeli assumptions regarding Arab strategic intentions ("total victory").[1] Erroneous conclusions about the Arab's general capabilities (insufficient for their strategic objectives).[1] The *erroneous assumption* in these cases is that the organisation knows the situation best and is better able to evaluate information than amateurs or outsiders.[1]
Dysfunctional momentum	We see the way the organisation was swept along in a tide of euphoria after the Six-Day War where the myth of the undefeatable Israeli armed forces was established.This myth become so rooted in the psyche of the nation that no accumulation of facts would change it.Any such change would have required a significant *mental interruption* (a *frame-breaker*) for it to have the required effect.
Plowman effect	During the period between the end of the Six-Day War and the conclusion of the War of Attrition we see a series of small events and decisions that mean that the situation at the end of the period was very different to the situation at the start but much that needed to adapt to the new circumstances had not.

In terms of *attribution error* (attributing your success to your own genius and failure to bad luck) we see evidence in both the descriptions of events provided by Stech and Lanir. Again in simplified terms, we see those who saw alignment between the correlation of their views and events being given credit greater than their luck may have justified and the reverse also being true. Those who were lucky were fêted and those who were unlucky were reduced in stature. The result was that the next time, those who had been lucky needed to be lucky again; a situation that cannot be guaranteed. The military relies heavily on the construct of the *commander's judgement* but woe betide any subordinate who questions that judgement; however, given *Feynman's numbers*, it would only be prudent for an organisation to prepare for the possibility that the commander is wrong. In contrast to relying on the judgement of a single person, we could lean more on group decision-making.

As with individual decision-making, group decision-making also comes with its own difficulties (*groupthink* and *risky shift* are but two examples). As a result, we need to look for ways to keep an open mind. An option here would be to use a device such as "three point accounting" that is used in financial management. This requires the organisation to monitor three options. These are the "best case", the "worst case" and the "most probable case". In this instance the "best case" would be if the scenario developed as expected by Israeli intelligence. The "worst case" would be if the scenario played out as espoused by the Arabs. The "most probable case" would lie somewhere in between. This technique requires the facts available to be evaluated against each and so should promote the possibility that the situation may develop in a way other than that prescribed by key opinion formers. It should be noted, however, that this technically is still vulnerable to the issues described above and so these must also be monitored at the same time.

Another step might be, rather than just relying on subjective judgement, decision-makers can use estimates of probability. These also range from simple subjective judgements (such as the *squirm test*) through scientific probability based on empirical events and finally to Bayesian probability. No matter what the method, and they all bring with them potential flaws that need to be addressed, there is still also the issue of whether the decision-maker(s) are able to assess their own ability and weaknesses objectively. The necessity to "know yourself" does not go away.

In reviewing the analytical method we highlight some immediate concerns that may have been addressed if they had been considered more systematically. Now it is time to look at how we might be helped to notice that natural instability within a system that makes it more prone to *crisis* over time.

The type of war

Within the *hypothesis for success* we express the concern that external forces may try to annihilate the State of Israel. While this remained central to the Israeli doctrine, in practice there was *drift* from this position. Lanir suggests that the *drift* from doctrine started soon after the end of the Six-Day War. He says "After the Six-Day War, Israel was not a nation that had an army but ... an army that had a nation".[2]

An explicit *hypothesis for success* may have made the Israelis re-evaluate whether the assumption of a "war of annihilation" held true or whether the Arabs now had more limited war aims. Lanir sees this assumption being central to "the myth of the undefeatable Israel Army" which in turn was a "central element in this conception". He goes on that in their eyes, to maintain it, the Israelis thought that they "must accomplish decisive victories in all wars. Less than a decisive victory would, in fact, be a moral victory for the Arabs, providing an incentive to challenge Israel's existence with another war".[2] The question for *foresight* is, where would the credible challenge to this assumption come from?

> *From an Egyptian perspective Nasser's death delayed preparations for the fourth stage until early 1973. Sadat reinvestigated the options of a "military solution". During a certain period, while it might appear that he had abandoned this path and was counting on a political solution that was not the case. Eventually he determined that a "military solution" was Egypt's only course of action. Sadat continued Nasser's four-stage plan. The basic consistency and continuity of Nasser and Sadat's strategic conceptions ... is seen in Egyptian military preparations and exercises. The Egyptian plan for the Yom Kippur War, "Improved Granite-2", was an updated version of the "Granite-1" plan prepared in early 1970.[2]*

> *Sadat came to the conclusion that it would be better and more satisfactory for the Egyptian people to fight a war and lose, than not to fight at all simply because defeat was likely ... honorable defeat was a preferable alternative to an inglorious peace. Dayan misperceived Sadat's goal, which was essentially political, not military: to establish a symbolic and real Egyptian stronghold on the east bank of the canal. Dayan's failure ... stemmed from not absorbing Sadat's message during the war of attrition – a war waged for political purposes using military means (another military orthodoxy derived from Clausewitz) ... However, the*

Egyptian tactical failure ... tended to divert (decoy) the Israelis from appreciating the Egyptians' intentions, and convinced them that Egypt could not make an attrition strategy pay off.[1]

Israel misread these signals because it failed to understand that Sadat was willing to sacrifice a lot for even a very small military achievement, which could then be used as leverage in the political negotiations that followed the war.

An explicit *hypothesis for success* may also have made the Israelis re-evaluate whether the assumption of manoeuvre warfare held true. Lanir says:

Israel considered the War of Attrition a victory. If the Six-Day War proved Israel's superiority in a general war, the War of Attrition demonstrated that even in static, partial, and defensive war, the Arabs had no hope to win against Israel.[2]

Here it can be seen that they saw evidence that they could beat the Arabs in any kind of war; the logic then becomes, "if we can beat the Arabs in any kind of war, why should we worry what type of war we will have to fight?" Lanir comments that:

What is so striking in retrospect is that the contradiction between the logic of the new deployment and the logic of the doctrine was not even recognized.[2]

Lanir goes on to explain that while the armed forces were built and trained for manoeuvre warfare, they were drifting towards static defence as they laid more and more emphasis on their defensive static positions on the Bar-Lev Line and in the Golan heights. A good question at this point is, "Why does this matter as the Israelis did win the military confrontation as they expected?" The answer lies in a hidden assumption; an assumption about the cost of the conflict.

The assumption held by the Israeli public was that any conflict would be won with a minimum of casualties amongst the citizen soldiery that made up their armed forces. The tactical (*micro level*) loss of the futile air and tank counter-attacks in the first days of the war, seen to be so necessary at the *macro level* where they enabled mobilisation to succeed, shocked the country and lead to much of the subsequent outrage. Would this have been different if the assumption had been made explicit in their *hypothesis for success*, thus causing them to pause and consider their options, we will never know. What they may have considered, however, is the implication of the nation's growing sensitivity to casualties.

Criticality of the warning

A critical assumption within the Israeli defence plan was the warning time that would be available:

> *The Israeli defense plans required at least a 48-hour warning of an Impending Arab attack, but sometime during 1971 or 1972 Israeli intelligence obtained authoritative information on the thinking of the Egyptian military chiefs under War Minister Sadeq.*[1]

Stech sets out the Israelis' proposition below. I have commented (in brackets) as to what may have been realised if such a statement had been constructed and tested beforehand. Stech says:

> *As the October war approached, (Israeli Intelligence's) reputation seemingly improved as a result of the premature mobilization in May 1973 ordered by Defense Minister Dayan which was opposed by Intelligence Chief Ze'ira. After this success (luck) it became even more difficult to question intelligence judgments (structural secrecy). The Military Intelligence Branch had "guaranteed" (hubris) the IDF at least 48 hours warning of an all-out attack, more than enough time for another pre-emptive air strike that, as in the 1967 war, would give the IDF control of the sky (erroneous assumption) and allow it to destroy the Arab attack (erroneous assumption). Also, Israeli intelligence enjoyed close contacts with US intelligence agencies, giving it access to the most modern technical intelligence-gathering resources (erroneous assumption) as well as those the Israelis themselves developed. Among these were mechanisms which Israeli intelligence believed would provide incontrovertible proof of an attack early enough to permit the "guaranteed" warning (hubris). This assumption was not questioned until October (structural secrecy).*[1]

With this and other sources they believed they had an insider's view of the Arabs' decision-making process. Not only did they perceive that they had this advantage but also the IDF believed that it would win the war even if this element in its war plans was not realised.

> *Until the Six-Day War, the issue of warning was a key component of IDF's security doctrine. IDF planning was based on provision of warning in order to execute a pre-emptive strike, an immediate counterattack or full deployment for defense. Following that war, however, Israel's strategic depth increased and its sensitivity to the*

danger of a surprise attack concomitantly diminished. Emphasis on warning as an important component of national security doctrine continued to appear in articles and speeches, but the IDF's strategic conception of war developments was no longer decisively dependent on the guarantee of a minimum warning time period.[2]

I comment further on this subject later in this section.

Criticality and recoverability

As we can see from what had gone before, it would appear that the Israelis experienced significant *drift* when it comes to the issue of what is critical. The survival of the nation was no longer the main issue. It would seem that this was now accepted reality by both sides. By failing to recognise this change, the subsequent mistake was to overlook factors that might have failed to minimise casualties within their own troops. This turned out to be a critical failing.

Also, as we have seen, the tactical (*micro level*) position was recoverable at the *macro level* although at a higher than expected cost. According to later analysis by Lanir, the cost escalated to the *mega level* as the Israelis continued to spend more and more on defence and this had a detrimental effect on their economy overall.

From this section we see how the *catalytic cube* can be combined with a *hypothesis for success* to tease out the implications of trying to fight, in this case, the wrong war. In addition we see where this sits within the overall analytical framework.

Air superiority

Within the *hypothesis for success* we have described the assumptions made about the critical role to be played in the next conflict by the Israeli Air Force. As this belief had set in by 1970, it is the role of *foresight* to test such a belief for its continuing realism.

The first step may just be to test the overall logic.

The story of the IAF (Israeli Air Force) success over the Arab air forces in 1967 had but one peer (the Nazi destruction of the Soviet Air Forces in a single day in 1941). No one on either side anticipated the remarkable surprise and effectiveness of the Israeli pilots' pre-emptive strikes.[1]

As the precedence for such a one-sided performance is so limited, one should question and challenge whether such an assumption remains valid to the point it becomes a key part of future strategy or whether the success during the Six-Day War should be accepted as just being good fortune on that day. At a *macro level* this question has to remain open to debate. The question for *foresight* is not "can we do it against" but "what make us sure we can?" Constructive scepticism should abound as this might be seen as another orthodoxy being ignored.

Also at the *macro level* is consideration of the future role to be played by pre-emptive strikes. The key assumption here is that a pre-emptive strike would take place. As we have seen, as a result of the bombing of the Nile Delta in 1970 there was a ceasefire. This leads to the re-engagement of the US and their support for Israel. This leads to them supplying more equipment to Israel and, in truth, this leads to the US wanting to be consulted before the Israelis engaged in further offensive military operations. In turn this leads to a diminishing prospect of the Israelis being able to use pre-emptive strikes at the start of the next war. This is a typical example of the *Plowman effect* at work. Articulation of this assumption, awareness of the *Plowman effect* and a method that reviews these assumptions may have brought the problem to light sooner that it did. Stech says:

> *The Israeli defense plans called for the ground forces … to contain the Arab ground attack while the IAF (presumably aided by striking pre-emptively …) would devote itself exclusively to destroying the Arab air defenses and air forces … By October 1973, however, it had become politically impossible for the IAF to preempt as it had so effectively in 1967. The US reaction to the IAF's deep bombing strikes into Egypt during the War of Attrition had made clear to the Israeli Cabinet that Israel would have to absorb the first blow or risk losing US support. These political realities seem not to have much influenced the IDF's precautions; … The original plan for IAF invincibility was useless, there were no others.*[1]

Here we see clear signs of *practical drift* with the clear dislocation between the espoused doctrine and allowed practice. The doctrine had become a *fantasy document*.

Also in the *hypothesis for success* is the assumption of air superiority. This can be seen to have had immediate implications at both the *mezzo* and *micro levels*; this issue managed to cascade upwards to the *macro level* in fairly short order when the war started. While evidence seen at the *macro level* would appear to depict the pattern of victories remaining constant up to 1970, this analysis would seem to ignore the *micro level* changes that had such a dramatic effect on the actual outcome. The question therefore becomes one of "what has changed at the *micro level* that may change the *macro level* outcome?"

Stech summarises these events and shows their own action that should have made them reconsider their assumption (in bold):

> While the incredible IAF successes of the 1967 and early War of Attrition supported the "invincibility" assumption, events from late 1970 to October 1973 should have weakened the dependence on IAF total superiority. The success of the IAF against the Egyptian and Syrian air forces during the War of Attrition, especially the bombing attacks near Cairo, led to a massive influx of highly sophisticated Soviet SAMs (surface to air missiles), guns, radars, and interceptors, forcing the **Israelis to halt its widespread bombing** so as to avoid directly confronting Soviet crews ... Gradually through 1970 the Soviet-Egyptian SAM belt was pushed closer and closer to the Canal. In late 1972 and early 1973 the Soviets added the ZSU-23/4, SA-6. SA-7 weapons ... to the older systems already in Arab hands thus completing an air defense belt that extended over both sides of the Canal.

As we noted earlier, this push forward was completed shortly after the War of Attrition ceasefire. It would be interesting to see which of these events were considered to be sufficient to warrant a review in addition to any ongoing threat assessment. Stech also tells us of the consequences for the Israelis. He says:

> When the October attack began the IAF was immediately pressed into support of the failing Israeli ground defenses, and was too preoccupied with halting ground attacks to deal effectively with, the air defense threats ... (this) permitted Egyptian jets to make short sharp strikes at the Israeli tanks, artillery, and communications which supported the Bar-Lev defences ... Although lacking air superiority, the Egyptian's jets nevertheless contributed to the Canal assault, then swiftly ducked behind the air defense screen ... The IAF plan for dealing with the Arab air defense required total concentration on this task, ruling out ground support. The critical need to block Arab ground attacks prevented this plan from being put into effect.[1]

We see that while the *macro level* assumption that they would be able to totally concentrate on the suppression of Arabs anti-aircraft defence proved to be erroneous, at the *mezzo level* they were aware of the problem.

> *The change in the effectiveness of Egyptian air defense came from the combined deployment of these missile types and the large quantities of ZSU-23 radar-controlled anti-airguns ... made it difficult to find breaches in its radar and firing coverage. Several days before the War of Attrition ended in summer 1970, the IAF lost five planes attempting to attack the Egyptian missile system. This closing note of the War of Attrition was deeply ingrained in the awareness of IAF commanders and pilots. During the three years between the end of the War of Attrition and the Yom Kippur War, destroying these systems became a key priority in Air Force training; new electronic means and tactical maneuvers were deployed to cope with missiles.*[2]

The link that was not made was the ability of the air force to concentrate on this task and its implication for its ground attack role.

> *... the Arabs mobile SAMs and guns, which thrust forward a defensive umbrella over the attacking ground forces, prevented the IAF strafing attacks needed to keep the Arab antitank forces from trapping Israeli armored columns ... The integration and complex organisation of the Arab air defence and its ability to fully absorb and dilute the IAF ... Only at a high cost in time, planes and pilots did the IAF learn to counter these capabilities, and only after the ground forces overran the SAM sites could the IAF again fly with impunity.*[1]

These two quotes raise a number of interesting issues about how this issue was analysed. The first, over which we can only speculate, is when reviews took place. One would see criteria such as significant ceasefire and the introduction of new capabilities providing *frame-breaker* moments. The second issue is again one where the all arms battle orthodoxy is challenged within the *hypothesis of success* and the fact that this should lead to difficult questions being asked. Finally we have another *Plowman effect* issue: in this case it is a question about whether debate about the air superiority battle silo was combined with the ground support role silo to determine the potential outcome when these two silos start to interact (in this case, when they call on the same resources).

Viability of "all-tank" tactics

Within the *hypothesis for success* we have described the assumptions made about the use of the extra territory won in the Six-Day War and the use of all-tank formations in manoeuvre warfare to disrupt then destroy enemy ground forces. Having set these assumptions they would also need to be tested. Stech explains that the:

> ... *all-tank tactics ... depended on adequate warning and mobilization. Further it assumed a war of movement: that the Arabs would attack to seize considerable terrain ... Finally the Israelis assumed that, because the fighting would be fast-paced and wide-ranging, Arab infantry would not keep up or would coordinate poorly and would pose little threat to the Israeli all-tank formation. Arab infantry would in any case be easily dealt with ... since the Israelis would have air superiority over their counterattacking forces and since the Arab soldier was known to be a good defensive fighter but a poor attacker.*[1]

In this instance Stech concludes that "All these assumptions were wrong in the Sinai".[1] The issues that Stech raised here can all be folded into the *hypothesis for success* and tested in the way described above. In this passage Stech also provides an example of Perrow's *Union Carbide Factor*; here we see multiple *erroneous assumptions* leading to the disastrous *precipitating event*. Stech goes on:

> *Israel had underestimated the effectiveness of the Arab defensive weapons and tactics and had assumed Arab tactics would be offensive. Although the Israelis lost tanks to the Arab ATGMs before (as early as July 1967), they continued to assume their tactics could deal with this threat and that the low quality of Arab infantry ruled out an effective, integrated antitank capability ... this (was) "a basic error of judgment". Nor did the Israelis anticipate the Arabs' effective use of night vision devices in night operations. In generally assuming the Arab attack could not get started, that the Bar-Lev defenses and tanks would prevent a Canal crossing, that Egyptian water-crossing efforts would be awkward and slow, the Israelis were unprepared to deal with the defensive tactics they faced in Sinai.*[1]

We can again see *practical drift* at work as "The 'All-tank'" concept, so effective in 1967, was obsolete in 1973";[1] this was recognised at the *micro* and probably *mezzo levels* but the problem was that this was not adopted at the *macro level*.

Overall, while the army had *learnt*, they do not seem to have anticipated or adapted the doctrine and organisations to encompass the necessary changes.

The universal issue of communications

While I have not articulated the assumption that the Israelis would have expected to have effective communications, this can be taken as a given. It always is. As communication is seen to be a *universal* issue, it is also safe to assume that the organisation will have experienced difficulties when it comes to the practicalities of communicating.

Stech says that "mishandling of information was not a primary factor in the October War disaster". He also says that there were "several instances of information handling difficulties" and that these "aggravated the situation". He added that "the combination of the 'fog of war', resulting from the failure of tactical communications, and the unexpected course of the Arab attack generated widespread confusion, and frustration in the Israeli high command and produced frequent disagreements on tactics and strategy".[1] The term "fog of war" is often applied to the military context but, as the phenomenon is *universal*, perhaps it should be thought of simply as the "fog of life" or just a "misty path"?

Stech points out that:

> *Perhaps the most paradoxical effect of ... centralization is the apparent fact that the mounting signals from the Southern Command were not integrated with those from the Northern Command. Such integration of information from disparate sources is one of the foremost justifications for centralized intelligence systems ... at no stage and at no level ... did any element link the Syrian buildup in the north with the unusual Egyptian activity and concentration in the south.*[1]

Stech seeks an explanation for this failure and in light of the US warning of a joint attack given on 24 September, he sees it as a "bureaucratic miscoordination"; I would label this *structural secrecy*.

Stech brings to our notice "a second difficulty in handling intelligence, the one-way flow of information from bottom to top. In other words, field tactical units collected and passed on information to General Headquarters and the Military Intelligence Branch but received little intelligence support in return". [1] In other words, that communications should be a two-way conversation but it was not. The result was that those at the front "lacked information, maps, air photographs – all of which were readily available to higher echelons". More critical, however, was that:

> ... when the higher Command and the Cabinet finally agreed war was imminent, warnings failed to reach the tactical units which were struck first: detachments on the Bar-Lev line were not warned and some soldiers manning the Mount Herman lookout posts were sunning themselves when Syrian artillery opened up ... Israeli artillery and tanks behind the Bar-lev line were destroyed by the Egyptian air and artillery attacks (as were) Israeli communications stations in Sinai. Even with the limited warning the Israelis had, the lowest levels were not alerted.[1]

Stech points out that:

> The Israeli forces had an excellent, highly sophisticated system of communications designed to keep the various levels of command fully informed ... yet the system somehow failed again and again to work as intended ... the divisional command and other higher echelons were under the misconception that the armored counterattacks (on October 6) were succeeding on the whole, and had an erroneous impression of the magnitude of the losses they were suffering. [1]

This suggests that perhaps we have to think again when it comes to communication. If we combine the plethora of work that questions whether we now rely on too much technology in many areas of our lives and the basic premise behind John Rockart's work on *critical success factors*, then we arrive at a basic question. If we cannot guarantee that every message gets through to its intended audience, then which ones must get through: which ones are critical? When lives literally depend on it, how do we guarantee that the key message is received and understood? This brings me back to the issue of *control bubble*.

With technologically sophisticated systems we have come to expect our communication system will work when required. We now express incredulity when a message does not arrive or when our systems do not function in the way we have come to expect. This daily habit of communicating adds to the illusion that communications is now a given and that our *span of control* is worldwide; any outages remind us of the limits of our *control bubble* and how quickly we can become just isolated from the outside world. When engaged in developing *foresight* we have to consider that we live in a *chaotic* world where "what can go wrong, will go wrong". This means that we must, in these circumstances, question our actual *span of control* and we must examine how quickly this span may reduce when things start to go wrong. We have to ask how quickly at the *mezzo*, *macro* and *mega levels* we might be reduced to being "a man in a box" isolated from the *micro level* only able to see what is around us as happened to the Israeli higher echelons at the start of the Yom Kippur War.

We also need to consider control at the *micro level* and how measures taken to add resilience may have their own *unintended consequences*. Lanir tells us of "the willingness of commanders at all levels to be personally responsible and dedicated in fulfilling their missions with self-reliance and self-initiative".[2] While I do not dispute that self-reliance and initiative being benefits, it also has to be accepted that they induce *chaos* (unforeseen patterns of activity) into the system. While *chaos* can be exploited to bring benefits, it does change the nature of the problem. It changes the function of higher levels of the hierarchy from being one of command to being one that facilitates communication. It changes from directing to one that helps those taking the initiative to coordinate their activities and to make the best out of the *chaos* that besets the contra-forces. As any discussion of the utility of *chaos* is outside the scope of this book, it is suffice to say that there would be two different paradigms now interacting at this point. Each of these will affect the *span of control* that could be exerted. The first paradigm is centred on direction and control and the second concerns *chaos* and coordination. I would suggest that if these two paradigms are to run in parallel, how this might be structured and work needs to have been discussed beforehand!

The types of discussion alluded to here are both difficult and alien to most organisations. The raising of such discussions is often countered with rebuke. This might be analysed against the scale provided by *Westrum's Continuum* which would, at best, suggest encapsulation if not suppression was at work. In the context of *organisational momentum* this is understandable. In terms of generating *foresight* this is likely to be counterproductive.

Failure of active learning

Up to this point in the discussion our focus has been on the enactment layer within the *catalytic cube*. It is now time to consider the other layers on this dimension. These being *learn*, *anticipate* and *adapt*. Both Stech and Lanir argue that it is too simplistic to contend that the Israeli failure prior to the Yom Kippur War was a simple failure of intelligence in that they did not know. Both provide sufficient evidence that this was not the case. They did know but the failure came within their ability to *anticipate* what would be different next time and to *adapt* accordingly. They provide examples where someone in the system knew but the information was not passed to those who need to use it. I would argue that it is also too simplistic to just put this down to a problem of *structural secrecy*. While it is an example of *structural secrecy* this does not help us in terms of developing *foresight*. The example provided concerns the Arab use of anti-tank and anti-aircraft missiles. Stech points to analysis that says:

> ... *there was much amiss behind the fact that Israeli armor was so heavily punished by the enemy's anti-tank missiles. The relevant Israeli military authorities knew the characteristics of these weapons, were aware that the enemy possessed them in large quantities, and had even devised ways to combat them: but somehow the practical conclusion of this information in terms of the composition of forces and battle field tactics were not followed up.*[1]

Lanir supplements this point. He says:

> *Another widely cited surprise in the war was (the) use of Sager anti-tank missiles ... Yet the existence and operation of these missiles by the Egyptian and the Syrian armies were well understood ... During the War of Attrition, the new tactics were tested against Israel armored vehicles. The IDF Intelligence Branch followed this development closely ... including not only technical information but also tactical operational procedures.*[2]

Lanir goes on:

> *In the winter of 1972–1973, three major border incidents occurred on the Syrian front. In the first incident, the Syrians suffered numerous losses, especially from Israel tank fire. In the second, the Syrians fired a barrage of 40–50 Sager missiles and succeeded in destroying an Israel tank for the first time since the Six-Day War. The IDF rapidly learned the lessons of the second battle; ... (the) OC Northern Command, ordered construction of special external armor plating for the Israel tanks to neutralize the efficacy of Sager missiles in future incidents. Consequently, during the third incident, which occurred several days later, despite the firing of numerous Syrian missiles, no Israel tanks were hit. The Israel Armored Corps Research Branch, which operates as part of the Armored Corps Command, distributed instructions among armored corps units, describing defensive tactics against personal anti-tank missiles. However, this technique was not sufficiently practiced.*[2]

We can see that activity on the *enact layer* had provided an operational lesson and precipitated work in the learning layer. This learning had developed new ways of working that should have been applicable to the next episode of enactment. However, as we see a failure to implement the solution, we have to assume that there was a failure in either or both of the *anticipate* and *adapt layers*.

We can see the same pattern when it comes to the Arab use of anti-aircraft missiles. Lanir says,

> another technological development that is claimed to be a surprise is the Egyptian surface-to-air anti-aircraft missiles. The Egyptian Army was equipped with some surface-to-air anti-aircraft missiles even before the Six-Day War. Although the Egyptians deployed about 30 batteries SA-2 and SA-2B missiles during this war, the Israel Air Force did not consider such missiles to represent a new substantial threat. During the War of Attrition, the Egyptians operated several new types of missile batteries, namely the SA-2C and SA-3. Indeed, the only new type of missile that appeared in the Yom Kippur War was the SA6. However its acquisition, too, was well known by Israel".[2]

As we discussed earlier, it was not the missiles themselves that had changed, it was the effectiveness in their deployment that had. This also suggests that the failure was not about learning itself but it was a failure in the *active learning* process.

Given that studies of *active learning* are still quite rudimentary at the time of writing this book, it cannot be a surprise that this problem befell the Israelis in 1973. Even today, the focus is on learning from incidents and why we fail to learn as a post-incident routine. As we see here, in terms of *foresight*, what is important is what we can learn from the past. However, because there are so many lessons, this issue becomes one of winnowing out the critical lessons pertaining to you and your circumstances. From this example we also suspect that the commander's focus is on the *enact layer*; this is clearly inadequate if effective *foresight* is to be achieved. A future area of research may be to embrace work done on the role of executives within learning organisations.

"The critical days"

During the *incubation period* we have seen that we can expect the organisation to oscillate in terms of tension and tempo that induces vulnerabilities to *crisis* into the system. As we have seen in the previous case of Pearl Harbor, post-incident analysis of *the critical days* leading up to the *crisis* can be clearly defined in *hindsight*. When it comes to *foresight* however, this period is not so easy to identify. For a start, as I described earlier, in many cases the period between *normal* and *abnormal chaos* is often less than 30 minutes. For *foresight* the questions become: how will we know we are in this period and 2) what contingencies do we need to have prepared to handle the situation?

How will we know?

In this case we see the Israelis are faced with some of the classic dilemmas experienced by people and organisations in these situations. In this case, within the same year, we see a rise of tension in their region; this occurred in May and again in October 1973. There are four possible explanations[4] for the period of tension in May. The first is that there was no build-up of forces and the Israelis just imaged it through their distorted lens. The second explanation was that there was an intention on the part of the Arabs to strike Israel but the mobilisation of Israeli troop deterred them. The third explanation is that the Arab deployment did not go as planned and so the strike was postponed. The final explanation is that the build-up was part of the Arab deception plan designed to produce the disarray that occurred with the Israeli higher echelons. This is akin to a burglar targeting a house with an alarm. Rather than defeating the alarm, the burglar convinces the owner that it is faulty and so they switch it off. The burglar does this by causing a series of seemly false alarms. In this case the alarm was not switched off; it was just that the police did not respond!

In terms that I have used earlier, this is a production versus protection dilemma. It concerns the resource cost of responding to a perceived warning rather than an issue with the warning itself. From a *foresight* perspective the issue is one of an *error of attribution* rather than a failure of the system. The problem for Israel was that, in simplified terms, it had a choice between whether it used its human resource to produce wealth for the nation or to protect itself. While in a different setting scale may allow a balance to be found between the two, faced with the circumstances as they were, the Israeli choice was actually binary: production or protection, for they could not do both. It is of interest to me that a similar scenario occurred in the 1990s in the conflict between the USA and the Soviet Union. The US used its industrial and economic power to entice the Soviet Union to spend so much on defence that it imploded. In the 1970s the Arabs seem to have been playing a variation on this scenario

---

4   These ideas where taken for http://www.globalsecurity.org/intell/library/reports/1990/LKA. htm, accessed 22 December 2014

with the Israelis. For this case I think there is sufficient evidence to rule out the first explanation and so we are left with three that are interrelated. I can only speculate but would suggest that the Israelis framed some of the issues around mobilisation incorrectly.

The first issue concerns misframing the *critical success factors* that related to the type of war that they would be fighting. In terms of a war of annihilation, the mobilisation in May 1973 made sense. When the real alternative to mobilisation is the destruction of the State, loss of economic production is very much a secondary consideration. Where the loss of production becomes an issue is firstly when it reaches the point that it may in itself cause the destruction of the State. Where the outcome is unlikely to be so extreme, then such a debate may indicate *drift* from the proposition implicit in the critical factor. That is to say, in this case, that more damage would be done to the State by mobilising than may potentially be caused by not mobilising. While matters of personalities (ego or hubris for example) or group dynamics (such as *new group syndrome, groupthink* or *risky shift*) might not be ruled out, these types of heated debate may also indicate that there is fundamental disagreement about some of the embedded assumptions that were not recognised.

The second issue of framing concerns the margins they gave themselves. One of their *critical success factors* that was key was giving themselves enough time to mobilise. I do not see any discussion of the *margin of error* that they had given themselves when it comes to determining the time of the strike. Nor do I see any discussion of the *safety margin* that they wished to give themselves when it came to making this judgement. In the text it would appear the Israeli leadership took account of neither and relied on the unrealistic expectations of perfect decision-making. We have to question the wisdom of "the 'guarantee' of at least 48 hours warning" being essential to the Israeli defense strategy.[1] To guarantee anything provides no *margin of error. Production pressure* is also likely to mean that the "at least" part of the guarantee is lost over time. The fact that "ten hours after the attack began the Egyptians had pontoon bridges and ferries in operation (half the time estimated before the war by Israeli intelligence)"[1] meant that there was 100 per cent error in the time taken to effect the crossing compared to the estimate supporting the case for them being formally considered. This suggests that a *margin of error* should have been considered as a routine part of the process.

The third issue of framing concerns Arab deception plans that present *decoy problems*. Given the first two issues of framing, the problem of deception is placed a distant third place. The possibility of annihilation of Israel would seem to justify categorisation as a *never event*; that is, it should be avoided at whatever cost is necessary. Having started to consider introducing the necessary margins into the mitigation process, the possibility of deception being attempted should be factored in and incorporated into the necessary margins. In the case of the Yom Kippur War, Stech describes how several Arab deceptions and a few coincidences provided *decoy problems* for Israeli attention. He says:

> The most successful Arab deception was the high" of tension and military mobilisation and exercises they created in the spring of 1973 which caused Dayan and Elazar to overrule Ze'ira and order a partial mobilization at great expense to Israel. Since no attack followed Ze'ira's estimate that the Arabs had had no intention of attacking was confirmed. Sadat's war of nerves dulled Israeli sensitivity to the Arabs' attack preparations and rehearsals, and created the "wolf cry" which strengthened the most complacent Israeli intelligence figure.

> The frequent conferences of senior Egyptian, Syrian and Jordanian political and military figures in the spring and summer of 1973 was attributed by the Israeli Military Intelligence Branch to the reopening of Jordanian diplomatic relations with Egypt and Syria. Consequently the shift of Syrian troops from the Jordanian border to the Golan line was seen in Israel as a goodwill gesture by Assad to Hussein, rather than a buildup prior to an attack ...

After a period in which the tension dropped, it started to build again.

> On 26 September Egyptian Foreign Minister Zayat arrived in Washington to reactivate the American mediation role in the Middle East. On 28 September Arab terrorists held up a trainload of Russian Jewish immigrants' enroute to Vienna and demanded that the Jewish transit camp at Schoenau be closed. ... Zayat's efforts were part of Sadat's deception plan, the terrorist incident may have been ... fortuitous. Israel's preoccupation with international and domestic terrorism between the 1967 and the 1973 wars was a constant distraction for the military and the Cabinet.[1]

The question regarding the framing of the May events is whether it is seen in isolation or as part of a whole. The human mind is prone to breaking down *complex* problems into digestible chunks. It is therefore quite understandable that the May events are treated by the Israelis as a discreet event. However, given the long-term nature of Nasser's four-stage plan, this would have been a mistake. This being the case, in terms of *foresight*, there is no difference between explanations two, three and four. They are all just evolution and oscillations in the tension of the *incubation period* of this *crisis*. In terms of *foresight* what is not important is analysis of who guessed correctly and who did not. What is important is how the events affected the way ahead. In this case the induced action increased the Israeli reluctance to mobilise next time with all the implications that this had. The events, whether they were a deception or a postponement of an attack, had the same outcome.

The final issue of framing is the effect our tendency to minimising emergent dangers has on our perception of events depicted in the data. Here again I can use Stech's words (my words are in brackets):

> The last element of the incubation stage of a disaster (that I have labelled the critical days) is the tendency to assume invulnerability, underestimate hazards, and overestimate the capabilities for dealing with them. When the occurrence of the disaster becomes undeniable, emergency measures are applied "too little and too late". Fears of false alarms prevent alarms being sounded. Disagreements about the significance of evidence pointing to danger leads to the underevaluation of warnings, particularly if the more complacent group is most powerful. Each of those problems contributed to the Israeli disaster.
>
> The Israelis clearly minimized the danger of an Arab military attack ... assuming an attack would be suicidal ... the Arabs would not attack. Because the IDF evaluated the Arabs as incapable of coordinated, surprise, and swift assaults both the Golan and Bar-Lev defense lines were thin relative to the forces facing them ... Ze'ira stoutly "explained away" evidence discrepant with his position: ... The financial costs of mobilization and the political costs of preemption prevented the cabinet from responding to these warning signals.

We can now understand that financial and political considerations may have affected the Israeli perception of the risks they faced. By understanding that these are issues may help other organisations to avoid them in the future. They might do this if they are prepared to reflect on the organisation's method of analysing problems. In terms of *foresight*, such issues may also be highlighted earlier by reference to and review of a central *hypothesis for success* in whatever form it may take. The key issue for *the critical period* is what damage may be caused if we do react compared to the potential damage that may be caused if we do not react. The tendency, however, is to collate the costs of reacting over time and thereby building up the sum of apparent waste. As probability theory and the idea encapsulated in the economic principle of *sunk cost* requires, previous experience has to be ignored but this can prove difficult to do! This issue needs to be considered at the review conducted after an event and not at the start of one. Such moments provide frame-breaking review trigger points.

What contingencies do we need to have prepared?
In this illustration we see a relatively long period of oscillation; Dayan put it at ten years. In this context, however, the speed of reaction can be presumed to be less than 48 hours as they asked for at least 48 hours' notice. An example at the other end of the scale is provided by the oil industry. In reading about the Deepwater Horizon accident, I was struck by the speed at which *normal chaos* became abnormal. For the depth of the drill the gas bubble would seem to take about four minutes to rise up the pipe and engulf the rig. The operators therefore had about two minutes to see, appreciate what was happening and act to avoid that disaster. While an operator might do this regularly, one slip, one lapse and disaster could occur. Even if you double that time, from the perspective of *foresight*, how many four-minute periods are there in ten years (being the life of the rig)? This would seem to change the probability calculation for a disaster considerably.

In this illustration the oscillation period of ten years takes second place to the mobilisation time of 48 hours. Given that it is the 48 hours that becomes critical, then all of the contingencies and necessary margins need to be based on this factor. I will discuss three. The first is the adequacy of the analytical capability and the application of the necessary margins. The second is the ability of the nation to mobilise rapidly enough to meet that standard and, finally, it is the adequacy of the operational plans to defeat any attack. Stech tells us that:

> The Israeli Cabinet relied heavily on their intelligence warning system even though the adequacy of this system – to predict an Arab attack – had been questioned at the highest" ... Israeli defense plans were premised on adequate warning which, in turn, was predicated on the operation of technical intelligence mechanisms.[1]

This would fall into the category of error that the historian Barbara Tuchman[5] labelled *folly*; the reliance on a plan you doubt. Stech explains that:

---

5   Tuchman (1984)

> *… no formal mechanisms existed (1) to arbitrate dis-agreements about*
> *warnings between the Defense Minister and Chief of Staff on the one*
> *hand and the intelligence chief on the other, and (2) to determine*
> *what mobilisation or pre-emption should follow the receipt of certain*
> *warnings. Formal standards seemed lacking for both the warning, and*
> *the operational elements of Israeli defense plans.*[1]

So we see some fundamental flaws in the plans which may justify them being
labelled *fantasy documents*. Stech continues:

> *No contingency plans provided for the actual-events: a warning that the*
> *attack would come in 15 hours (in fact, the attack came in 11 hours). That*
> *is, when faced with a far less timely (and even then, inaccurate) warning*
> *than expected, the Cabinet was forced to debate what steps to take.*[1]

Here we see "at least 48 hours" turning out to be 11 hours; this gives us a margin
of 37 hours and enhances my argument that one needs to be considered. In this
quote we also have evidence of the *perfect world* paradigm. What is described
as the *perfect world* paradigm can be seen when there is the suggestion that all
disruptions and unwanted events can be avoided through proper planning and
a careful execution of that plan. Also implicit in this paradigm is that perfection
should constitute the expected norm. This paradigm therefore extends further
to posit that all would be fine if *mistakes* are not made; that is, things will only go
wrong if *mistakes* are made. This paradigm ignores unexpected outcomes that
can derive from normal activity occurring as planned. It does not understand
that these unexpected outcomes may be due to *interactive complexity* nor does
it accept the reality of human fallibility and therefore that perfection is, in all
probability, an unrealistic expectation.

In addition to the assumption that a warning can be delivered exactly
as required is the fact that they had "no contingency plans provided for the
actual events". This will come as no surprise to students of *crisis* studies. The
flawed assumption is that you can write a plan that will match future events;
this supports the case for contingencies providing generic guidance that can be
readily adapted to the circumstances as they emerge.

Throughout both the texts by Stech and Lanir is the sense of how important,
how critical, mobilisation was. It was the linchpin between peace and war on
which everything else depended; it is an example of the critical nature of the
transition between *operational modes*. However, despite it being considered to be
critically important, the viability of the plan receives very little debate. One may

surmise that this factor had not been discussed previously because Dayan had to ask: "What is the difference between mobilization of these units in the evening – if the war actually opens – or now, in the morning?"[2] As the answer of "12 hours" represents 25 per cent of the warning time, this lends weight to the importance of this factor. Fortune (luck) seems to have been with the Israelis on this occasion as "despite this brief warning, reserve detachments reached the northern and southern fronts within 24 hours of the outbreak of war".[2] Lanir says that this conformed to original IDF reserve mobilisation plans. He explains that:

> *The main mobilization occurred on Yom Kippur, the only day of the year during which daytime call-up is as effective as nighttime call-ups, since most Israelis are at home or in the synagogue. Thus the potentially adverse effect of brief warning on the reserve call-up process was counteracted by an especially rapid call-up, proceeding at twice the pace assumed in mobilization exercises.[2]*

The result was that both the divisions in the south and in the north were mobilised on day 2 (7 October). To be balanced, we do have to question whether this was Israeli good luck or poor planning by the Arabs; might they have foreseen this? Given the war aims of the Arabs, this was not critical to their planning. As we read on we can see more *folly* probably caused by *drift* and the *Plowman effect* in that before the war an "immediate full mobilization of the reserves became less probable as a result of the need to consult the Americans first ... American support was considered more valuable than the harm of calling up only part of its forces and conducting war without a preventive strike".[2]

When viewing the Israeli battle plans from the perspective of *foresight* and within the paradigm of *normal chaos*, the plausibility of the plans becomes questionable. Stech says, "The 'all-tank' tactics ... depended on adequate warning and mobilization".[1] This required all the components of the plan up to this point working as designed. We have to consider this to be a very unlikely eventuality; a more constructive perspective would seem to be one that considers how much variation from the design could occur before the plan would cease to be an effective guide to future operations. Stech continues:

> *The Israeli defense plans called for the ground forces ... to contain the Arab ground attack while the IAF ... would devote itself exclusively to destroying the Arab air defenses and air forces ... when the October attack began the IAF was immediately pressed into support of the failing Israeli ground defenses, and was too preoccupied with halting ground*

attacks to deal effectively with, the air defense threats. The original plan for IAF invincibility was useless, there were no others, and the IAF was committed to battle day-by-day, even hour-by-hour until the Israelis had turned the tide. Summarily, Israel's plans for her armored forces were inapplicable ... and inflexible and unworkable (because the attack that came was not what was expected).[1]

Lanir looks at the counterattack contingency. He states:

In the first two days of fighting, Israel's military leadership attempted to confront the fundamental change as if it were experiencing only situational difficulties by allocating more and more forces in order to stabilize the lines ... The counterattack of ... (the) reserve division on October 8th was a complete failure, providing a clear demonstration that the surprise was not the main reason for Israel's chaotic response during the first days of the war. Rather, that was caused by the distortions of an obsolete doctrine. On the same day, Israel conducted another counterattack on the Golan Heights. The need to conduct two simultaneous counterattacks on two different fronts may have been seen at the time as a necessity. However, it clearly contradicted the doctrine.[2]

We see that rather than *macro level* contingencies providing the critical contra move, they were created by people operating at the *micro level*.

The two turning points in the Yom Kippur War that enabled Israel to recover from its chaotic situation ... (were) mainly the results of actions taken by Israel's combat commanders. The first one was the discovery of the Second and Third Egyptian Armies ... Daring to rely on this fragile bridgehead, Israel built up an offensive force on the west bank of the Suez Canal, behind the main Egyptian army deployment. The other turning point ... in the midst of battle, an Israel armor unit reached a ground-to-air missile installation and destroyed it with tank guns ... Once the missile position ceased to function as a system, each missile battery become even more vulnerable to air attacks.[2]

The contingency plans that the Israelis had in place did not work. Should the Israelis have foreseen this? Maybe not. Should they have prepared for the possibility, definitely. In each case the plan was based in the *perfect world* paradigm where you expect things to go as planned. This can be the only explanation for the battle plans being constructed in the way they were. The *normal chaos* paradigm suggests that by phase 2 of any plan some of the prerequisites for success will not be in place. Local actors need to assess what can continue and what will need to be changed. By phases 3 and 4 expectations that plans will be proceeding as designed are more likely to be a wish than reality and so flexibility and adaptability now becomes critical.

STAGE 3

Prior to the *precipitating event* we can only speculate when it will or is likely to occur and what form it will take. However, even in *hindsight* and after a great deal of analysis, while generally possible, it can still be difficult to determine what the *precipitating event* was and when it occurred. As we can see in the texts provided, this is even more difficult to discern at the time. If the ambiguity of *the critical days* is the *mega level* problem, the identification of the *precipitating event* is the *micro level* version.

In this case, however, even in *hindsight* it is difficult to be exact as to when the event occurred. At one point Lanir says it was "1355 hours, when the enemy opened fire along the entire front" and in another he says, "the war actually began …, at 1358". These timings need to be compared with the estimate made on the day that fighting would start at 1800 hrs. This gives us a *margin of error* of four hours in the estimate. Lanir adds that when "commanders of the Bar Lev Line strongholds received their orders to be on full alert only after 1200 on October 6 … (there was no) indication that war was to break out within less than two hours".[2]

We can also see that even when you are in Stage 3, you may not realise it. We are given illustrations of where the message did not get through. For example: "detachments on the Bar-Lev line were not warned and some soldiers manning the Mount Herman lookout posts were sunning themselves when Syrian artillery opened up".[1] Another example is that the code word "Dovecote", which meant immediate operation of the stronghold along the canal, was received at 1430 hrs, 30 minutes after the war had begun.[2]

The issue is, when do you realise you have a new problem (the *crisis*) and start to react to it. What we see here is an illustration of the moment of increased vulnerability as you are transforming between modes. In this case it might be characterised as transforming between *normal* and *abnormal chaos*. Alternatively is might be seen as moving from *high tempo* (or routine operations if you have been caught out really badly) to *crisis*/emergency mode. This is just an issue of the labels you like to use. The key point here is to recognise it has happened so that you can start to react.

STAGES 4 AND 5

In Stages 4 and 5 we see the interaction of the contra-forces at work. In terms of *foresight* we need to *anticipate* how the *crisis* might develop and how these developments might be countered. As this is not a book about *crisis management* I will not dwell on these stages. In this case we see what was prepared, what capabilities were to hand and where the Israelis improvised (often referred to in the academic literature as *bricolage*), and we might made judgements about how well they improvise. We also see frequently that the side that comes out ahead is the one that performs less badly; this is not meant as a criticism but just as a reflection on the reality and that *chaos* is actually normal. I will let Stech and Lanir finish their narrative:

> ... the Egyptians recognised the formable nature Israel's capability and so their future plans "stressed surprise explicitly to keep the Israeli armour out of the fight until the bridgeheads over the Canal were established and (their) tank and air defense traps were ready". These traps, seen as being a "meat grinder", destroyed 140 Israeli tanks during their first counterattack because the Israelis failed to adapt to the changing situation.[1]

> In the first two days of fighting, Israel's military leadership attempted to confront ... only the situational difficulties by allocating more and more forces in order to stabilize the lines. This response involved many losses ... by October 8, Israel managed in the canal front to turn over its initial quantitative inferiority into superiority, it still had failed to translate it into military achievements ... On the same day, Israel conducted another counterattack on the Golan Heights ... (while) the Adan Division was in the midst of its attack and it was already clear that they had severe difficulties, the second reserve division ... stood watching ... with only the foggiest knowledge of where it would confront the main enemy force ... this was a different kind of war, in which the Egyptian infantry could stand against Israel's army. The confusion, disorder, and misreading of the situation by headquarters ... characterized the situation ...: "A division commander who did not know what was going on reported to a front commander who knew less, who in turn reported to a Chief-of-Staff who knew less than either ... it was the man who knew the least who made the crucial decisions".[2]

> *During the first three days of the war, what saved the IDF from defeat was the tremendous ability of its low-level combat commanders to initiate and improvise ... in chaotic situations. ... By their own initiative, some of them "requisitioned" crews and tanks from the vestiges of retreating units, confiscated ammunition from trucks that were on their way to units in the front that probably did not exist anymore, and thus improvised new fighting units and returned to (the) fight ...[2]*

> *The two turning points in the Yom Kippur War that enabled Israel to recover from its chaotic situation ... and to move from chaos into a new order and from defense to offense were ... the results of actions taken by Israel's combat commanders. The first one was the discovery of the Second and Third Egyptian Armies ... The other turning point ... an Israel armor unit reached a ground-to-air missile installation and destroyed it with tank guns.[2]*

> *It was not until the afternoon of Monday, 8 October, that Mendler (Sinai Armored Commander), Gonen [Southern Commander] ... understood the new threat posed by the Egyptians. From the initial crossings on 6 October until late on the 8th, Military Intelligence kept informing Gonen that the Egyptians were ready to "break" at any moment. Gonen's repeated orders of attack can be attributed in part to the continued underestimation of the enemy by military intelligence.[1]*

In terms of Clausewitz, the Israelis were fighting the wrong war as, for them, the paradigm had once again changed.

In his work Stech reminds us that Turner describes this stage as the "first stage adjustment" where there is "the application of ad hoc adjustments to the post-collapse situation so that the major features of the failure can be recognized and dealt with ... and (that) prolonged analyses are not undertaken, but only the minimal recognition of changed circumstances necessary to deal with the immediately pressing problems". He adds "some of the afflicted cannot make even these adjustments and continue to deny the failure" as we see happened in the South for the first three days of the war. The point here for *foresight* is that this is not the time for deep analysis, this is the time for action. However, without adequate analysis and preparation beforehand you will not have the tools available to you when you need them.

Stech concludes this section by saying,

> *The story of how the Israelis improvised their defenses in the face of the Arab assaults and regained the military initiative in the October War bears witness to the adequacy of their rescue and salvage efforts. The details of this readjustment have little bearing on the application of disaster theory to intention estimation failures.*

I disagree. It is the application of this disaster theory to *foresight* that enables us to see how the parts interact and thus enable us to avoid *fundamental surprise*.

STAGE 6

And so we return to the learning process and the *full cultural readjustment*, or as full an adjustment as the local politics will allow. Here we have to *anticipate* how we might benefit most when learning from a future *crisis* and so I have to return to one of my main points of this book. The question is where the greatest value lies; does it lie in the lessons a particular case has to teach the future or is greater value to be gained by those involved harvesting appropriate lessons from the past? I would argue to place greater priority on the latter learning. This requires a whole new approach to learning from such incidents. It is about the more effective refinement, dissemination and application of what we already know being given priorities over the marginal improvement we have to gain by learning from the most recent events. While this may be academically stimulating, it has only marginal *practical utility*. Having said that, we may still like to consider the lessons learnt from these events in order to highlight two important issues when it comes to *foresight*. The first is the division into lessons that are applicable at the *micro* to *mega levels*. The second is the use of the *active learning* dimension of the *catalytic cube*.

The *micro level* will have produced lessons about weapons systems, tactics and the personal abilities of their enemies. At the *mezzo level* will have been lessons about operational level issues. At the *macro* level and *mega levels* the Agranat Commission[6] made the usual types of recommendations that changed structures within the defence establishment and at government level and blamed individuals for their shortcomings. Whether they improved the systems or just changed them is for others to decide. There is one lesson that is worth examining in slightly more detail as it applied equally to all layers. It is the issue of shock. Stech writes:

---

6   http://www.knesset.gov.il/lexicon/eng/agranat_eng.htm, accessed 23 December 2014

> *Golda Meir ... wrote (1975): The shock wasn't only over the way in which the war started, but also the fact that a number of **our basic assumptions were proved wrong** [emphasis added] ... the circumstances (in the opening days of the war) could not possibly have been worse ... [T]he word "trauma", most accurately describes the national sense of loss and injury (that persisted – through and after the war).*[1]

Lanir adds: "Although Israel finally won the war militarily, the realization that Israel's limited strength constituted an insufficient response to Arab threats undermined Israel's self-image".[2] We might suspect that the leaders and the country were having, what Wieck calls, a *cosmological episode*! Referring back to the shock that Cohen and Gooch described the US as experiencing after Pearl Harbor, this may be better understood by viewing it this way.

Learning is part of a process. In a later article[7] on this subject Lanir looked more at our ability to learn about *fundamental surprises*; I see this construct being akin to mine as they both are premised on the sufferer having the incorrect perspective to cope with the data that confronts them. He describes three phases of understanding the nature of the phenomenon. The first I would equate to my *perfect world* paradigm. Lanir sees three phases of development.

In the first one the premise was that there is a known norm of actions that can prevent any kind of surprise. This notion was based on the presumption that "the truth" lies in the information and therefore in the absence of failures of information retrieval, analysis and distribution, no surprise would occur. When a surprise occurred, deviations from this norm were seen as explanatory causes of the surprise. The distinction between types of surprises was not understood as between "'situational' and 'fundamental', but by their magnitudes – 'tactical', 'operational' or 'strategic'". He says that the "Agranat Commission that investigated the Yum Kippur case (1973) represents this line of thought ... Therefore, their recommendations were to replace the intelligence officers who were blamed responsible and to improve the process of 'connecting the dots'".

Lanir sees this process as following the line of recommendations given by the American Investigation Commission into Pearl Harbor (1941) and the Commission that investigated the 11 September 2001 case. I would go

---

7   http://www.articlesbase.com/economics-articles/fundamental-surprise-israeli-lessons-2784076.html, accessed 8 December 2014

further and say it is the dominant paradigm for all the public inquiries and commissions that I have examined. Like the counterparts everywhere "the Commission explicitly attempted not to fall victim to the tendency to be wise after the event, but (others) conclude(d) that to some extent they succumbed to the all too human tendency of distinguishing more clearly between signals and noise with hindsight than would have been possible at the time".[1]

Lanir sees the "second phase of explanations was mainly raised by academic critique on those committees. They emphasized the need to shift the focus from the information handling to human basic thinking errors".

He cites Roberta Wohlstetter's pioneering book *Pearl Harbor: Warning and Decision* (1962)[8] and Richard Heuer's[9] book *Psychology of Intelligence Analysis* (2005). I would also cite Professor James Reason,[10] Sidney Dekker[11] and Garry Klien.[12] These and many other works provide essential material in order to understand the practical issues, however they do not in themselves help promote *foresight*.

His final phase "of understanding the nature of the Fundamental Surprise phenomenon derives from the question: why are armies subject to fundamental surprise even in cases where the intelligence provides the fundamental warning, and why are they reluctant to perform the reframing processes long after they were fundamentally surprised?"

This is much the same question Cohen and Gooch were asking in their work on military misfortune. Lanir "suggests that the focus the study of Fundamental Surprise should be expanded from the realm of the intelligence to encompass the organizational mind set and how it changes" as I try to do here.

This finally brings me back to the *active learning* dimension of the *catalytic cube*. It may be easier and more comfortable for senior managers and the executive to focus on the *enact layer* of activity. While this may be understandable it also has to be recognised that it will leave very important aspects of their system unmonitored. If they do not monitor the other layers of the *active learning* processes then they cannot know whether they are incubating major problems for themselves and their organisations within these areas. In terms of *foresight*,

---

8   Wohlstetter (1962)
9   Heuer (1999)
10   Reason (1990); Reason (1997); Reason (1998); Reason (2008)
11   Dekker (2011)
12   Klein (1998); Klein (2009); Klein et al. (2005)

to do today is not enough. In areas that are critical, they have to be aware of gaps as they emerge, be aware of what is being done in order to learn how the gaps may be closed, *anticipate* how the world may change around them, adapt so they are ready to act appropriately when called on to do so. As in other areas, success does not just happen. It needs resources and sponsorship.

Using the Cube

Up to this point we have looked at the use that can be made of the re-imagined *Disaster Incubation Theory*. Our last stage in this method of *foresight* is to look at how the *catalytic cube* may be incorporated into this method. Here we have to return to Mark Baker's work on the different levels of sophistication available within management controls. While his work has shown that benefits can be derived from greater levels of sophistication, as with all things these levels each bring their own problems as well. His work emphasises the need for organisations to utilise these tools at the most appropriate level. I will therefore describe four levels at which the *catalytic cube* may be used.

At the lowest level of sophistication we may view each of the areas within each gridded layer as a specific problem space that needs to be addressed. This may be done as a mental exercise or it may be committed to paper. As the complexity of the problem and the need to communicate the ideas to others increases, then the necessity to make the cube explicit also grows. We can see the cube as being a derivative of the two by two matrix common to many such tools. It provides four options for consideration. This number of options falls comfortably under the threshold of nine provided by Miller's *magical number 7 (+2)*. If we grow the square to a three by three matrix we reach Miller's upper threshold of nine being reached. If this becomes a cube we now have 27 problem spaces; if each cube dimension has four categories we end up with 64 problem spaces. The issue then becomes one of recognising that the problem has many more components than Miller's construct suggests that the human mind can consider at any one time. By accepting this premise, decision-makers have to accept that they have to start prioritising their effort. An option may then be to delegate various problem spaces to others while ensuring someone is responsible for each problem space. The cubes also highlight the fact that each problem space produces boundary issues with adjacent and linked cells. Whether these issues are being addressed may be annotated using a coding system.

The second level is to mark each problem space within the cube with a "traffic light" or colour-coded system; in Figure 4.1, for example, I have used pattern as a substitute for colour as only black and white options were available. In the case of Figure 4.1 the patterns were to denote the level of harm that the organisation is able to sustain in a particular space. These ranged from *critical harm*, through *serious damage* and *containable disruption* to normal disruption. In practice these details will be determined by what the management wish to monitor.

Three levels may use the cube alongside a legend which lists the projects or activities associated with each problem space. Making linkages between these spaces may provide a further level of sophistication.

The fourth level may be to produce a schematic diagram showing these linkages such as the one used to produce the iconic map of the London underground rail network. This can be used to depict the existing entities and the relationship between them. The fourth level may be to produce a cube that maps the presumed causal links between the activities. This will depend on your knowing the causal link relationships and having the mental and technical capability to produce such a diagram.

The *catalytic cube* provides one way to visualise problems and the links between them. It is open to each user to decide the level of sophistication that they wish to apply to their process.

Conclusion

The conclusion to this chapter is also the conclusion to this book. We have seen how, with a little bit of imagination, Turner's *Disaster Incubation Theory* can be used to facilitate *foresight*. However, more interesting to me is the realisation that we do not start at the beginning. We enter the process at some point dictated by the moment we decide to engage with the issue at hand. It is then our choice how much effort we spend looking back before we start to look forward. We look back in order to understand the context, to learn lessons from the past, to determine what may have made us the way we are and what we have put in place to prevent the unwanted occurring or preparing to react to events when they occur. When we look at what unwanted events may occur, we need to extract from the multitude of possibilities those that are critical and assess the rate at which they are likely to emerge. Within this discussion we need to consider the frequency at which such events are likely to reoccur within our system: that is, the oscillation rate. Once a baseline is established, it is then possible to track how changing expectations, context and means may have weakened a once adequate defence at any one of a number of significant levels within our organisation. This needs to be done for each *critical task*.

Next we see that we have to look forward in order to be clear about what we are trying to achieve and how activity at each of the critical levels helps lead us to that success. Within this process we also need to consider how a beneficial act at one level may produce adverse effects at another. We need to be clear about our strategy for delivery, which I have called the *hypothesis for success*, which needs to link together the goals, the method of delivery and the resources required with those available. We need to assess whether what we plan to do can realistically be expected to deliver what we want, in the way we suggest and within the resources we have. On top of this we need to assess what actual control we have over the process and therefore to determine what else we might be able to do to deliver what we want. Within this process we need to assess the barriers and pitfalls that might prevent success as we must also assess the potential for unintended adverse consequences being generated by our activities. We also need to consider the issues we need to take an interest in as they have been recognised to cause problems.

Like all systems, this process has its limitations. It requires hard work, it is often counter intuitive, and it is demanding of the most precious resource – executive time and effort. This demand therefore leads back to questions about what is critical for it is only these issues that can be expected to be allocated such a resource. In addition, we have to accept that *risk discourse*, in itself, has limitations. Just because people discuss a problem does not mean that they will arrive at the appropriate solution: discussion by itself can be used as a way of avoiding the taking of action. In the context of the Yom Kippur War we have seen how intelligent, experienced and knowledgeable people debated the issues and still arrived at an erroneous position. In the case of the Yom Kippur War, the key players failed at the *mega level* to mobilise their forces at exactly the right moment. They had subsequent success, this time at the *macro level*, and won the military campaign against their Arab neighbours, however they also failed at the *mega level* when they lost the Sinai as a result of the peace settlement. For discourse to succeed it requires not only intelligent, experienced and knowledgeable people but they must also understand the technicalities of their subject in enough detail to be able mitigate their own bias and to foresee the potential for *unintended consequences* to emerge. To assist their deliberations, it would help if they have a framework, such as the *catalytic cube*, that not only stimulates their thinking but also facilitates *cross-understanding* between those concerned.

As we do not live in a perfect world, we have to consider what we might realistically achieve with proper use of *foresight*. This may not be near the utopia that the *perfect world* advocates as being possible. At the very least *foresight* should reduce the number of times we are confronted by the unexpected. While this may not seem much, given the number of occasions that post-incident inquiry reports say this occurs, it would offer a considerable advance on the present situation. We might also hope to see an increase in the number of appropriate contingency plans that assist organisations to manage their *crisis* more effectively. We may see more unwanted occurrences being prevented but these occurrences are under reported and so are more difficult to appreciate. To the question of whether we should expect perfection, the answer is clearly "no". Even advocates of high reliability accept accidents will happen. This leads to the question whether, if we cannot prevent all accidents, it is worth the effort required to try. Each organisation can only answer this question for themselves; the answer will depend on whether they view the cost of not doing so as being acceptable.

Again taking lessons from the empirical work carried out by Mark Baker within his organisation, we can see that the tools suggested here do not have to be used as a comprehensive package. Mark's work took one limited section and derived direct commercial benefit from its application. He saw evidence that even the use of one question could bring benefit: he cites the question of *who cares* as the one that had the greatest resonance for his organisation and described how it had stimulated energetic and constructive debate. The aim of all of these tools is to reduce the potential for *fundamental surprises*. However, as Lanir points out, *fundamental surprises* build up over a long period of time, they are created during a long *incubation period* that offers opportunities for early diagnosis. Lanir has concluded that:

> *One approach to performing such diagnosis is to commit oneself to constant study of ... (an organisations) shared model of its self in relation to its environment. Implementing that commitment would require the development of novel methodologies.*

> *A second approach is to examine the signs of fundamental surprises, going beyond the tendency to learn just the immediate lessons.*

> *A third lesson is to exploit positive surprises as well as negative ones for their potential for learning, even though they do not cause political or social crisis.*

A fourth component is being aware of environmental changes that might have fundamental implications.

I hope that this book will help this process of reflection as it looks to provide a way of thinking rather than a solution. It does not look to prevent every symptom but to enable risk factors to be identified more easily. I see it as a way of trying to make sense of complexity by providing a suitable analytical framework which may require us occasionally to send yourself a *postcard* of misty path to help continuously maintain our focus on *foresight*. It is up to us all to find solutions to the problem we face in the situations we find ourselves.   ·

For Christmas I was given the autobiography of General David Richards. As I read his book, I could not help but see examples of what I have discussed in this book. I do not however suggest, nor do I believe, that these issues are unique to the military. It is just that the military is subject to greater scrutiny from insiders and external armchair experts than seems to be the case for other walks of life. In the case of General Richards it is also that he was unusually honest! I have chosen a few examples to share here.

He describes the dysfunctional relationships between senior officers[13] as they jockey for influence within the Defence structure. He describes how his military perspective clashed with those of civil servants, diplomats, politicians and even the military of other nations as what they cared about differed and so brought them into conflict.[14] If the internal dynamics described in this book were present within the Israeli Ministry of Defence before the Yom Kippur War, it would go a long way to explain what happened. In addition he seems to have often found himself in a position where "there was no effective process of coordination".[15] It is also clear that he supports the military orthodoxy that you should never underestimate your opponent[16] and applied this to opponents both internal and external! These issues can all be part of what comes under the label of *failure to launch*.

The *catalytic cube* helped to prompt some obvious questions. For example, General Richards talked of his role in developing strategic planning doctrine and the part played by consideration of "ends, ways and means".[17] This type

---

13 Richards (2014:170 and 187)
14 Richards (2014:185)
15 Richards (2014:187–188)
16 Richards (2014:318)
17 Richards (2014:201)

of explicit hypothesis links the outcome required to how it will be achieved and the capability required into a realistic and realisable whole. I see this as being akin to goal, method and resources that are central to any *hypothesis for success*. What he does not do, however, is link the need for coherence at the strategic (*macro level*) plan to the tactical (*micro*) level where he sees a role for "tools, rules and resources". At another point in the book he describes his role in the writing of a campaign plan (*macro level*) for operations in Northern Ireland. He then says that "this would mean doing things that tactically (*micro level*) were frustrating or didn't appear to make much sense".[18] The question this would raise is whether this clash was recognised at the time and, if so, was there an effective effort to communicate to the *micro level* the logic behind what made sense and the *macro level*? I can say, as someone serving there around that time, if it was recognised and they did try to explain this dilemma, they failed. Later during his time in Afghanistan it is clear that he becomes very much more aware of the links between tactical (*micro level*) and strategy (*mega*) levels as politicians tried to micro-manage the campaign. Here again we can see a use for the *catalytic cube* for it leads us to ask, if the politicians are concerned at the *micro level* who is focusing on the *mega level* spaces?

In his book, General Richards spends quite a lot of time on the issue around the *control bubble*. For example, he describes the role of Chief of the Defence Staff[19] as being one with responsibility but without power. He had also experienced this problem during his time in Afghanistan where he had to live by the LIC Principle (listen, influence, coordinate).[20] He also clearly recognised that this bubble could burst at any time. He seems to have developed his own management style to cope with this eventuality. Unlike many people who espouse the orthodoxy that "no plan survives first contact" with the enemy,[21] but then go on to insist on ever more *complex* and detailed plans, General Richards seems to espouse and live by the concept of mission command both for himself and his subordinates. To enable this to happen he saw the need to carefully craft his "intent"[22] as guidance as to what was expected and acceptable. Once he had made his intent clear he had to leave his subordinate commanders free to deliver in the way the saw fit.

---

18   Richards (2014:80)
19   Richards (290–291 and 299)
20   Richards (2014:193)
21   Richards (2014:188)
22   Richards (2014:160, 192 and 318)

If I was to draw a cube in this case, there would be some interesting discussion over what was critical. It is clear that he used the idea of "vital national interest"[23] as a pragmatic test of criticality. He also spoke of the critical importance of media and psychological operations to the success of current military operations. These are not factors considered by any of the other cases used here: this reinforces my point that what is critical will change case by case and, while previous experience may provide a guide, it should not be followed slavishly without further thought. There is, however, one item that he emphasises on a number of occasions; that is the idea "Clout, not dribble".[24] This espouses the importance of exerting sufficient military force to achieve your aim; in terms of a *critical task* I would phrase as "providing sufficient force to ensure the objective is achieved at an acceptable cost". Despite repeating this phrase a number of times, it does not appear in the index and so it is difficult to determine how important this factor is to him.

Finally, in terms of *foresight*, we see a number of quotes and assertions that resonate with what has gone before in my previous cases and so raise some concern. For example, General Richards says, "I was not concerned about the danger of state on state warfare – it was unlikely in the short to medium term".[25] This reminds me of Moshe Dayan's assertion less than a month before the Yom Kippur War and so I do hope that this assumption is regularly reviewed, especially in light of his veiled barb made with reference to the future reliance on the reserve force.[26] General Richards exposes the problem of what I have labelled the rate of *crisis* oscillation; on a number of occasions he talks about the changing defence environment and the actual timeframes required to deliver a military effect as opposed to the ones desired by politicians.[27] The impression given is the view in Whitehall is focused on the short-term direct threat. In terms of *foresight* they are less concerned with the medium term, the medium-length oscillations over the decades. There also appears to be far less concern over the long term, the long oscillation as seen in the rise and fall of empires which are also at play in the overall picture.

General Richard's book does seem to explicitly accept that *chaos* is normal and that we have to learn to manage our lives and our organisations within this context. We must, however, leave that debate for another book.

---

23 Richards (2014:311)
24 Richards (2014:160, 236 and 315)
25 Richards (2014:312)
26 Richards (2014:299)
27 Richards (2014:322)

Epilogue

In this book I have described a method, inspired by Turner's *Disaster Incubation Theory*, to promote *foresight*. Those readers who have made it this far will know that what I have presented does not offer a quick or simple solution. The method described is complex, circular and requires a significant expenditure of time and other resources to implement. I make no apology for this. To understand why, I have to return to the issue that underlies all my work. The focus of my research is the *failure of foresight*; to be more accurate, it is how we may prevent such failures.

While risk management offers ways to assess and prevent potential failures, this work starts with the implicit question, "What is the scope of work required to prevent *failures of foresight*?" Therefore, while this work does offer a new approach to addressing this problem, I am now even more certain that failure is inevitable at some time. These failures are driven by the law of large numbers rather than their being due to any specific *"cause and effect"* relationship, an issue that had blighted the *high reliability* verses *normal accident debate*. In this book I have started to explore the multifaceted nature of any system and the *complex* relationships between its parts. These relationships are truly *complex* and they can generate many unexpected outcomes, some of which are very significant and disruptive but many are manageable as part of everyday business. This latter group often passes unnoticed. This complexity generates patterns of activity that we do not really understand and, as such, can be seen as being *chaotic*. Such *chaos* can therefore be considered to be the norm. Within this paradigm, a paradigm of *normal chaos*, we can start to understand that *foresight* may be both fleeting and fragile.

As *foresight* is both fleeting and fragile, while we may achieve it on some occasions, I would suggest that we should consider ourselves lucky when we do. When we do, we might recognise that what has occurred is a fortunate correlation between what our educated guess determined would occur and what actually did. With practice, experience, suitable technology and better data, we may improve our forecasting. That is, the rate of correct correlation may increase in favour of the forecaster. However, we only have to look at weather forecasting to realise how far we still have to go and they do not have to cope with the pernicious human factor.

This should not be taken as a council of despair. We should continue to try; we must continue to try. This is, however, a challenge to commentators or the heads of inquiries who criticise practitioners for having a *failure of foresight*. The challenge for them is, before they offer such glib criticism, to show not only how, without *hindsight* and in the context that the failure occurred, such a failure was possible to avoid but also that it would have been reasonable to give it the priority necessary above all the other issues that faced those involved at the time.

Bibliography

Adams, J. (2007), "Risk Management: It's Not Rocket Science ... It's Much More Complicated", *Risk Management*, Vol. 54, No. 5, pp.36–40.

Ashby, W.R. (1956), *An Introduction to Cybernetics*, Chapman and Hall, London.

Aven, T., Vinnem, J.E. and Wiencke, H.S. (2007), "A Decision Framework for Risk Management, with Application to the Offshore Oil and Gas Industry", *Reliability Engineering and System Safety*, Vol. 92, pp.433–448.

Barton, M.A. and Sutcliffe, K.M. (2009), "Overcoming Dysfunctional Momentum: Organizational Safety as a Social Achievement", *Human Relations*, Vol. 62, No. 9, pp.1327–1356.

BBC, "Cliff hero resigns in safety row", http://news.bbc.co.uk/1/hi/england/tees/7183017.stm, accessed 6 November 2010.

Bierly III, P.E. and Spender, J.-C. (1995), "Culture and High Reliability Organizations: The Case of the Nuclear Submarine", *Journal of Management*, Vol. 21, No. 4, pp.639–656.

Black, R. and Baldwin, J. (2007), "Really Responsive Risk-Based Regulation", *Law and Policy*, Vol. 32, No. 2, pp.181–213.

Boin, A., Hart, P., Stern, E. and Sundelius, B. (2005), *The Politics of Crisis Management*, Cambridge Press, Cambridge.

Brown P. and Heyman, B. (2012:422): "Perspectives on the 'Lens of Risk' Interview Series: Interviews with Joost van Loon and Ortwin Renn", *Health, Risk and Society*, Vol. 14, No. 5, pp.415–425.

Bourne, M. and Bourne, P. (2011), *Handbook of Corporate Performance Management*, Wiley, Chichester.

Bourrier, M. (2005), "An Interview with Karlene Roberts", *European Management Journal*, Vol. 23, No. 1, pp.93–97.

Boyer, E.L. (1990), *Scholarship Reconsidered: Priorities of the Professoriate*, Carnegie Foundation for the Advancement of Teaching, Menlo Park, CA.

Bozeman, B. (2011), "Toward a Theory of Organizational Implosion", *The American Review of Public Administration*, Vol. 41, No. 2, pp.119–140.

Bullen, C.V. and Rockart, J.F. (1981), "A Primer on Critical Success Factors", *Sloan WP No.1220–81*, MIT.

Burlando, T. (1994), "Chaos and Risk Management", *Risk Management*, Vol. 41, No. 4, pp.54–61.

CAIB (2003), *Columbia Accident Investigation Board Report*, Washington, DC (also see: http://caib.nasa.gov/, accessed 1 April 2012).

Cannon, D.R. (1999), "Cause or Control? The Temporal Dimension in Failure Sense-Making", *The Journal of Applied Behavioral Science*, Vol. 35, No. 4, pp.416–438.

Chang, J. and Halliday, J. (2006), *Mao, The Unknown Story*, Vintage, London.

Clarke, L. and Perrow, C. (1996), "Prosaic Organizational Failure", *American Behavioral Scientist*, Vol. 39, No. 8, pp.1040–1056.

Cohen, E. and Gooch, J. (1990), *Military Misfortune: The Anatomy of Failure in War*, Free Press, New York.

Constantinides, P. (2013), "The Failure of Foresight in Crisis Management: A Secondary Analysis of the Mari Disaster", *Technological Forecasting and Social Change*, Vol. 80, pp.1657–1673.

Corley, K.G. and Gioia, D.A. (2011), "Building Theory about Theory Building: What Constitutes a Theoretical Contribution?", *Academy of Management Review*, Vol. 36, No. 1, pp.12–32.

Dekker, S. (2011), *Drift into Failure*, Ashgate, Farnham (Kindle Edition).

Dekker, S., Cilliers, P. and Hofmeyr, J.-H. (2011), "The Complexity of Failure: Implications of Complexity Theory for Safety Investigations", *Safety Science*, Vol. 49, pp.939–945.

Donaghy. R. (2009), *One Death is too Many Inquiry into the Underlying Causes of Construction Fatal Accidents*, Stationary Office, London.

Dooley, K. and Van de Ven, A. (1999), "Explaining Complex Organizational Dynamics", *Organization Science*, Vol. 10, No. 3, pp.358–375.

Drummond, H. (2011), "MIS and Illusions of Control: An Analysis of the Risks of Risk Management", *Journal of Information Technology*, Vol. 26, No. 4, pp.259–267.

Dudezert, A. and Leidner, D.E. (2011), "Illusions of Control and Social Domination Strategies in Knowledge Mapping System Use", *European Journal of Information Systems*, Vol. 20, No. 5, pp.574–588.

Dunbar, R. and Garud, R. (2005), "Data Indeterminacy: One NASA, Two Modes" in Starbuck, W.H. and Farjoun, M. (Eds), *Organization at the Limit*, Blackwell, Oxford.

Durand, R. (2003), "Predicting a Firm's Forecasting Ability: The Roles of Organizational Illusion of Control and Organizational Attention", *Strategic Management Journal*, Vol. 24, No. 9, pp.821–838.

Durand, R. (2004), "Can Illusion of Control Destroy a Firm's Competence?", in Tsoukas, H. and Shepherd, J., *Managing the Future*, Blackwell, Oxford.

Edmondson, A.C., Roberto, M.A., Bohmer, M.J., Ferlins, E.M. and Feldman, L.R. (2005), "The Recovery Window: Organizational Learning Following Ambiguous Threats" in Starbuck, W.H. and Farjoun, M. (Eds), *Organization at the Limit*, Blackwell, Oxford.

Farjourn, M. (2005), "Organizational Learning and Action in the Midst of Safety Drift", in Starbuck, W.H. and Farjoun, M., *Organization at the Limit*, Blackwell, Oxford.

Fink, S. (1986), *Crisis Management: Planning for the Inevitable*, Backimprint, Lincoln, NE.

Fischbacher-Smith, D. and Fischbacher-Smith, M. (2013), "Tales of the Unexpected: Issues Around the Development of a Crisis Management Module for the MBA Program", *Journal of Management Education*, Vol. 37, No. 1, pp.51–78.

Flournoy, A.C. (2011), "Three Meta-Lessons Government and Industry Should Learn from the BP Deepwater Horizon Disaster and Why They Will Not", *Boston College Environmental Affairs Law Review*, Vol. 38, Rev. 281, pp.281–303.

Furniss, D., Back, J., Blandford, A., Hildebrandt, M. and Broberg, H. (2011), "A Resilience Markers Framework for Small Teams", *Reliability Engineering and System Safety*, Vol. 96, pp.2–10.

Ghaffarzadegan, N. (2008), "How a System Backfires: Dynamics of Redundancy Problems in Security", *Risk Analysis*, Vol. 28, No. 6, pp.1669–1687.

Goldoff, A.C. (2000), "Decision-making in Organizations: The New Paradigm", *International Journal of Public Administration*, Vol. 23, No. 11, pp.2017–2044.

The Guardian (2007) "Boy drowned as police support officers 'stood by'" http://www.guardian.co.uk/uk/2007/sep/21/1, accessed 5 November 2010.

Grint, K. (2008), "Wicked Problems and Clumsy Solutions: the Role of Leadership", *Clinical Leader*, Vol. 1, No. 2, BAMM Publications.

Hale, A. and Heijer, T. (2006), "Is Resilience Really Necessary? The Case of Railways", in Hollnagel, E., Woods, D. and Leveson, N. (Eds) *Resilience Engineering: Concepts and Precepts*, Ashgate, Farnham.

Hancock, D. (2004), "Tame Problems and Wicked Messes: Choosing between Management and Leadership Solutions", *RMA Journal*, July/August.

Hancock, D. (2010), *Tame, Messy and Wicked Risk Leadership*, Gower, Farnham.

Hancock, D. and Holt, R. (2003), *Tame, Messy and Wicked Problems in Risk Management*, Manchester Metropolitan University Business School, Manchester.

Heimann, L. (2005), "Repeated Failures in the Management of High Risk Technologies", *European Management Journal*, Vol. 23, No. 1, pp.105–117.

Heuer, R. (1999), *Psychology of Intelligence Analysis*, Center for the Study of Intelligence, Central Intelligence Agency.

Hirschhorn, L. (1993), "Hierarchy versus Bureaucracy: The Case of a Nuclear Reactor", in Roberts, K.H. (Ed.), *New Challenges to Understanding Organization*, Macmillan, New York, pp.137–149.

Hocke, P. and Renn, O. (2009), "Concerned Public and the Paralysis of Decision-making: Nuclear Waste Management Policy in Germany", *Journal of Risk Research*, Vol. 12, No. 7, pp.921–940.

Hollnagel, E. (1993), *Human Reliability Analysis, Context and Control*, Academic Press, London.

Hollnagel, E. (2008), "Investigation as an impediment to Learning", in Hollnagel, E., Nemeth, C.P. and Dekker, S., *Remaining Sensitive to the Possibility of Failure*, Ashgate, Vol. 1, pp.259–268.

Hollnagel, E. (2009), *The ETTO Principle: Efficiency-thoroughness Trade-off: Why Things That Go Right Sometimes Go Wrong*, Ashgate, Farnham.

Hopkins, A. (2011), "Risk-management and Rule-compliance: Decision-making in Hazardous Industries", *Safety Science*, Vol. 49, pp.110–120.

Houghton, S.M., Simon, M., Aquino, K. and Goldberg, C.B. (2000), "No Safety in Numbers: Persistence of Biases and Their Effects on Team Risk Perception and Team Decision making", *Group and Organization Management*, Vol. 25, No. 4, pp.325–353.

Huber, G.P. and Lewis, K. (2010), "Cross-Understanding: Implications for Group Cognition and Performance", *Academy of Management Review*, Vol. 35, No. 1, pp.6–26.

Huff, A.S. (2000), "Citigroup's John Reed and Stanford's James March on Management Research and Practice", *Academy of Management Executive*, Vol. 14, No. 1, pp.52–64.

Jaques, T. (2010), "Embedding Issue Management as a Strategic Element of Crisis Prevention", *Disaster Prevention and Management*, Vol. 19, No. 4, pp.469–482.

Johnson, G. and Scholes, K. (1997), *Exploring Corporate Strategy*, Prentice Hall, Hemel Hempstead.

Kaplan, R.S. and Norton, D.P. (2004), *Strategy Maps Converting Intangible Assets into Tangible Outcomes*, HBS, Boston.

Katzenbach, J.R. and Smith, D.S. (1993), *The Wisdom of Teams*, Harvard Business Press, Boston.

Keil, M., Depledge, G. and Rai, A. (2007), "Escalation: The Role of Problem Recognition and Cognitive Bias", *Decision Sciences*, Vol. 38, No. 3, pp.391–421.

Klein, G. (1998), *Sources of Power*, MIT Press, London.

Klein, G. (2007), "Performing a Project Premortem", *Harvard Business Review*, Sep, pp.18–19.

Klein, G. (2009), *Streetlights and Shadows*, MIT Press, London.

Klein, G., Pliske, R., Crandall, B. and Woods, D. (2005), "Problem Detection", *Cognition, Technology and Work*, Vol. 7, No. 1, pp.14–28.

Klinke, A. and Renn, O. (2001), "Precautionary Principle and Discursive Strategies: Classifying and Managing Risks", *Journal of Risk Research*, Vol. 4, No. 2, pp.159–173.

Lagadec, P. (1993), *Preventing Chaos in a Crisis*, McGraw-Hill, Maidenhead.

Langer, E.J. (1975), "The Illusion of Control", *Journal of Personality and Social Psychology*, Vol. 32, pp.311–328.

Lanir, Z. (1983) "Fundamental Surprise – The National Intelligence Crisis" a Hebrew text later translated into English and published at http://praxis.co.il/AbstractFS.htm, accessed on 13 March 2014.

LaPorte, T.R. and Consolini, P.M. (1991), "Working in Practice But Not in Theory: Theoretical Challenges of 'High-Reliability Organizations'", *Journal of Public Administration Research and Theory*, Part-J, Vol. 1, pp.19–47.

Latané, B. and Darley, J.M. (1970), *The Unresponsive Bystander: Why Doesn't He Help?*, Appleton-Century Crofts, New York.

Lauder, M.A. (2011), *Conceptualisation in Preparation for Risk Discourse: A Qualitative Step toward Risk Governance* (Doctoral Thesis), Cranfield University.

Lauder, M.A. (2013), *It Should Never Happen Again*, Gower, Farnham.

Leveson, N. (2004), "A New Accident Model for Engineering Safer Systems", *Safety Science*, Vol. 42, pp.237–270.

Lindblom, C.E. (1959), "The Science of 'Muddling Through'". *Public Administration Review*, Vol. 19, No. 2, pp.79–88.

Lissack, M.R. (1997), "Of Chaos and Complexity: Managerial Insights from a New Science", *Management Decision*, Vol. 35, No. 3, pp.205–218.

Mainelli, M. (2005), "The (Mis)behavior of Risk Managers: Recognizing our Limitations", *The Journal of Risk Finance*, Vol. 6, No. 2, pp.177–181.

Manning, P.K. (1998), "Information, Socio-Technical Disasters and Politics", *Journal of Contingencies and Crisis Management*, Vol. 6, No. 2, pp.84–97.

Massingham, P. (2010), "Knowledge Risk Management: A Framework", *Journal of Knowledge Management*, Vol. 14, No. 3, pp.464–485.

McNamara, R. (1999), *Argument without End*, Public Affairs, New York.

Miller, G.A. (1955), "The Magical Number Seven, Plus or Minus Two, Some Limits on Our Capacity for Processing Information", *Psychological Review*, Vol. 101, No. 2, pp.343–352.

Mintzberg, H., Ahlstrand, B. and Lampel, J. (1998), *Strategy Safari*, Prentice Hall, London.

Mitroff, I., Shrivastava, P. and Udwadia, F.E. (1987), "Effective Crisis Management", *The Academy of Management Executive*, Vol. 1, No. 3, pp.283–292.

Moore, C., Beck, H. and Buchanan, D.A. (2013), "Mr Mitcham's Lens: Post-incident Change and the Investigation Trap", *Fifth Annual Seminar on Improving People Performance in Healthcare: Understanding Organizational Errors in Healthcare*, Dublin City University Business School, Friday 6 September 2013.

Oloruntoba, R. (2013), "Plans Never Go According to Plan: An Empirical Analysis of Challenges to Plans during the 2009 Victoria Bushfires", *Technological Forecasting and Social Change*, Vol. 80, pp.1674–1702.

Pearson, C.M. and Mitroff, I.I. (1993), "From Crisis Prone to Crisis Prepared: A Framework for Crisis Management", *Academy of Management Executive*, Vol. 7, No. 1, pp.48–59.

Peng, M.W. and Dess, G.G. (2010:287), "In the Spirit of Scholarship", *Academy of Management Learning and Education*, Vol. 9, No. 2, pp.282–298.

Perrow, C. (1984 and 1999), *Normal Accidents: Living with High-risk Technologies*, Princeton University Press, Princeton, NJ.

Pidgeon, N. (2012), "Complex Organizational Failures Culture, High Reliability, and Lessons from Fukushima", in *The Bridge Fall*, National Academy of Engineering.

Plowman, D.A., Baker, L.T., Beck, T.E., Kulkarni, M., Solansky, S.T. and Travis, D.V. (2007), "Radical Change Accidentally: The Emergence and Amplification of Small Change", *Academy of Management Journal*, Vol. 50, No. 3, pp.515–543.

Rasmussen, J. (1997), "Risk Management in a Dynamic Society: A Modelling Problem", *Safety Science*, Vol. 27, No. 2/3, pp.183–213.

Reason, J. (1990), *Human Errors*, Cambridge University Press, Cambridge.

Reason, J. (1997), *Managing the Risks of Organizational Accident*, Ashgate, Aldershot.

Reason, J. (1998), "Achieving a Safe Culture: Theory and Practice", *Work and Stress*, Vol. 12, No. 3, pp.293–306.

Reason, J. (2008), *The Human Contribution, Unsafe Acts, Accidents and Heroic Recoveries*, Ashgate, Farnham.

Renn, O. (2004), "Perception of Risks", *The Geneva Papers on Risk and Insurance*, Vol. 29, No. 1, pp.102–114.

Renn, O. (2008), *Risk Governance*, Earthscan, London.

Roberts, K.H. and Bea, R. (2001), "Must Accidents Happen? Lessons from High-reliability Organizations", *Academy of Management Executive*, Vol. 15, No. 3, pp.70–78.

Roberts, K.H. and Rousseau, D.M. (1989), "Research in Nearly Failure-Free, High-Reliability Organizations: Having the Bubble", *IEEE Transactions on Engineering Management*, Vol. 36, No. 2, pp.132–139.

Roberts, K.H., Madsen, P.M. and Desai, V.M. (2005), "The Space Between in Space Transportation", in Starbuck, W.H. and Farjoun, M., *Organization at the Limit*, Blackwell, Oxford.

Rochlin, G.I. (1991), "Iran Air Flight 655 and The USS Vincennes", pp.99–125, in La Porte, T.R (Ed.), *Social Responses to Large Technical Systems*, Klinver, Netherlands.

Rockart, J. (1979), "Chief Executives Define Their Own Data Needs", *Harvard Business Review*, Harvard.

Roe, E. and Schulman, P.R. (2008), *High Reliability Management*, Stanford Business Books, Stanford.

Roger Commissions (1986), Report of the Presidential Commission on the Space Shuttle Challenger Accident, Annex F. See: http://history.nasa.gov/rogersrep/genindex.htm, accessed 5 September 2012.

Richards, D. (2014), *Taking Command*, Headline, London.

Rijpma, J.A. (2003), "From Deadlock to Dead End: The Normal Accidents-High Reliability Debate Revisited", *Journal of Contingencies and Crisis Management*, Vol. 11, No. 1, pp.37–45.

Rittel, H.W.J. and Webber, M.M. (1973), "Dilemmas in a General Theory of Planning", *Policy Sciences*, Vol. 4, pp.155–169.

Roux-Dufort, C. (2009), "The Devil Lies in Details! How Crises Build up Within Organizations", *Journal of Contingencies and Crisis Management*, Vol. 17, No. 1, pp.4–11.

Sagan, S.D. (1993), *The Limits of Safety*, Princeton University Press, Princeton, NJ.

Senge, P., Kliener, A., Roberts, C., Ross, R. and Smith, B. (1994), *The Fifth Discipline Fieldbook*, Nicholas Brealey, London.

Shaluf, I.M., Fakharul-Razi, A., Aini, M.S., Sharif, R., Mustapha, S. (2002), "Technological Man-made Disaster Precondition Phase Model for Major Accidents", *Disaster Prevention and Management*, Vol. 11, No. 5, pp.380–388.

Shrivastava, P., Mitroff, I.I., Miller, D. and Miglani, A. (1988), "Understanding Industrial Crises", *Journal of Management Studies*, Vol. 25, No. 4, pp.285–303.

Silverstein, M.E. (1992), *Your Right to Survive*, Brassey's, Washington.

Singh, J.P. and Parikshit, D. (2002), "Risk Management, Nonlinearities, and Chaos", *Singapore Management Review*, Vol. 24, No. 2, pp.47–58.

Skogdalen, J.E., Utne, I.B. and Vinnem, J.E. (2011), "Developing Safety Indicators for Preventing Offshore Oil and Gas Deepwater Drilling Blowouts", *Safety Science*, Vol. 49, pp.1187–1199.

Slovic, P. (2000), *The Perception of Risk*, Earthscan, London.

Smith, D. (2002), "Crisis for Health Care Not by Error, But by Design – Harold Shipman and the Regulatory", *Public Policy and Administration*, Vol. 17, No. 4, pp.55–74.

Smith, D. (2003), *For Whom the Bell Tolls: Imagining Accidents and the Development of Crisis Simulation in Organisations*, University of Liverpool Management School, Liverpool.

Smith, D. (2005), "Business (Not) as Usual: Crisis Management, Service Recovery and the Vulnerability of Organisations", *Journal of Services Marketing*, Vol. 19, No. 5, pp.309–320.

Smith, E. (2013), *Luck*, Bloomsbury, London.

Snook, S.A. (2000), *Friendly Fire: The Accidental Shootdown of US Black Hawks over Northern Iraq*, Princeton University Press, Princeton, NJ; Oxford.

Snowden, D.J. and Boone, M.E. (2007), "A Leader's Framework for Decision Making", *HBR*, Nov, pp.1–8.

Stech, F.J. (1979), *Political and Military Intention Estimation* (US Office of Naval Research Report: N00014–78–0727), Mathtech. Inc., Bethesda.

Steinzor, R.I. (2008), *Mother Earth and Uncle Sam: How Pollution and Hollow Government Hurt Our Kids*, University of Texas Press, Austin, TX.

Stoner, J.A.F. (1968), "Risky and Cautious Shifts in Group Decisions: The Influence of Widely Held Values", *Journal of Experimental Social Psychology*, Vol. 4, No. 4, pp.442–459.

Sutcliffe, K.M. (2005), "Information Handling Challenges In Complex Systems", *International Public Management Journal*, Vol. 8, No. 3, pp.417–424.

Sydow, J., Schreyogg, G. and Kock, J. (2009), "Organizational Path Dependence: Opening the Black Box", *Academy of Management Review*, Vol. 34, No. 4, pp.689–709.

Taleb, N.N. (2007), *The Black Swan*, Penguin, London.

Toft, B. and Reynolds, S. (2005), *Learning from Disasters: A Management Approach*, 3rd edition, Palgrave Macmillan, Basingstoke.

Trompenaar, F. and Hampden-Turner, C. (1999), "First Class accommodation", *People Management*, April, pp.30–37.

Tsoukas, H. and Shepard, J. (2004), *Managing the Future*, Blackwell, Oxford.

Tuchman, B. (1984), *The March of Folly*, The Folly Society, Bury St Edmunds.

Turner, B.A. (1976), "The Organizational and Interorganizational Development of Disasters", *Administrative Science Quarterly*, Vol. 21, September, pp.378–397.

Turner, B.A. (1978), *Man-made Disaster*, Wykeham, London.

Turner, B.A. (1994), "Causes of Disaster: Sloppy Management", *British Journal of Management*, Vol. 5, pp.215–219.

Turner, B.A. and Pidgeon, N. (1997), *Man-made Disasters*, Butterworth-Heinemann, London.

van Asselt, M.B.A. and Renn, O. (2011), "Risk Governance", *Journal of Risk Research*, Vol. 14, No. 4, pp.431–449.

Van de Ven, A.H. (2007), *Engaged Scholarship*, Oxford Press, Oxford.

Vaughan, D. (1996), *The Challenger Launch Decision*, Chicago Press, London.

Vaughan, D. (1999), "The Dark Side of Organizations: Mistake, Misconduct, and Disaster", *Annual Review of Sociology*, Vol. 25, pp.271–305.

Weick, K.E. (1987), "Organizational Culture as a Source of High Reliability", *California Management Review*, Vol. 29, No. 2, pp.112–127.

Weick, K.E. (1988), "Enacted Sensemaking in Crisis Situations", *Journal of Management Studies*, Vol. 25, No. 4, pp.305–317.

Weick, K.E. (1989), "Theory Construction as Disciplined Imagination", *Academy of Management Review*, Vol. 14, No. 4, pp.516–531.

Weick, K.E. (1993), "The Collapse of Sensemaking in Organizations: The Mann Gulch Disaster", *Administrative Science Quarterly*, Vol. 38, No. 4, pp.628–652.

Weick, K.E. (1998), "Foresights of Failure: An Appreciation of Barry Turner", *Journal of Contingencies and Crisis Management*, Vol. 6, No. 2, pp.72–75.

Weick, K.E. (2004), "Normal Accident Theory as Frame, Link, and Provocation", *Organization and Environment*, Vol. 17, No. 1, pp.27–31.

Weick, K.E. (2005), "Making Sense of Blurred Images", pp. 159–177, in Starbuck, W.H. and Farjourn, M. (Eds) *Organization at the Limit*, Blackwell, Oxford.

Weick, K.E. (2007), "The Generative Properties Of Richness", *Academy of Management Journal*, Vol. 50, No. 1, pp.14–19.

Weick, K.E. (2011), "Organizing for Transient Reliability: The Production of Dynamic Non-Events", *Journal of Contingencies and Crisis Management*, Vol. 19, No. 1, pp.21–28.

Weick, K.E. and Bougon, A. (1986), "Organizations as Cause Maps", pp.102–135, in Sims, H.P. and Gioia, D.A. (Eds) *Social Cognition*, Jossey-Bass, San Francisco, CA.

Weick, K.E. and Sutcliffe, K.M. (2007), *Managing the Unexpected: Resilient Performance in an Age of Uncertainty*, 2nd edition, Jossey-Bass, San Francisco, CA.

Weinstein, N.D. (1987), "Unrealistic Optimism about Susceptibility to Health Problems", *Journal of Behavioural Medicine*, Vol. 10, No. 5, pp.481–95.

Westrum, R. (1982), "Social Intelligence about Hidden Events", *Knowledge: Creation, Diffusion, Utilization*, Vol. 3, No. 3, pp.381–400.

Westrum, R. (2004), "A Typology of Organisational Cultures", *Quality and Safety Health Care*, Vol. 13, No. 2, pp.22–27.

Wohlstetter, R. (1962), *Pearl Harbor: Warning and Decision*, Stanford University Press, Stanford, CA.

Wohlstetter, R. (1979), "The Pleasures of Self-Deception", *Washington Quarterly*, Vol. 2, No. 4, pp.54–63.

Woods, D.D. (2005), "Creating Foresight: Lessons for Enhancing Resilience from Columbia", in Starbuck, W.H. and Farjoun, M., *Organization at the Limit*, Blackwell, Oxford.

Yang, X. and Haugen, S. (2014), "A Fresh Look at Barriers from Alternative Perspectives on Risk", *Probabilistic Safety Assessment and Management PSAM*, 12 June 2014, Honolulu, Hawaii.

Yin, R.K. (2003), "The Role of Theory in Doing Case Studies", in *Applications of Case Study Research*, 3rd edition, Sage, London, pp.3–27.

Index